# MISSION 51%

BY

HASAINUL ARAFINE CHOUDHURY

Chennai • Bangalore

CLEVER FOX PUBLISHING
Chennai, India

Published by CLEVER FOX PUBLISHING 2026

ISBN: 978-93-7500-496-7



## Disclaimer

# DEDICATION

---

*To my father, whose stories ignited my imagination, and to my mother, whose steadfast presence carried me through my darkest hours.*

*To my maternal uncles and aunts, who enriched my childhood with wisdom, and to my brothers and sisters, my wife, and my son—your love and faith were my anchor.*

*To the selfless people and organisations—friends, relatives, and medical professionals—who stood by me through dialysis, vision loss, surgeries, transplant rejections, burn injuries, ICU stays, and severe infections, offering strength when I had none.*

*It was only your support and God's mercy that allowed me to write this book.*

# PREFACE

This book did not begin with a message. It began with a memory.

A small-town showroom. Dust on the glass. Targets scrawled on a whiteboard—impossible, unrelenting. The pressure of numbers that never seemed satisfied. The sweat on his back as he chased one customer after another. Rejections piling up. Frustration is settling in. And then the quiet effort to gather himself and begin again.

*Mission 51%* follows Arjun Chowdhury, a young sales executive navigating the unforgiving rhythms of the small-town automobile market. What begins as a pursuit of market share slowly becomes something else—a test of character under strain.

In business, success is often measured in percentages, margins, and monthly reports. But beyond those figures lie private battles: doubt that lingers after closing hours, accusations that threaten reputation, loyalty stretched thin, and moments when ambition collides with vulnerability.

For Arjun, the mission to cross fifty-one percent is not merely professional. It becomes a measure of endurance—of how far one can be pushed without surrendering integrity, and how many times one can fall and still rise.

This is not a story about sales alone. It is about pressure, misjudgment, resilience, and the fragile balance between ambition and humanity. It is about the cost of standing firm when circumstances demand compromise.

If these pages resonate, it will not be because they offer answers, but because they reflect something familiar—the quiet determination to continue, even when the odds feel heavier than the will to persist.

**– Hasainul Arafine Choudhury**

# CONTENTS

# CHAPTER 1
# The Call

The night's silence broke in the early hours of July 22, 2014. My phone rang—loud, insistent—dragging me from sleep. Half-awake, I reached for it—3 a.m. The hour felt wrong, unnatural. The pale glow of the screen washed the room in an eerie light.

A panicked voice came through the rain, hammering the tin roof. The noise made it hard to hear, but I caught enough to know something was wrong. That call would pull me into one of the strangest nights of my life.

It was Mr. Pintu Haldar, a fleet customer of our dealership.

"Arjun Da, my brother… It's me, Pintu. I've met with an accident. Near Rocky Island…"

His words cut through the rain. This wasn't business. His voice was broken, desperate.

"My driver, Noor… he lost control. We hit something. He's badly hurt. I think he might be dead, Da."

I sat up at once. My heart thudded. This wasn't just a road accident—it was a fight for life.

"How is Noor now?" I asked.

"He's critical," Pintu said, trembling. "There's blood everywhere. I tried calling him, shaking him… he won't wake up. Please… help us."

At that moment, I wasn't just a dealership man. I was his only hope.

"I'm coming," I said. "Hold on."

He kept talking, pouring out his panic.

"The windscreen shattered. I was thrown out. My left hand's broken. The truck's jammed between rocks. Noor's trapped inside—I tried, Da… I really tried…"

Thunder swallowed his voice.

"Don't worry," I said, gripping the phone. "Stay calm. Have you called the police?"

"I tried. No one answered. The Rocky Island bridge is about a kilometre back, but I don't know where exactly I am. It's pitch dark. No lights. No cars. I've called everyone—no one's answering. I'm alone here, Da."

"Alright. Share your GPS location," I told him.

"Yes… wait…"

Seconds dragged. Then—buzz. His message arrived.

"I sent it, Da. Did you get it?"

"Yes. I'm leaving now."

I paused. "What are you doing out there?"

"Arjun Da," he said weakly, "I was carrying poultry for the Siliguri market. I left early to get a better price. But the cages broke—the chickens are everywhere. I've lost everything…"

He hesitated, then whispered, "This area's near the forest. People say leopards come down at night."

His fear shifted from human to primal.

"I'm scared, Da. I'm bleeding. Noor isn't waking up. Please… come fast."

"Listen," I said, keeping steady. "If you can move, find a safer place. If not, stay low and keep your phone close. I'm on the way."

When the call ended, a rush of determination filled me. I threw on my clothes and grabbed the keys to the dealership's demo truck.

As I opened the door, Ma—my mother—stood in the hallway, half-asleep in her white saree, her face tight with worry.

"Arjun, where are you going at this hour?" she asked sharply.

"One of our customers—Pintu Haldar—met with a serious accident near Rocky Island," I said. "He and his driver are badly hurt. There's no one else."

Her face paled. "Rocky Island? In this weather? It's pouring! Can't the police handle it? Why must it be you?"

"Because right now, he's alone—bleeding, terrified, begging for help. I can't turn him away, Ma."

Thunder rolled across the sky. She looked up at the roof, then back at me, eyes full of fear.

"I'm your mother, Arjun. That road cuts through the forest. What if something happens?"

I stepped closer and touched her shoulder.

"Your blessing will keep me safe," I said softly. "Baba always said—never ignore a cry for help. If I don't go, he wouldn't forgive me. And neither could I."

Her eyes filled with grief and pride. She sighed, went to the kitchen, and came back with glucose biscuits and water.

"Here. Take these. Don't argue."

I touched her feet. She placed a trembling hand on my head.

"Go, help your customer," she whispered. "God will watch over you. But next time, Arjun—I'll hide your keys if I must."

A small smile tugged at my lips.

"I'll be back, Ma. Promise."

And with that, I stepped into the storm—her blessings in my pocket, her fear heavy behind me.

CHAPTER 2

# When the Forest Tested Steel

The rain poured down, soaking the earth. Droplets struck my raincoat like tiny arrows. Lightning flashed, frogs croaked, and the ground squelched underfoot. It was a wild night for a rescue.

I reached the demo truck. In the lightning, the Turbo Cheetah crouched like a predator ready to leap. My heart raced. I slid the key into the ignition. The engine roared to life, loud and alive, its growl echoing through the storm.

I pulled onto the highway. The wipers fought the rain, each stroke a drumbeat of urgency. I checked Pintu's GPS—he was forty-two kilometres away, near Rocky Island in Samsing.

With both hands tight on the wheel, I pressed the accelerator. The truck surged ahead, water spraying from its tyres. I passed Singimari and Baulbari. Next was Moulani. Beyond that lay the forests of Gorumara, where elephants and bison often blocked the road.

The rain eased to a drizzle. I picked up speed. For a moment, hope rose with the engine's roar. But soon, the downpour returned, blinding me. Near Moulali, I hit a deep pothole and slowed to a crawl. Frustration burned inside me.

Then my phone buzzed.

"Arjun Da?!" Pintu's voice cracked with panic. "Where are you? How long?"

"I'm near Moulali. Hold on—I'll be there in thirty minutes."

"Thirty minutes?!" His cry pierced me. "I don't know if I have thirty minutes!"

His words cut deep. "I'm trying, Pintu Da. Just hold on."

The line went dead.

I called the local police. One ring. Two. Three. No answer.

The road grew darker as I entered Gorumara forest. Shadows pressed in from all sides. The headlights cast a pale yellow glow, barely slicing the rain. Every pothole was a trap, every shadow a living thing.

The storm was alive. And somewhere ahead, in that wild darkness, Pintu was waiting—bleeding, desperate, alone.

As I left Lataguri, the forest thickened. Trees stood like dark sentinels, their branches swaying under the storm. I switched on the fog lamp. Its beam cut through the gloom, showing each curve—and hinting at what might wait in the shadows. Out here, even a second's mistake could be fatal.

The rain lashed harder. I shifted into third gear, gripping the wheel tighter. The Turbo Cheetah growled, steady against the storm. Fear and duty wrestled within me. I heard Ma's trembling voice: That road cuts through the forest… anything can happen. She was right. Anything could. Yet I had no choice.

Suddenly, I slammed the brakes. The truck skidded, tyres shrieking. In the fog lamps' beam, something thick and glistening moved—a giant python, sliding across the road. My heart raced. For a second, I imagined its coils crushing metal, the jungle swallowing me whole. Then it vanished into the dark, and the road called me on.

The storm offered no mercy. My chest felt tight. The glove box rattled. I opened it with one hand. Beneath stray papers was a forgotten pack of cigarettes. I hadn't smoked in weeks, but it felt like the only anchor I had.

I lit one. The flame flickered, trembling like my heart. Smoke filled my lungs—bitter, hot. It dulled the fear for a moment. I remembered Baba's words: Never ignore a cry for help, even in the dark. The ember glowed. I pressed the accelerator harder.

The truck surged—sixty, seventy, eighty. The storm pounded the windows, but I felt alive, almost defiant. Until the forest answered back.

They appeared out of the mist.

A herd of elephants—massive, glistening with rain. Their tusks gleamed, their trunks lifted high. The night itself seemed to bow before them.

My blood froze. I slammed the brake. The truck skidded, rain spraying like shattered glass. The wheels screamed. For a moment, I wasn't in control—the storm and road had taken over. The truck twisted, then stopped. Barely a hundred meters from the herd.

Silence. The world held its breath. Man and beast. Machine and nature.

Then, a trumpet ripped the night. The herd stirred—panic spreading—and suddenly they charged.

The ground shook. Their eyes blazed. Their trunks whipped the air, their tusks gleamed like blades. They were fury itself, bearing down on me.

My heart pounded so hard I thought my ribs would break. I saw Ma's face—her warning, her tears. Would this be the last time she saw me?

I slammed into reverse. The Turbo Cheetah screamed backwards, mud flying. My hands trembled, but I held on. In the rearview mirror, the elephants grew larger, unstoppable.

Every trumpet pierced me like a dagger. My throat went dry. Not here, not tonight. I can't die here. Pintu is waiting. Ma is waiting.

Through the rain, I saw it—a narrow side track, half-swallowed by jungle. I didn't think. I spun the wheel, slammed it into drive, and the truck leapt forward. Tires skidded, mud sprayed, and I burst onto the hidden path.

The GPS flickered. A new line appeared. Via Tila Bari. A snake-like trail twists into the forest.

I followed it, heart pounding, hands damp on the wheel. For miles, the track wound through trees and mist. Every bend felt like the last—until the forest suddenly parted, revealing familiar ground.

Malbazar Road. The way to Rocky Island.

I exhaled, trembling. The storm still raged, but I was alive. Ahead, Pintu was waiting.

But the trial wasn't over.

Rain hammered down. Visibility dropped to nothing. The truck skidded near the edge, wheels fighting for grip. I clenched the wheel, battling storm and soil. Behind me, the echo of elephants roared, pushing me forward.

A thunderous crash shook the trees. I looked back—my blood ran cold. A herd charged with unstoppable force, each step powered by raw muscle. Panic surged. One mistake could be fatal.

The road ahead twisted like my thoughts. The ground trembled. Trumpets cut through the storm—they weren't just chasing; they were hunting.

Deeper in the jungle, the path turned to muck. My Turbo Cheetah crawled at 20 km/h, every bump testing endurance. I gritted my teeth and pushed on.

A jolt rocked the truck. One massive elephant loomed close, trunk reaching out. Could my little machine survive even one hit?

Weighing only 1,800 kilos, the Turbo Cheetah was nothing beside them. Yet it didn't give up. It had something the beasts didn't—engineering and speed. Its high clearance held steady through deep holes. Agility became its armour.

Once mocked for its turning radius and chassis, the Turbo Cheetah now proved its worth—on the worst road imaginable, chased by giants. It was my savior.

I'd tried to sell it with brochures and numbers. No one saw its soul. Here, deep in the forest, it wrote its own story. It seemed to say:

I'm not flawed. I'm built for this. I am the best in class.

The elephants roared again. I turned onto Tila Bari—a pothole-filled gamble. The truck twisted and slid but never faltered. It wasn't just surviving; it was proving its worth.

As the beasts faded behind, swallowed by trees, I realised this wasn't just a ride. It was a statement—a promise that the Turbo Cheetah could carry us forward in Mission 51%, not just as a truck but as a symbol of strength and purpose.

The ground shook again. A deafening trumpet split the night. Two elephants charged from opposite sides. Panic struck. I slammed the accelerator. The engine roared, wind whipping through the cabin. The jungle blurred. My heart pounded.

Each bend tested me. Gravity pulled at the truck, daring it to fail. I kept going, eyes sharp, hands steady.

The trail turned cruel—potholes gaping like traps. The truck hit one hard; mud splashed, coating the windshield. Tires spun in the muck. Still, the Turbo Cheetah fought on.

The wipers carved the rain in a frantic rhythm. Every second was a battle. The jungle pressed close, alive and watching. It was just me and the truck—my only chance of escape.

Shadows moved ahead. Elephants again, their dark shapes shifting through the storm. I pushed harder, widening the gap, but the road worsened.

A violent jolt threw me forward. The truck sank into a waterlogged ditch. Tires spun helplessly. I tried forward, reverse, again and again. The engine groaned. Rain hammered the roof. Then came a trumpet—loud and angry.

I froze. Another blast, closer. My breath stopped.

The jungle fell silent except for thunderous feet—elephants, charging.

I pressed the accelerator, praying for the Turbo Cheetah to move.

The phone rang. "Ma" flashed on the screen. Her name pulsed like a heartbeat. I answered, her voice trembling through the speakers.

"Arjun, where are you? Are you safe?"

I sealed the windows, wiping sweat from my brow. "I'm fine, Ma. Heading to the customer's place. Don't worry—I'll be home soon."

Shifting to four-wheel drive, I slammed the accelerator. The engine snarled. "Don't worry, Ma! I'll be back soon!"

The Cheetah responded like a beast unleashed. It climbed out of the ditch, torque transferring flawlessly. But the phone rang again. Ma.

Inside the cab, tension mounted. Wipers thrashed. Wheels fought the slick ground. An elephant loomed in the rearview mirror.

If Ma heard everything, panic would consume her. But silence wasn't an option.

"Arjun, what's happening? This noise… something's wrong!" Her voice cracked.

Taking a sharp curve, I muttered, "Just a bumpy patch, Ma. I'm trying to reach fast."

"Don't lie. I know you're in trouble."

An elephant slammed into the truck, throwing it into a tree. The brakes clutched the road, saving us from tipping.

"Tell me now! Or I'll get the neighbors to find you!"

"Ma, it's the Lataguri road. Elephants… they're chasing me. I'm trying to get away."

Silence. Then her fury exploded.

Her worry for her son had sharpened into anger, cutting through every word she spoke.

"I told you—leave this cursed job! One day it will kill you!"

"But Ma, it pays our bills…"

Her words crashed like thunder.

"Why aren't you studying for the government jobs?"

She couldn't possibly understand the deadly danger I faced in the jungle. I stayed quiet, hiding the harsh reality outside my vehicle.

Her voice rose, sharp with anger.

"Prepare for civil service, primary teacher, or even a clerical post—anything is better than this madness!"

Even amid the chaos, she dreamed of a safer world for me.

"Ma, if everyone joined government jobs, who'd build India's business future?"

Her voice hardened. "You don't need to carry the weight of the nation. From tomorrow, you're studying. That's final."

The Cheetah danced through mud and bends with cat-like grace. It shook off the dirt like a shield, its headlights slicing through the rain.

"Okay, Ma," I said, dodging branches and doubt. "From tomorrow, I'll start. Study for exams... I promise."

Another blow. The truck hit a tree. Pain flared. I cried out, "Oh Ma…!" The brakes screeched.

"What happened?!" she yelled.

"Nothing. A pothole. Please, rest. I'll be home early."

The line went dead. I exhaled.

The Cheetah was more than metal. Muscle and memory. Precision and traction. My comrade in chaos. The forest twisted like a maze—but we were built for this.

I wondered again—why do people doubt this machine? Why is it so hard to sell something so reliable?

It felt like the Cheetah heard me. As if it too had something to prove.

"You're brilliant," I whispered. "You can win Mission 51%."

The brakes answered, steady and sure. Every system felt in tune with me.

We weren't just escaping elephants—we were fighting fate itself.

Five giants thundered at my side. Nature and machine clashed in mud and motion. I pushed harder. Slowly, they disappeared into the shadows. Gone.

The Cheetah's engine roared—not in fear, but in victory.

We hit the main road. Headlights sliced through the dark. The forest leaned closer, silent and watching.

I gripped the wheel tightly. The road curved toward Rocky Island. I trusted my instinct and followed.

CHAPTER 3

# The Broken Cage

The phone rang—Pintu Haldar, voice raw with fear.

"Arjun Da! Where are you? Five leopards—circling us. They'll pounce. Come fast, Dada—please!"

In Bengal, "Dada" is more than a name; it is a call for help. I turned the wheel hard, gravel spraying.

"I'm close, Pintu Da! Don't panic," I shouted.

"Noor's unconscious—his head's bleeding. The cage is smashed, and the chickens are everywhere. The leopards are watching, Da." His breath sounded like a broken radio.

I pressed the accelerator. Rain slapped the windshield. Tea gardens blurred by, diesel and earth mixing into the air. The Cheetah growled beneath me—steady, angry, alive.

The GPS blinked: five kilometres. My heart hammered in time with the engine. Every second mattered.

When my headlights finally cut through the dark, Pintu stood in the road, ringed by three leopards. Their eyes shone, cold and patient. Chickens ran in flurries. The cage lay wrecked. Pintu swung a branch, blood on his hand, rain on his face.

I hit the brakes. The Cheetah stopped between him and the predators. I smashed on the horn and flashed the high beam. The noise sliced the jungle; the leopards hesitated, then melted back into shadow.

I ran out, boots sinking in mud. Pintu wouldn't look at me. "You're late, Arjun Da," he said—anger and grief caught together. "They took everything."

No time. Noor.

The crashed vehicle lay on its side in a ditch. I yanked open the door. Noor slumped, temple torn, blood warm against his hair. "Water…" he breathed.

"Hold on," I said. "We'll move you."

Pintu wrapped his bleeding hand and climbed down. Together we hauled Noor free—mud clinging, rain beating. He was heavy and limp; every step a fight.

Then the leopards returned, closer, growls threading the rain. "They're back," Pintu whispered.

"Get Noor to the truck," I ordered. "I'll cover you."

We staggered to the Cheetah. Noor collapsed onto the rear seat; I pulled a tarpaulin over him and slammed the door. Behind us, the pack crept forward, eyes bright as knives.

Pintu stood, branch raised, rain soaking through him. "This ends tonight," he said, voice low and fierce.

I checked the engine, hands steady now. The Cheetah was more than metal; it was shelter, a promise. We had come this far—now we held the line.

I switched on the fog lights—halos cutting through the storm. The engine's hum rose like a war drum. Soaked and bruised, watching a man defend what little he owned from nature's hunger, I understood—

this wasn't a rescue.

It was a stand.

Five leopards emerged—sleek shadows slicing through the rain. Not just beasts, but raiders, eyes lit with hunger. Chickens scattered in panic, feathers strewn across the mud like fallen stars.

They lunged at Pintu Da, growls lost in the roar of rain. Some vanished with prey clutched in their jaws; others circled back. With nothing but a branch, he fought on. Fear had no place left in him. Each swing pushed the darkness back an inch.

In the glare of headlights, the image burned—one man in the storm, soaked to the skin, fighting for his fragile cargo. Fat white broilers glowed like ghosts in the gloom.

"Pintu Da! Get the birds into the truck cage!" I shouted. "The back's low—use the wires to seal it!"

"Right, Da!" he called back, breath ragged but steady. "Take the branch—keep them off!"

He ran for the truck; I took his place, gripping the branch like a sword. Blood and rain mingled on the road, a red stream running between my boots. The leopards came again—cunning, greedy, relentless. A hundred chickens floundered through the mud, their wet feathers slowing them down.

I fought on, swinging, shouting. The road had turned into a battlefield—predators circling, feathers flying, courage holding the line.

Each blow was an answer to fear. This wasn't about poultry anymore—it was about survival, dignity, and debt. Pintu Da had taken a loan for that truck. It was his livelihood, his hope. If the leopards won tonight, he'd lose everything.

Driven by that truth, he worked faster—tying wires, fixing latches, rebuilding his cage as if stitching together his future. His left hand was fractured, his face streaked with rain and pain, yet he did not stop.

The rain fell harder, relentless. Pintu Da looked like a soaked crow in a storm—shirt plastered, hair stuck to his forehead—but his will didn't waver. Chickens darted in terror; he caught them by their legs, two at a time, shoving them into cages.

I circled the area with the branch, guarding the line. Mud sucked at my boots. We just had to save the birds—and Noor, his favorite—before the next strike.

Then came the scream.

We froze. From the forest's edge, five glowing eyes reappeared—silent, hungry. They'd tasted chicken before and wanted more.

One leapt. Teeth flashed, feathers burst into the air. Chaos followed—birds screeching, feathers flying like snow. The leopards tore through the cages, wild with hunger.

Pintu vanished, then reappeared with an iron rod. Without a word, he charged. The leopard didn't see him coming.

The rod cracked across its back. The beast shrieked and vanished into the dark.

But it wasn't over.

The cries of the flock mixed with the leopards' growls — a wild chorus in the jungle night. One tried to sneak in again. Pintu Da raised the iron rod high. Soaked, trembling, furious—but fearless. The leopards paused. They saw something in him: a man who would not step back.

He hurled the rod. It struck the ground with a dull thud. The leopards scattered, their glowing eyes fading into the trees.

Pintu Da stood still, chest heaving, rain running down his face. Most of the chickens were safe. He no longer felt the pain in his fractured hand, tied in a blood-soaked handkerchief. Fear and exhaustion had drowned everything else. In that moment, in the middle of the forest, Pintu Da was no longer a chicken seller.

He was a hero.

We worked fast. He gathered his flock, cradling each bird like a fragile truth, locking them inside the cage. But blood still dripped from his hand — red against the rain.

In the back seat, Noor lay curled and half-conscious, his face tight with pain, blood crusted under his nose and brow — the scars of a brutal night.

The rain eased to a drizzle. Dawn rose over Rocky Island, light spilling on the wet earth. The air smelled of fresh soil. Birds sang. The world shook off its terror and blinked into hope.

Both Noor and Pintu Da were bleeding. I begged them to go to the hospital. But Pintu Da's burden seemed heavier than pain.

He slipped a packet of khaini from his pocket, rubbing the flakes with his injured hand, tucking them under his tongue. The sting steadied him.

"You're hurt," I said.

He spat to the side, voice rough. "No, Dada. I must get my chickens to Matiali farm."

"You need treatment first," I insisted.

"Our wounds will heal," he said, calm but firm. "If I lose my chickens, I lose everything."

"Pintu Da," I said softly, "I've informed the police. They'll handle the truck and the birds. Please come."

He shook his head. "Just tow my truck with a rope."

"Your truck's in a ditch," I warned. "My demo can't pull that weight."

"If you have a strong rope," he said, "let's try. I'll reverse while you pull."

Fear prickled through me. The load could wreck my engine. But his eyes were desperate. Then he raised his hands—not in protest, but surrender.

"Dada… this is all I have. If I lose this truck, I lose my life."

His voice cracked. I saw not a farmer, but a man trying to hold on to dignity.

Silently, I took out the towing cable. Hooked one end to his truck, the other to mine.

"Get inside," I said.

"Wait," he called. "We need traction."

He grabbed a spade, cleared the mud from the wheels, and wedged bricks and stones beneath them. His moves were quick, mechanical — the reflex of someone who'd fought too many battles with broken tools.

When he finished, he tossed the spade aside. The sound rang through the quiet dawn. The birds clucked nervously, feathers damp. Yet the morning held a strange calm, as if the world watched two men defy the impossible.

Pintu Da jumped into his seat and slammed the door.

"Arjun Da! Start your vehicle—pull!"

Engines roared. Mud splattered. The chickens screamed in panic as the tyres spun, digging deep. Pintu Da gritted his teeth, shifting gears again and again. He was trying to save his world — and no one else would do it for him.

Then he turned to me, voice cracking with desperation.

"Please help!"

His plea pierced through the rain and noise. I jumped into my driver's seat and twisted the key. The 2400cc engine of the Turbo Cheetah roared alive—a metallic growl rolling through the misty dawn like a wild beast answering a cry.

The truck surged forward, tyres gripping the soaked earth. The rev counter rose past 2000 rpm, the hum of the engine beating with my pulse—urgent, unbroken.

We fastened the thick towing cable between our trucks. As it tightened, the air itself seemed to strain, a cord stretched between despair and hope. Pintu Da reversed; I pushed forward. The road fought us—mud sucking at the wheels, tyres spinning, debris flying.

The vehicles groaned together, one dragging, one rising. Mud exploded outward. Pintu Da gritted his teeth, foot hammering the pedal. Inch by inch, his truck began to move.

The roar of our engines filled the air—a rough, mechanical symphony. Burnt rubber mixed with the sharp smell of feathers and rain. Then, suddenly—release.

His truck jerked free, crashing onto the road with a thud. Chickens shrieked. Feathers flew. He steered aside, engine sputtering, then silence.

A wide grin spread across his face—broken teeth gleaming, eyes shining. He stepped out, drenched and trembling, but alive. The first rays of the sun touched his soaked shirt, and the world finally breathed again.

I switched off my truck, lit my last cigarette, and exhaled slowly. "Well done," I said. "Your chickens are safe."

"Yes, Da!" he said, joy trembling in his voice. "If you hadn't come, we'd be finished. Thank you!"

He took out his familiar khaini packet, rubbing the tobacco between thumb and finger—a ritual of calm after chaos.

"Let's go to the hospital," I said. "Noor's too weak."

He nodded. "Yes, Da. Let's go."

I clapped him on the back. "It's my job to make sure you're all safe."

Just then, a sharp honk split the dawn. A police jeep screeched to a stop. An officer stepped out, eyes still heavy with sleep. His gaze swept over the muddy road and stopped at Pintu Da's battered truck.

"Whose truck is this?" he barked.

Pintu Da stiffened. "Sir, it's mine."

"Documents," thc officcr said.

Pintu Da hurriedly fetched them—insurance, license, pollution certificate—hands trembling.

The officer studied each page, slowly and suspiciously. "This truck's been in an accident. Anyone hurt?"

"No, Sir," said Pintu Da. "Just minor injuries."

"Why didn't you go to a hospital?"

"Sir, we got stuck in the rain. Leopards attacked. We lost many chickens. This man—Arjun Da—saved us."

"Who's Arjun?"

I stepped forward, putting out my cigarette. "Good morning, Sir. Arjun Chowdhury."

The officer smirked. "Ah, the famous Truck Man. Selling trucks at dawn?"

"No, Sir. I came because my customer called for help after the accident," I said evenly.

"Such dedication," he said with a sneer. "Or maybe another reason?"

"I represent Darjeeling Auto Works, an authorized Rana Motors dealer. Helping customers is part of my job."

He turned back to Pintu Da. "Bring this truck to the station. We'll file a report."

"Sir, please," said Pintu Da, voice cracking. "Let me settle my chickens first. The leopards killed many."

The officer's face didn't soften.

"Sir," I said, stepping in. "Let him finish. He'll come."

"Let me do my job," he snapped. "People like him don't return."

"I give you my word," I said quietly, "on behalf of my company."

But he wasn't convinced. I saw panic rising again in Pintu Da's eyes. I couldn't abandon him—not after what we'd survived.

One name flashed in my mind—Mr. Amol Das, MLA and proud owner of five Turbo Cheetah Trucks. I took out my phone and dialed his number.

"Good morning, Sir. This is Arjun. I need your help."

"What happened? It's early."

"Sorry for the call at this hour, Sir. One of our customers had an accident. There was a leopard attack. He's hurt, and his truck is damaged. The police are harassing him now."

"What's the problem?"

"The officer insists he must come to the station immediately. But the driver is unfit, and the livestock is at risk. Please, Sir, intervene."

"Arjun, the police have to follow protocol."

"I understand, Sir. But maybe they can allow medical treatment first and temporary care for the livestock?"

Mr. Das sighed. "I trust you. Let me see what I can do."

Back at the site, tension was still high. Noor, the driver, was barely conscious. I pleaded again.

"Sir, look at them. They're injured. Please let them get treatment first."

"You should have informed us earlier," the officer snapped. "Why wait? I need to question your motives."

"Sir, we called Chalsa Station at 4 a.m. A constable promised help, but no one arrived. You can check the logs."

Just then, the officer's phone rang. He stepped aside, and we heard snippets: "Yes, Sir… No, Sir… I understand…"

When he returned, his attitude had changed.

"Mr. Arjun, my apologies. My team didn't act quickly. Please, take your customer to the hospital. He can come to the station later."

"Thank you, Sir. He'll go after treatment."

Mr. Das had come through.

That's the power of true customer relationships.

The police jeep pulled away.

We secured the chickens at Pintu Da's Matiali farm and rushed to Malbazar Medical Centre.

I stayed until Noor and Pintu Da were stable. Noor, still groaning, gave me a faint smile. "Thank you," he whispered. Blood crusted around his nose, and damp hair clung to his forehead, but his eyes shone with gratitude.

Pintu Da sat silently, his handkerchief clenched, drained but safe. Pintu Haldar turned to me, his voice filled with heartfelt thanks. "Arjun Da, thank you. Today, because of you, our lives and my poultry are safe. If you ever need help, just call me. I'll be there."

I climbed into my Turbo Cheetah Truck and drove off, waving to Pintu and Noor. They stood there, smiling and waving back, their gratitude clear.

It was 9 a.m. in Malbazar. My Siliguri meeting was at 10. I wouldn't make it in time. Mr. S.K. Aggarwal, our irritable boss, would likely explode.

But as I sped along, cool wind brushing my face, I felt a deep sense of peace. Those smiles, that relief—I hadn't just done my duty. I had done something profoundly human.

My thoughts drifted back to a training session with Vikram Singh, our Territory Manager. During the session, he had been guiding us on how to achieve Mission 51%. I remembered asking him, "Sir, is this sympathy or empathy?"

He had smiled. "Sympathy says, 'I'm sorry for your pain.' Empathy says, 'I feel it with you.'"

Bikash had nodded. "Sympathy sees the wound. Empathy shares the hurt."

"Exactly," Singh had said. "Empathy builds trust. That's what matters."

Partha had grinned. "We're not just truck sellers. We become family."

Raju had smirked. "And then, they won't go anywhere else."

Singh had beamed. "That's The Drive Beyond the Funnel—selling trust, building relationships that last."

CHAPTER 4

# We Need Closers, Not Dreamers

I reached home around 10:30 a.m. Mother scanned me from head to toe, worry clouding her eyes. Once sure I wasn't hurt, she switched straight to scolding.

"What brings you home so early? You could've been out meeting customers."

Trying to calm her, I said, "You're the world's best mom. Don't be upset. Tell me what needs to be done."

"There's nothing. Just eat your breakfast," she said, voice firm yet soft.

As I got ready for a bath, I called out, "So, what's for breakfast?"

Her reply came sharply. "What groceries did you buy? It's been five days since you went to the market. There's roti and potato fries—make do with that."

Guilty but grinning, I shouted back, "Don't worry! I'll get everything today."

"I'm sure," she muttered. "You always say that."

After Father's death, her pension was halved. She stretched every rupee with quiet dignity.

When I finally sat to eat, the dry roti stuck to my throat—a fair punishment for my neglect. Work had swallowed everything else.

She appeared again, her tone softer. "Don't worry. You give me money; I'll manage. You focus on work."

"I'm sorry, Mom," I said. "I'll buy everything today."

"No need. Just give me the cash," she replied gently but firm.

It was 22nd July. Funds were low—as always. First week, you're a king; last week, you count coins. I had ₹800 left. I handed her ₹400 and kept the rest for emergencies. She understood the routine. She always did.

I stepped out, climbed into the demo truck, and waved goodbye. The sky was clear, the roads familiar. Siliguri was 45 minutes away.

Just past Fatapukur, my phone rang—it was Isha.

"Hi Arjun! Good morning! Where are you?"

"On my way to the office," I said.

"Really? The meeting started at 10. It's noon!"

"I'll reach by 1. Mr. Aggarwal won't spare me—I'm ready for the fire," I laughed.

"Don't joke. Come fast. He's waiting for the review."

"I think Mr. Sushil Kumar Aggarwal should rebrand himself as Mr. Teekha Kumar Aggarwal. Every meeting with him feels like a grill."

"Be serious, Arjun. And try being punctual for once," she said and hung up.

I pressed harder on the accelerator, thinking of my boss—short, fair, forever frowning behind thick glasses. His dyed hair fought age; his temper fought reason. Nearing sixty, with two unmarried daughters and retirement closing in, he carried the weight of both home and office.

I reached by 1:30 p.m. The meeting was over. Some colleagues lingered outside, smoking or sipping tea. They waved—not judging, just surviving.

Inside, Mr. Aggarwal sat behind a fortress of files. His assistant Nilesh worked quietly beside him.

"Good afternoon, sir," I said.

Without looking up, he asked, "What's the time?"

"1:30 p.m., sir."

"And the meeting?"

"10 a.m., sir."

He looked up, eyes cold. "We're under pressure to meet targets, and you stroll in at 1:30? This isn't casual work, Arjun."

"I understand, sir. But there was an emergency. Mr. Pintu Haldar called at 3 a.m. I went to help."

"Did that help our sales?" he snapped.

"Sir, he owns five TCTs. I did what was right."

"You work for Darjeeling Auto Works, not Pintu Haldar," he said sharply. "Stay focused."

I disagreed silently. For me, customer satisfaction was the job.

"I'll manage better next time," I said quietly.

"Well, you're marked absent today," he concluded.

I exhaled. "If helping a client at 3 a.m. doesn't count as work, I don't know what does," I muttered as I left.

Outside, colleagues glanced up. I smiled faintly and walked away, my backpack hanging low.

Opposite the office stood our usual tea shop. I went in and bought a packet of cigarettes. Just a little farther was "Subhas Udyan"—a quiet park where the city's chaos faded into chirping birds and rustling leaves.

I walked there, settled under a tree, and lit the cigarette. Smoke rose slowly, curling into the still afternoon air. It wasn't ideal, but it helped me breathe. My shoulders began to loosen.

My shoes, old and worn out, bore the stains of rain and rocky paths. After last night's rescue in Rocky Island, they were worse off. But they told my story—of effort, of grit. I wore them like a badge of honour. Sadly, effort isn't always recognized.

As I sat beneath that tree, the park offering its quiet comfort, I let my thoughts drift. The clouds parted above, and a warm ray of sunlight touched my face. It was the kind of day that forced you to pause, to remember how it all began.

The crows cawed, birds chirped, and the breeze stirred. It felt like the world was listening.

And for a moment—just one—I felt a little less alone.

My mind goes back to 2010, my final year of college. Graduation promised freedom, yet I felt the weight of duty. That November, my father retired, and suddenly my future wasn't only mine—it belonged to the family.

In May 2011, fate struck harder. My father, Saibal Chowdhury, died in our small home. A Group C employee all his life, he spent everything on debts and daily needs. Retirement left him restless; illness took him swiftly. That night, when he begged to go to a private hospital, I had no money. The government ward was all I could offer. He didn't return. With him, the balance of our lives collapsed.

Grief turned to guilt, then survival. It was just Ma and me now. She gave me courage even as her health weakened. I earned my first ₹500 tutoring two students—awkward but determined. Teaching grew into something more; it showed me resilience. Neighbors recommended me, but money was never steady.

Then came insurance sales, thanks to Subir Saha, who saw potential where I saw only need. "Sales isn't taught—it's discovered," he said. I learned fast—closing deals, facing rejection, winning small prizes. But the market was harsh. Clients wanted rebates; I had none to give. Still, every policy sold meant food on the table.

Yet I longed for stability. Government jobs were still the dream, though rejection was routine. Over tea one March afternoon in 2013, my friend Sunil sighed that corruption blocked every door. We sat silent, helpless against a tilted system.

Then a newspaper ad caught my eye: "Join a Leading Car Dealership." Temporary job, three months, sales executives. But it stirred something—cars, engines, possibility. I told Sunil; he urged me on.

That evening, I shared it with Ma. She frowned; she'd hoped for a government post. I held her hand and said, "Ma, this is a start. I need to stand before I can rise." She nodded, eyes moist.

That night, under the hum of the ceiling fan, I wrote my résumé and read the ad again. For the first time in years, I felt a spark of hope.

On the morning of my first interview, I had no formal trousers, no polished shoes—just a faded blue shirt, black jeans, and dusty sandals. My hair was wild; I hadn't shaved. Still, I told myself it would do.

By 7:30 a.m., I was on the crowded bus to Siliguri, swaying in the press of bodies and sweat, holding one thought—that today could change something. Ma stood at the door as I left, silent, her eyes saying what words could not.

At Darjeeling Auto Works, the dealership buzzed—cars gleamed, trucks stood like sentinels, salesmen moved fast. Eight of us had come for the same role. We waited, half strangers, half companions, each of us holding the same fragile dream in our chest.

I waited all day, the hours stretching longer than expected. My turn finally came at 4:00 p.m.

The interview room belonged to Mr. S. K. Aggarwal, the Sales Manager. His presence filled the room even before he spoke. A metal ashtray on his desk held a half-smoked cigarette, still fuming faintly. A young clerk, head down, typed away on the left side of the room.

"Ah, Mr. Arjun," Mr. Aggarwal greeted, his voice gravelly and unimpressed. "Take a seat. Let's begin."

"Thank you, sir," I replied, steadying my breath.

He dove straight in. "You're here for the commercial vehicle sales role. Why should I consider you—a fresher—over someone with experience?"

I leaned forward slightly. "While I haven't worked in this sector yet, I've spent the last year in insurance sales. It taught me negotiation, resilience, and the importance of understanding a client's needs. I even won an award for meeting last year's policy targets."

He exhaled, unimpressed. "Insurance and vehicle sales are worlds apart. You do know that?"

"I do, sir. But I believe the core of sales—listening, empathy, persistence—remains the same. I'm a fast learner, and I adapt well."

He leaned back, narrowing his eyes. "Confidence is good. But this isn't a game of words. We need closers. What happens when a tough customer rejects you?"

I didn't flinch. "I listen harder. Rejection often hides an unmet need. I treat it as feedback and adjust my approach accordingly. Patience, sir, paired with persistence, can break most walls."

There was a pause. Then, almost mocking, he asked, "Why should I hire you over someone with years in the automobile industry?"

I took a breath. "Experience is valuable, but it can come with blind spots. As a fresher, I bring a clean slate. I'm eager to learn, not married to any old habits, and I can bring in ideas unshaped by the industry's clichés. With training, I can become a valuable long-term asset."

He chuckled—a dry, almost dismissive sound. "Ideas? We're not hiring dreamers. We need people who can sell trucks, not poetry."

His words stung, but I didn't break.

"Give me the chance, and I'll prove I can do both," I said quietly. "I'll sell your trucks and make sure they stay remembered."

He looked at me without a flicker of expression. "We'll see. You may go. My team will contact you."

As I stepped out, the stale air of the office gave way to the dusk-drenched buzz of the city. My heartbeat was a drum, part fear, part fire. He was tough. But I had spoken my truth.

The next two days drifted by like mist—routine, slow, laced with waiting. I went about my chores, not mentioning the interview too much, though I replayed it in my head a hundred times. Somewhere in my gut, I felt a flicker—he might have liked me, even if just a little.

On the third evening, Ma asked, her voice tentative, "Did they call?"

"Not yet," I said, masking the uncertainty with a smile. "They said seven days."

She nodded, eyes downcast. The weight of monthly expenses was written on her face. She didn't say it, but I knew—this job meant more than a paycheck.

On the seventh day, each ring of the phone felt like a call from fate. When it finally came, my hands trembled as I picked it up.

"You've been shortlisted for the final round," the voice on the line said.

I didn't say much, just whispered a thank you.

When I told Ma, her face lit up—not wildly, but gently, with a quiet pride that made my throat tighten.

Interview—Round Two,

March 28th, 2013.

The rain had washed the roads clean but left potholes full of muddy reflections. I tiptoed through them, careful not to let the water ruin my only decent pair of clothes.

At the Maynaguri bus stand, I ran into two old friends—Amol and Haru.

"Where are you off to so early?" Amol asked, surprised.

"Last round of my job interview," I replied, unable to hide the hope in my voice.

"What kind?" Haru asked. He was prepping for civil services—confident, focused, and already on a different path.

"A car dealership in Siliguri. Commercial vehicle sales executive."

Amol raised an eyebrow. "Sales job? You were always a bright student. Why not try for a government position?"

"No job is inferior," I said. "Every job done with dignity earns money and respect."

He frowned. "Sales is like begging from door to door. You deserve better."

Haru added sharply, "You'll become a hawker. Don't expect us to call you a friend if that's where you end up."

I smiled, a calm, knowing smile. "You two have time, choices. I don't. My Ma needs me to stand on my feet. I can't wait for something perfect—I need something now."

The bus arrived, splashing water onto our shoes. I climbed aboard with a silent prayer and a hopeful heart.

The clock struck 10:30 a.m. as I stepped into Darjeeling Auto Works, the air dense with the damp scent of a night-long rain. Puddles glimmered in the potholes, and vehicles splashed through them with carefree haste. I tiptoed between them, clutching the edges of my trousers to protect them from the dirty water. The showroom buzzed with activity, yet felt strangely impersonal. I made my way to the reception desk to confirm my attendance for the interview.

There, my eyes met Miss Isha Sharma.

Something in her gaze—calm, observant, and quietly radiant—arrested my steps. She wasn't just beautiful; she possessed a presence that seemed to slow time. The other candidates noticed it too, their first-day anxiety momentarily giving way to silent admiration.

"Good morning," she greeted, her voice crisp yet gentle, paired with a smile that felt like sunlight breaking through the grey.

"Good morning," I replied, suddenly conscious of my soaked sleeves.

Her eyes, large and almond-shaped, shimmered with curiosity. Her fair skin seemed to reflect the soft white lights of the showroom, and her posture—straight, assured—told of someone who had long learned how to command a room without raising her voice. Isha's presence didn't just lighten the space; it shaped it.

I took a seat nearby, trying to appear composed, but my mind kept circling back to her voice—a melody that lingered even in silence. As the morning wore on, I asked, "Excuse me, could you tell me about my interview with Mr. Rakesh Chetri?"

She glanced at her schedule, dialed a number, then nodded. "The GM will see you after lunch—at 3 p.m.," she said, her voice soft as a breeze through leaves.

"Thank you," I said, barely masking the eagerness in my tone.

Time passed like molasses. I returned to the desk under the pretext of requesting a glass of water. It was partly true—I was parched—but mostly I was drawn to the rare ease in her presence.

"May I know your name?" I asked, more timidly than I intended.

"Isha," she answered with a smile, then surprised me with, "You're Arjun, right?"

"Yes, Arjun," I confirmed, a flicker of delight in my chest.

"Where are you from?"

"Maynaguri."

There was a pause, not awkward, just brief enough to allow curiosity to flourish.

"Do you know the expected salary for this role?" I asked.

"That will be discussed by the boss. Just wait till 3 p.m., everything will be clearer then," she said, her reassurance tinged with professional detachment.

The phone rang. I watched as concern flickered across her face. She murmured an apology and disappeared into the corridor after mentioning Mr. S. K. Aggarwal.

I knew Mr. Aggarwal from the day of my first interview. Mr. Aggarwal—an uncompromising and arrogant figure, respected but feared. I couldn't help but feel a pang of sympathy for Isha as she responded to his call.

After a long wait, I was finally summoned.

The General Manager's office was on the upper floor. Around thirty employees worked in departments like accounts, sales, finance, and old vehicles. The absence of air conditioning didn't bother anyone; fans kept the environment manageable.

I entered Mr. Rakesh Chetri's office. He remained seated but welcomed me warmly from his chair.

"Good morning! Please take a seat. I'm Mr. Rakesh Chetri. What's your name?"

"Good morning, sir. I'm Arjun Chowdhury," I replied, my nerves somewhat easing.

"Lovely to meet you, Arjun. Tell me a bit about yourself—where you're from and your academic background."

"I'm from Maynaguri, and I studied economics," I said.

"Economics! Interesting choice," he remarked. "Tell me about your family."

"Just me and my mother."

His tone softened. "Are you truly interested in this opportunity?"

"Absolutely, sir. I'm eager to learn and grow in this role."

He outlined the job responsibilities: a three-month temporary position under a senior sales executive, focused on generating leads. Three sales conversions were expected from those leads.

It sounded demanding, but not impossible.

"I'm ready for the challenge," I responded confidently.

"Salary will be ₹8000, plus travel allowance and phone reimbursements."

Though modest, the offer felt like a door opening. "I'm happy with that. It's a good start."

"Once you finish here, please meet Mr. S. K. Aggarwal. He'll guide you on the remaining formalities."

"Thank you, sir," I said, rising with a mixture of excitement and trepidation.

Mr. Aggarwal's office felt heavier, both in air and atmosphere. A cigarette burned in his ashtray, the smoke curling around him like armor. He didn't look up.

"May I come in, Sir?"

"Come in," he said curtly.

I stood waiting. He didn't offer me a seat.

"What brings you here?" he asked while flicking ash into a tray.

"Mr. Chetri asked me to meet you."

"What did he say?"

"That I've been selected for a temporary role."

"Welcome to the battleground of sales," he muttered.

"What salary did he promise?"

"₹8000, with allowances."

"Too much for a fresher. Should've been ₹5000," he said, shaking his head.

"Will there be an offer letter?" I ventured.

"No need. You're a temporary lead generator. Report to Mr. Prakash Roy. He'll handle your leads. For each successful sale, you'll get ₹1000 as an incentive, in addition to your pay."

"Understood, sir."

"Start in the field tomorrow. Training will follow. Here's Prakash's number. Now go."

I left without another word.

Back downstairs, the rain had eased. The sound of cars hummed outside, and golden slants of evening sun pierced the glass walls.

Isha approached again, her voice breaking through the haze. "How was your interview?"

"Good. Mr. Chetri was very kind," I replied.

"He's the best boss anyone could ask for," she beamed.

"Could you share Mr. Prakash Roy's contact details?"

She noted them down for me.

"How is he to work with?" I asked.

"Not bad—helpful. You'll learn a lot."

Her words were simple, but the warmth in her tone lingered as I stepped away. The mingling scent of damp earth and petrol hung in the air, but it was her voice I carried home.

By 10 p.m., I returned home with groceries—sugar-free sweets included, in celebration of the job. My diabetic mother greeted me with joy.

Over dinner, we talked about the people I met, the challenges ahead, and the hope that shimmered between us like a shared secret.

Some might scoff at a sales job with an ₹8000 salary.

But for me, it felt no less significant than cracking a government exam. It was a start—not just of a career, but of something deeper. A new chapter, written with resolve.

CHAPTER 5

# *Walking on Worn Soles*

On July 22, 2014, I was drained after being scolded by my boss, Mr. S. K. Aggarwal. During training, we had been taught to win trust, not just sales—to reach Mission 51% through genuine connections. I remembered what Vikram Singh once said:

"When you show real empathy—celebrating their joy or sharing their grief—you build relationships that last."

But Mr. Aggarwal never believed in such things. His style was harsh, proud. Even if I started work before dawn, he'd still mark me absent. Feeling defeated, I went to the park to clear my mind.

We treated our product—the Turbo Cheetah Truck—like a plain but beloved son. It had strengths but many flaws: cracked chassis, poor mileage, and high maintenance. Rana Motors held only a 20% share, yet the target was 51%—an impossible dream unless we cared for customers beyond the sale. But how could I make Mr. Aggarwal see that?

I lit a cigarette and watched the smoke fade into the monsoon sky. Clouds parted, letting in thin rays of light. I sat quietly, letting the weather soothe me.

April 3, 2013—my first day in the field. I called Mr. Prakash Roy, the senior executive from Jalpaiguri. I got his number from Isha. When I called at 8 a.m., he sounded half-asleep.

"Hello?"

"Good morning, I'm Arjun," I said.

"Who?"

"I've been appointed by Mr. Aggarwal for the Jalpaiguri district."

He paused, then replied, "Meet me at 10 a.m. at the Jalpaiguri pickup stand."

After breakfast, I left Maynaguri and reached Jalpaiguri by ten. I called, but he didn't answer. By the fourth try, his phone was off. Frustrated, I waited till 11:30, then called Isha.

"Isha, I've been waiting over an hour."

She laughed. "That's Prakash for you—never on time. But don't worry, he'll come."

I sipped tea at a nearby stall, questioning my decision to join this job. At 11:50, Prakash finally called:

"Where are you? I'm coming."

At 12:15, he arrived on a motorbike—a stocky man in a tight polo shirt, jeans stretched over his belly. He handed me brochures, price lists, and schemes. "Meet customers, explain the vehicle," he said.

Before I could ask more, three drivers approached. Prakash slipped on his sunglasses, started his bike, and said, "Arjun, do what I said. Report by evening." Then he vanished in a trail of dust.

The drivers surrounded me.

"Where's Prakash?" one asked sharply.

Before I could reply, another said, "That cheat ran away."

A third glared. "You from Darjeeling Auto Works?"

"Yes, I just joined."

"I'm Panchu. Three of our trucks have cracked chassis. Prakash promised replacements. Nothing's happened."

"If he doesn't fix it, we'll tie him up tomorrow," another threatened.

I called Prakash in panic. He replied coolly, "You're new. Ignore them. Move to another market."

I followed his advice, visiting three more stands, but found nothing. I returned home defeated.

Mom asked, "How was your first day?"

"Good," I said. She probably thought I worked in an office, like my father. But the truth felt heavier. Still, I had to make this work—for my future.

The next day, I went to the Dhupguri market. Heat pressed down, engines roared, horns blared. Sweat stung my eyes. At the truck stand, a few small vehicles waited for renters. Across the road stood the heavy-load trucks.

To steady my nerves, I ordered a tea. Then I approached Mr. Shakil Alam.

"Hi, I'm Arjun from Darjeeling Auto Works."

"Which company?"

"Rana Motors' dealership."

"You new in sales?"

"Yes."

"I don't need a vehicle," he said flatly.

I moved to another driver, Debu, sitting in his truck, listening to music.

"Brother, I've been waiting three days. No work. Can't pay my EMI. Sorry, not buying."

His words stayed with me—the weight of their struggle matched mine. I met five more drivers. None were interested.

Prakash had said the stands were full of leads. All I found was uncertainty.

I reached the side of a truck parked beneath a large tree. A group of drivers and owners was huddled together on the load body, playing cards. I approached with a polite smile.

"Hello, I'm from Darjeeling Auto Works, the authorized dealership of Rana Motors."

The five men paused, eyes shifting toward me. One of them squinted.

"New sales executive?"

"Yes," I replied, trying to keep my tone upbeat. "I joined this month."

Another, in a curious but wary tone, asked, "Where are you from?"

"Maynaguri," I said, expecting a warmer response. But the atmosphere stiffened. The heat of the summer suddenly mirrored the mood.

One man threw down his cards and barked, "That guy Prakash came like you and sold me a Turbo Cheetah Truck. Within five months, the engine broke down. Still waiting for a replacement. Where is he now, hiding?"

I took out my diary and pen with shaking hands, trying to stay composed. "Sir, I'm noting down your complaint. I'll inform my senior manager—"

"Manager? That arrogant Aggarwal?" another interrupted. "He won't lift a finger for us."

Another driver snapped, "Don't waste our time, man. We're not getting any hires today, and now you come to sell us more problems?"

Embarrassed and disheartened, I quietly walked away from the Dhupguri market.

On the bus ride home, my thoughts spiraled. I had just started this job, and already the ground felt like it was crumbling beneath me. My salary was commission-based—no sales meant no pay. I needed to sell four vehicles this month to earn anything. But how could I sell a product that customers already hated?

At home, my mother greeted me with a gentle smile, thinking I'd spent the day in an office like my father once did. She had made snacks and tea, just like she used to for him. Her pride in me stung.

"How was your day, Arjun?" she asked warmly.

I forced a smile. "Good, Ma. The office environment is nice. Colleagues and bosses are supportive."

She beamed. "I know one day you'll become a big officer."

Her innocent faith deepened my guilt. I turned on the television and kept switching channels, trying to mute the noise inside my head.

At 8 PM, Prakash called.

"Hi Arjun, how was your day?"

"Good," I replied, hesitating.

"How many leads today?" he asked.

"Leads?"

"Customers who might buy—those are leads," he clarified.

"Didn't find a single one."

"What's the issue? I sell four to five vehicles a month in that market," he said.

"The market's dead against the Turbo Cheetah. They've had bad experiences. It's tough to convince anyone."

Prakash didn't respond with empathy. His voice turned stern. "I don't care. Tomorrow, I want two *hot* leads—customers ready to buy this month." Then he hung up.

His tone shook me more than his words.

The next morning, I got up early. My shoes, old and cracked at the sole, had already been repaired twice in just ten days. The wear and tear told their own story—of endless walking for insurance business, of markets entered and exited, of rejection after rejection. Yet, they remained my only armor.

I reached the Jalpaiguri pickup stand by 8:30 AM. Around thirty market load operators were waiting for hires. The stand secretary was managing the queue, his voice sharp and commanding.

I greeted him, "Good morning, sir."

He barely looked at me. "Who are you?"

"I'm from Darjeeling Auto Works…"

Before I could finish, his face hardened. "Your Turbo Cheetah? It's making our lives miserable. Get out of here before someone loses their temper."

Fear swept through me. I stepped aside quickly. At that moment, my phone rang. Mr. S.P. Aggarwal.

I picked up. His voice was already cold. "Where are you?"

"In Jalpaiguri, sir."

He scoffed. "Still at home?"

"No, sir, I'm at the truck stand."

"What are you doing there? Gossiping?"

"No, sir. I'm visiting customers."

"How many customers have you met?"

"About ten, sir."

"And how many hot leads?"

I hesitated. "None so far. Most customers aren't happy with our truck."

There was silence—then the storm.

"If everyone's unhappy, how do we sell 30 units a month? You're just another useless hire! If people are unhappy, fix it. I want three sales this month. And after ten days, bring all your visit details to my office."

Click.

The line went dead.

I stood there, under the same tree, drenched in sweat. But this time, it wasn't just the heat. It was stress, self-doubt, and the sting of humiliation trickling down my cheeks like sweat.

With no training, no support, and unrealistic expectations, I felt abandoned. My shoes scraped the gravel as I turned to leave—another market, another desperate hunt. In ten days, I had met almost 300 customers. Almost all of them were either uninterested or postponing their plans. I kept walking.

Every day, my shoes aged. Every day, I aged.

And every night, I feared I might not get paid. That my mother's smile would fade. That my dignity would dissolve under the weight of unmet targets.

And still, the next morning, I laced up those worn-out shoes.

And kept walking.

After ten long days in the field, I returned to the Siliguri showroom with Prakash for our performance review. Mr. S. K. Aggarwal was seated behind his desk, cigarette smoke curling around him like a judge's gavel ready to fall.

He glanced at Prakash first.

"Prakash, how many sales have you made from Arjun's leads?"

Without hesitation, Prakash replied smoothly, "Sir, there's no strength in those 300 leads. No customer was willing to purchase this month."

It was a clean lie, delivered without blinking. He hadn't even checked. For the first time, I witnessed how some people survive reviews—not with truth, but with practiced deception. I knew Prakash well. He was hardly sincere in his work. His reputation in the market was anything but respectable.

Mr. Aggarwal's glare now shifted to me.

"Arjun, you were hired on a three-month probation. If you fail to sell nine vehicles during this time, we won't be able to keep you permanently."

It sounded harsh—almost like a threat—but he wasn't wrong. The terms had been clearly stated in the job advertisement. Crushing the remainder of his cigarette into the ashtray, he exhaled a sharp breath of smoke and stared at me.

"What will you do now?"

I steadied the fear crawling up my spine and replied, "Sir, I will sell. But I need proper training to understand the vehicle and the sales process."

Turning to Prakash, he asked, "You haven't trained him?"

Prakash, ever the seasoned player, replied casually, "Yes, sir I've already given him two days of training and provided all the sales documents."

I knew exactly what that meant—two brochures and a price list. That was his version of training. No product knowledge, no understanding of the industry, no guidance. Everything I had learned about selling came from my previous boss in the life insurance sector, not from this dealership.

Mr. Aggarwal lit another cigarette, his tone now sharper.

"Why are you saying you haven't received training? Don't give excuses, Arjun. I don't care about anything else—I need three Turbo Cheetah Truck sales this month. Or your salary will be on hold."

The words hit me like cold steel. A knot tightened in my stomach, but I managed to reply with a dry throat, "I'll try my best, sir."

As I turned to leave the showroom, Isha called from the reception desk.

Her voice, soft and honeyed, floated through the air and touched something aching inside me. I walked toward her, pulled by the gentleness in her smile. The ceiling fan hummed above her head, stirring her hair in light, hypnotic waves. Her forelock swayed slightly, brushing against her forehead. She looked at me with concern.

"Upset?" she asked gently.

"Why?" I responded, surprised.

She tilted her head slightly and pointed to Mr. Aggarwal's cabin. "Most people walk out of that chamber like that."

Then she laughed. The sound of her laughter spilled like sunlight breaking through clouds—it was warmth I hadn't felt in days.

I stepped closer to her desk. A faint scent of jasmine lingered in the air—perhaps from her. Her face, almost angelic, seemed to glow softly in the showroom light. She stood up slightly and said, "Don't worry, Arjun. That chamber is the hottest zone in our dealership. Everyone comes out burned."

She smiled again, the kind that made burdens momentarily lighter.

Then, with a glance over my shoulder, she whispered, "Go now. Otherwise, he'll start reviewing us, too."

She was trying to save me—not just from the boss's wrath, but from drowning completely in my despair. Despite the pull I felt toward her, I had to leave.

The next seven days were a blur of desperation. I combed through the markets, knocking on every door, visiting every transport stand, meeting every driver, every truck owner, every trader. I needed a sale—no, I needed salvation.

My brown skin darkened under the unforgiving sun. I lost five kilos. Meals became an afterthought. Sleep shrank to four restless hours a night. The only thing circling in my head was how to keep my job, how to earn my salary.

At home, my mother noticed.

"Arjun, what's going on? You look exhausted. Is everything okay?"

I didn't want to worry her. "Just work, Ma. New job, a bit of pressure."

"Take care of your health," she said, and went back to her chores.

I tried watching TV, flipping through the channels. But the noise couldn't drown out the storm in my head. Next month's grocery bill haunted me. The unpaid electricity bill loomed. My world was slowly caving in under pressure.

Yet, in all that chaos, flashes of Isha's smile kept returning—like unexpected rain on scorched earth, a memory that gave my burning mind brief shelter.

The next day, as usual, I was wandering through the rural market, meeting one person after another. My shirt clung to me with sweat, my steps heavy with exhaustion. Suddenly, an acquaintance stopped me and asked, with a smirk on his face:

"Why are you roaming around like a beggar?"

The words struck me deep in the heart.
*Do I really look like a beggar?*
*What would my mother think if she saw me like this?*

In the blink of an eye, a dozen questions raced through my mind. I was still staring at him when he repeated himself:

"What happened? Why are you roaming about like a beggar here?"

Trying to gather my composure, I answered with pride, "Actually, I'm from Darjeeling Auto Works, the authorized dealership of Rana Motors."

But he showed no sign of respect. He simply spat his paan and betel on the ground, revved his bike, and sped off without another word.

The ignorance stung more than the heat of the sun.

At 2:30 PM, my phone rang. The name flashing on the screen felt like a cool splash of water on my burnt-out body and mind. It was Isha—the only one, after my mother, who truly cared for me.

"Arjun, have you had your lunch?" she asked, her voice soft and concerned.

I hadn't eaten anything, but I forced a smile and lied, "Yes, Isha. I've had my lunch."

"Have you?" I asked in return.

"Yes, Arjun, I have," she replied gently.

Then she asked, "Any hot leads for the month?"

I sighed. "No. Not a single customer wants to buy. The month is ending, and Aggarwal keeps warning me that I won't be paid if I don't meet my target."

My frustration must have been obvious. She tried to soothe me.

"Be patient, Arjun. You'll see results soon. Just stay strong."

Then she changed the topic. "By the way, Mr. Vikram Singh, the territory manager from Rana Motors, is visiting our dealership on the 3rd of May. There's going to be a training session for all the sales executives—new and old. Mr. Rakesh Chetri will be joining too."

Curious, I asked, "Why is this a special training?"

She replied casually, "I don't know. They were talking about something called 'Mission 51%.'"

"Mission 51%? What's that?" I asked, intrigued.

"Maybe some new project," she guessed, but she didn't seem sure.

She ended the call, and I sank back into my frustration. Not a single lead. Not one potential buyer. My only tools were the vehicle brochure and a laminated price list. Still, I was pouring everything I had into the field, hoping to find my diamond in the dust.

By 4 PM, I was sitting on a cement bench under a tree, exhausted, reviewing the last month of effort. I had worked hard—no doubt about that. But something was missing. I needed to find that missing piece.

Across the street was a cigarette shop. I walked over and asked for one.

The shopkeeper handed me a fancy cigarette worth ₹30—perhaps thinking I was a corporate executive. I shook my head. "Give me the cheapest one, please. ₹5."

Like every smoker, I knew cigarettes were poison. But today, I needed one poison to kill another. The stress was unbearable.

Sitting on that rough bench, puff after puff, I felt a little lighter. My mind began to open up. Ideas started forming. Maybe there was a way forward.

Then at 4:30 PM, my phone rang again. I crushed the cigarette in a hurry. It was Mr. S. K. Aggarwal. His name alone tightened the stress in my chest.

"Good evening, Sir," I said, trying to sound alert.

"What are you doing?" he asked, his voice thick with sarcasm.

"I'm in the market, visiting customers," I replied, trying to defend myself.

He laughed—mocking, cold.

"You've been roaming the market for 25 days. How many vehicles have you sold?"

His question was a knife. But he didn't stop there.

"I told you on the first day—you're not fit for this job. And now I know I made a mistake hiring you."

I swallowed my pride and replied, "Sir, I've visited nearly 400 prospects. But none have shown interest. Most say they're not looking to buy right now."

He snapped, "If that's true, then how are we selling over 30 Turbo Cheetahs every month? Who's buying those?"

It was harsh—but not entirely wrong.

With my voice low, I admitted, "Sir, I don't know how to find the right customers. Please guide me."

"Move!" he barked. "Move in the market! You're not moving enough. You're not selling because you're not moving!"

That was his only form of training—yelling at me to move.

"Yes, Sir. I'll move more," I said, defeated but determined.

He paused, then added, "Anyway You have to attend two days of training in the Siliguri showroom. You must attend the training on time along with all data. And remember, if you do not meet this month's target, you will not get your salary."

Depressed and frustrated, I dug into my pocket, searching for a five-rupee coin—just enough to buy my next cigarette. My fingers wrapped around the last coin I had. I pulled it out, handed it to the shopkeeper, and lit the cigarette.

Two puffs in, and the sky had already dimmed. Evening had arrived. But my thoughts weren't on the fading light. I was still consumed by a single worry: where would I find my next prospect?

Then it struck me—this was the right time. In rural areas, evening meant people came out to the market, finished with the day's labor, ready to relax, shop, and talk. The marketplace was starting to buzz. People were buying groceries, sipping tea, and chatting in small groups.

I decided to use this crowd to my advantage. Somewhere among them, perhaps, was the customer who could make my month—who could secure my salary and give me a lifeline.

I walked through the chaos, trying to engage one person after another, pitching our product with whatever confidence I could gather. My voice had to compete with the murmur of the crowd, the vendors calling out prices, the clatter of utensils from roadside stalls.

Just then, my phone rang. I fished it out and answered the call, stepping aside into a quieter corner.

"Good evening, Prakash," I said, trying to sound composed.

"Where are you?" he asked.

"In the market. Just trying my luck," I replied.

"Don't stress so much, Arjun," he said. "Go home and get some rest."

For someone I'd always thought of as rough around the edges and negative in nature, Prakash's voice carried an unexpected warmth. It felt like someone had cracked open a door to let in a little comfort.

"What else can I do, Prakash? It's already the 25th. I haven't made my sales target. Mr. Aggarwal called me an hour ago—he said if I don't close a deal soon, I won't get my salary."

I couldn't hold back anymore. The frustration poured out of me. The pressure was overwhelming, and in that moment, I needed someone to just listen.

Prakash was silent for a second. Then he said, calmly, "Take it easy, Arjun. This is what sales is like. It's stressful. But it gets better after a while. You'll get used to it."

"But how do I manage my family expenses if I don't get paid?" I asked, my voice faltering. "This job was all about the salary. That's why I joined."

I was being raw, honest—laying my fears bare.

There was a pause. Then came words I didn't expect.

"Don't worry," Prakash said. "I'll give you one sale from my side."

I was stunned. For a moment, I thought I had misheard him.

"You'll... give me a sale?"

He chuckled. "Yes, man. It's okay. You've helped me before with leads. Now it's my turn."

I didn't know what to say. I had judged him too quickly, written him off. And yet here he was, reaching out when I needed it most.

"Thank you, Prakash," I said, my voice thick with emotion. "Really. I didn't expect this from you."

"It's no big deal, buddy. I know you'll be killing it in a few months. And then, you'll return the favor," he laughed.

"And don't miss the training on the 3rd of May. It's important for all of us. Might just change how we look at sales."

With that, he ended the call.

I stood there for a while, holding the phone, letting his words settle. Amid the noise of the market, something inside me felt quieter. Lighter. I had found a little hope—in the most unexpected place, from the most unexpected person.

CHAPTER 6

# Filling the Blind Spots

On the morning of May 3rd, 2013, I arrived at the Siliguri office long before the city had fully stirred. The air carried a nervous stillness, as if the day itself held its breath. Anticipation coiled inside me, quiet but alive. I had no idea what lay ahead—only a name circled in my thoughts: *Mission 51%.*

Isha was already there.

She sat at the reception, her eyes lifting as I entered. That smile—gentle, knowing—met me like sunlight breaking through morning fog. When I approached, she rose, her presence calm and unhurried, and welcomed me with a grace that felt almost unreal. A strange warmth bloomed inside me, wordless and sudden, as if some forgotten part of me recognized her.

With professional poise and personal ease, she began the introductions.

"Arjun, come, meet the team," she said, leading me into the office. "This is Bikash Lohar—he handles the Darjeeling territory."

Bikash, lean and fair, nodded with a warm smile. "Welcome, Arjun."

"And this is Partha Banerjee—he's our Siliguri lead. And Rahman from Malda. Both kings in their zones." She grinned.

They welcomed me with courteous nods. But when she introduced Raju Roy from Coochbehar, something shifted. His eyes lingered on me a second too long. He smiled, but it was measured—a smile laced with questions I hadn't asked yet.

We made small talk, but there was a tremor beneath the surface. Everyone seemed distracted. The air around us wasn't just about new beginnings—it was thick with unspoken concerns.

Soon, I understood why.

The conversation, scattered and strained, kept circling back to two things: the erratic temperament of Mr. S. K. Aggarwal and the unresolved issues with the Turbo Cheetah Truck. The team felt cornered, unsupported—left to defend a product without the tools to do so.

At 9 a.m., Mr. Rakesh Chetri appeared at the entrance. "Let's move to the conference room," he instructed. We stood, gathered our files, and followed.

Behind us, footsteps echoed—a deliberate, dragging rhythm. Mr. Aggarwal was coming. Laptop in hand, face unreadable, he followed like a man herding reluctant cattle.

On the first floor, we entered a large conference room—the largest I'd ever seen in a dealership. One by one, we took our seats. The air buzzed with curiosity and anxiety. What *was* Mission 51%?

Mr. Chetri remained focused on his laptop, likely preparing a report for the managing director. At 9:15, Mr. Aggarwal stood. His presence filled the room—tall, seasoned, exuding authority laced with fatigue.

He began.

"Good morning, team," he said, voice low and heavy. "This training is not just routine. It's a mission. A long-pending target. Yes, the market is difficult. Yes, our product faces challenges. But that's no excuse. We fight back."

A pause. Then—

"You've all heard of Mission 51%. Mr. Vikram Singh from Rana Motors will take you through it in detail."

Just then, a knock on the door broke the flow. Prakash stood at the threshold, disheveled, breathing hard. Red streaks of paan and betel juice lined his lips. His shirt clung to his back. He looked like someone who had just sprinted through a monsoon.

"May I come in, sir?" he asked, panting.

Mr. Aggarwal turned slowly. His professional mask fell, revealing the man beneath—sharp-edged, unforgiving. His lips curled back like an animal baring its teeth.

"It's 9:25. You're *twenty-five minutes late*, Prakash. When will you take your job seriously?"

Prakash lowered his gaze. "Sorry, sir. It won't happen again."

Aggarwal opened his mouth to continue the scolding, but Mr. Chetri interjected, calm but firm. "Mr. Aggarwal, let him in. Let's continue."

Prakash slipped in and took the seat beside me. A strong scent—part perfume, part sweat—rose off him. I leaned away slightly. Isha, noticing, silently switched on the AC. Cold air flowed in, and I exhaled, thankful.

Mr. Aggarwal resumed.

"Our General Manager, Mr. Rakesh Chetri, will lead the marketing session. Mr. Atunu Chakrabarty, along with Selim Khan from Rana Motors, will cover service operations. I will begin with auto basics."

Bikash, ever curious, raised a hand. "Sir, what exactly are auto basics?"

Aggarwal's eyes narrowed.

"Two years in the industry, and you still ask that?" His voice was calm, but it struck like a whip. "Basic automobile engineering, Bikash."

He turned to the projector and connected it to his laptop. "Isha, change the slides," he instructed.

As the presentation began, something shifted. The gruff manager became a teacher. His voice, once harsh, now carried authority rooted in experience. He spoke of combustion cycles, torque ratios, chassis layouts—as someone who had lived those machines from the inside out.

For fifteen years, he had worked in the belly of the industry. Manufacturing plants. Assembly lines. Blueprints and bolts.

And now, in this quiet room, he shared that world with us—one slide at a time.

GM Rakesh Chetri sat in the back of the room, holding a steaming cup of tea while tapping on his laptop with quiet intensity. At the front, Mr. S. K. Aggarwal, with a habitual tug on his loose white trousers and an adjustment of his thick glasses, signaled the beginning.

His voice, rough yet commanding, sliced through the conference room. "Alright, team. Let's begin. Today, we're covering the fundamentals of auto basics. If you grasp this well, even your most technical customers won't be able to confuse you."

Before the seriousness could fully settle in, Partha—grinning as if he were in on a private joke—interjected with an air of practiced charm.

"Sir, sometimes customers ask things I don't quite know. But I've got a method—just nod wisely and say, 'Excellent query, sir!'"

A ripple of laughter ran through the room, a welcome release from the stiffness. But Mr. Aggarwal wasn't amused. His eyes narrowed, scanning the room before landing on Rakesh Chetri, who raised a calming hand.

"Partha," Chetri said with a mock-serious tone, "if nodding sold vehicles, we'd be running a bobblehead factory."

The laughter doubled, but beneath it, I sensed a subtle shift. The room fell quiet again. A reminder: this was still a performance review in disguise.

I reflected on my own induction. Prakash, my mentor, had taught me little beyond pricing sheets and color options. And Mr. Aggarwal—he might have the degrees and years, but his leadership was mechanistic, like a gearbox stuck in second. His entire sales pitch to the team was simple: 'Keep moving, boys. You should be seen in the market, not in the office.'

Aggarwal resumed, turning to Bikash. "Tell me—what is engine combustion?"

Bikash, ever straightforward, responded. "Sir, when the engine burns fuel and moves the car forward."

Aggarwal raised an eyebrow. "So if I burn my toast, my kitchen should start rolling down the highway?"

Laughter again—quick, restrained.

Rahman, who held a diploma in automobile engineering, chimed in, rescuing the moment. "Sir, combustion is when air and fuel mix inside the cylinder, ignite, and generate power to move the engine."

Aggarwal nodded. "Good. Now, who can explain mileage?"

I sat straighter, eager. "Mileage is the distance a vehicle travels per litre of fuel. If a car gives 20 kmpl, it can cover 20 kilometers on a litre."

Before my words could even land, Prakash leaned forward. "Then my bicycle has the best mileage. Zero fuel, unlimited range!"

Isha turned, her voice a playful dagger. "By that logic, walking wins. Infinite mileage, no traffic jams."

The room cracked up again. But Mr. Aggarwal snapped back to his original frown. "Enough."

Just then, Heeru Da entered, carrying a tray of tea and biscuits. He moved around the room with quiet reverence, placing cups gently.

When he reached Prakash, a hushed exchange followed:

"What's for lunch today?" Prakash whispered.

"Chicken," Heeru Da replied in a dry whisper.

"Free?"

"Yes."

The knowledge of a warm chicken curry lunch did more to lift the room's spirit than any motivational quote could have. I made a mental note: small comforts mattered.

Post tea-break, Aggarwal resumed, lifting his glasses again. "Now let's talk about torque. Partha, define torque for us."

Partha, ever unserious, said, "Torque is the power to push through traffic while I honk endlessly."

Chetri sighed. "If honking gave torque, every auto-rickshaw would be a Ferrari."

Partha's grin faded. He shrank into his chair. Prakash, however, leaned in, his voice steadier now. "Torque is the rotational force that helps the vehicle move, especially under load or uphill."

Aggarwal nodded. "Correct. And payload?"

I jumped in. "Payload is the maximum weight a vehicle can safely carry — passengers plus cargo — over and above its own empty weight."

Aggarwal looked up, a faint smile breaking the stern lines of his face. "Good. Prakash and Arjun—well done. Arjun, as a newcomer, your learning curve is impressive."

I felt something unfamiliar stir in me—pride.

The laughter, the lessons, even the teasing had all led to this moment: a nod of approval, the first glimmer that I belonged.

After that Mr Aggawal thoroughly explained about torque and Payload.

In the meantime, Mr. Vikram Singh entered the conference room. His face was sweaty from the summer heat, but he greeted everyone with a warm, "Good afternoon."

Noticing the discomfort, Isha quietly reduced the AC temperature to cool the room. The presentation slide changed to the next topic: **vehicle suspension**.

A subtle yet captivating fragrance from Vikram Singh's perfume filled the air, leaving a quiet impression. He pulled out his laptop from his bag, a faint smile appearing beneath his well-groomed beard. Looking at Rakesh Chetri, he said, "My flight was delayed. Sorry, Rakes!"

"It's alright, Vikram. Please, have a seat," Rakesh replied courteously.

Standing tall at 6'2", the Territory Manager from Rana Motors had impressed me from day one. With his calm and professional demeanor, he turned to Mr. S. K. Aggarwal and said politely, "Please go ahead with the training."

"Sure, Vikram," Mr. Aggarwal replied with a smile. "Now, let's talk about suspension. What does it do?"

There was a short silence until Bikash, ever straightforward, said, "Sir, it's what keeps our backs from turning into jelly on bad roads!"

Everyone laughed. Mr. Aggarwal nodded in amusement. "Not wrong! Suspension absorbs shocks and keeps the vehicle stable. Now, what are the types of suspension?"

He moved between questions and explanations with ease, making the session lively. I had to admit—his style made auto basics feel interesting.

Rahman, our technical expert, replied confidently, “Sir, there’s independent suspension, where each wheel moves separately, and rigid suspension, where the movement of one wheel affects the others.”

“Correct,” said Mr. Aggarwal. “SUVs are usually built with stronger suspension systems for rough terrain, while sedans focus more on comfort.”

He paused to sip water. As he did, Vikram Singh turned to us.

“How’s the training going, guys?”

“Good, sir,” said Bikash simply.

Vikram nodded. “We arranged this training after noticing a few knowledge gaps. Hopefully, it’ll help you handle the market better.”

Mr. Aggarwal cleared his throat and resumed. Before explaining anything new, he always started with a question. It kept us alert.

Then his eyes settled on me.

“What is the chassis, Arjun?”

Thankfully, I had looked this up recently. “Sir, it’s like the skeleton of the vehicle. Everything is built on it.”

He smiled. “Good. And what’s a wheelbase?”

Prakash answered this time. “Sir, it’s the distance between the centers of the front and rear wheels. A longer wheelbase means more stability. A shorter one makes the vehicle easier to turn.”

Rakesh Chetri looked pleased. “Exactly, Prakash. That’s why buses have long wheelbases, and rickshaws can turn in a small space.”

Mr. Aggarwal then explained various types of suspension systems—independent, non-independent, MacPherson Strut, Double Wishbone, Multi-Link, Solid Axle, Leaf Spring, Torsion Beam. His deep knowledge truly impressed us.

Still, the past month in the field had left me with real concerns. I raised my hand.

"Sir, why does the chassis crack in our Turbo Cheetah vehicle?"

Mr. Aggarwal hesitated and tried to shift the topic. "Our service manager will address these issues in his session."

But Vikram Singh interrupted gently. "Mr. Aggarwal, please answer his question."

"Okay, Mr. Vikram. I will," he replied.

Turning to me, he explained, "Arjun, yes, the Turbo Cheetah truck has been facing chassis crack issues. But most of the time, it's because of overloading. The vehicle is designed for a payload of 1,200 kg, but many owners carry over three or even four tonnes."

He paused before continuing, "Repeated overloading creates extreme stress on the ladder-frame chassis. That's what causes the cracks."

But **Raju Roy**, the star salesperson from Darjeeling Auto Works, representing the Cooch Behar district, wasn't in a celebratory mood despite his top sales record for the Turbo Cheetah Truck. The very success that earned him accolades had now become his burden. With rising customer complaints and recurring product issues, he was struggling. In some parts of his assigned territory, things had escalated so badly that he faced physical intimidation—assaulted by angry customers and frustrated drivers.

Raju stood up, his voice steady but laced with frustration. He asked the kind of question most managers dread.

**"If overloading is the issue, then why aren't the chassis of competitor vehicles cracking? They carry the same loads."**

The room fell into an uneasy silence.

Even Mr. Vikram Singh, representing Rana Motors, had no immediate answer. The truth hung heavy in the air—it was a valid concern. Everyone knew this was a genuine product issue. Attempts had been made to address it, but the problem persisted. The cracks, both literal and metaphorical, were becoming harder to cover.

Mr. Rakesh Chetri stepped in to diffuse the tension.

"Raju," he said calmly, "no matter the product's limitations, it's our job to support our customers and find ways to resolve their issues. That's how trust is built in the long run."

Then, turning to Vikram Singh, he added diplomatically, "Anyway, our service manager will be addressing these matters in detail during his session."

Mr. Vikram Singh nodded and asked all of us to go for lunch.

CHAPTER 7

# Hunters and Cultivators

We rushed to the dealership canteen, driven less by order than hunger. Faces lit up at the sight of food—eager, restless, almost wild. Prakash darted to Heeru Da, plate in hand, forgetting even the small ritual of washing up.

The spread was generous—chicken, rice, and a few humble sides. We ate as if time had stopped. Since it was free, Prakash and Raju went for seconds, reclaiming what life had once denied.

Outside, the sun pressed hard on the concrete roof, sealing the heat inside like a furnace. After lunch, our shirts clung to our backs, and even our handkerchiefs had surrendered.

The bosses dined apart, their laughter drifting from the garden. Mr. Aggarwal, Mr. Vikram Singh, and our ever-smiling GM, Mr. Rakesh Chetri, stood in a loose circle, puffing cigarettes and sharing easy jokes—the quiet brotherhood of men who led from the shade.

Behind the canteen, we—Arjun, Bikash, Prakash, Rahman, Raju, and Partha—found a patch of shadow and stretched our few minutes of freedom.

"That chicken was divine," Prakash said, licking his fingers.

"Too spicy," Raju groaned, fanning his mouth.

Partha chuckled. "Says the man who ate three rounds of rice."

Laughter broke out—a brief, bright escape from the day's weight.

Rahman pulled out his khaini pouch, kneading it in his palm before passing it around. One by one, we took a pinch, sliding it between lip and gum—our quiet ritual. Bikash lit a Wills King.

"Premium stuff," Prakash teased. "Let me have a puff."

"Just one stick," Bikash grinned. "We'll share it like gold."

Then my phone rang.

"Hello, Sir?"

"Arjun, where are you all? Come to the conference room. Now."

It was Mr. Aggarwal—calm, but commanding. The laughter froze. Cigarettes dropped. We wiped our hands and marched back inside.

Back to the Grind

The blast of air-conditioning hit like mercy. The room smelled faintly of tea and detergent, and of bodies that had worked too hard. Mr. Vikram Singh was typing rapidly. Mr. Aggarwal had stepped out. At the front, our GM, Mr. Chetri, adjusted the projector.

"Hope you all enjoyed your lunch?" he said with a smile.

"Yes, Sir!" we answered in unison.

"Good. Let's begin. Marketing and enquiry generation first—then retail finance."

He clicked to the first slide. The afternoon haze still clung to our eyes, but there was no time for drowsiness. The next lesson had begun.

Neat, cheerful, and brimming with energy, Mr. Chetri carried himself with ease. "Alright, team! What does marketing mean in our world?"

I raised my hand. "It's about promoting our trucks and finding leads."

"Good," he nodded. "But it's more than that. Marketing brings the customer to us—enquiry generation keeps them coming."

Bikash leaned forward. "Sir, what are the main sources of enquiries?"

"Walk-ins, cold calls, ATL, BTL, digital—each a thread in the funnel," he said. "Marketing creates interest. Sales converts it."

"What's a sales funnel exactly?" I asked.

"Excellent question, Arjun," he smiled. "That's Mr. Vikram Singh's domain."

Prakash raised his hand. "Sir, do local influencers really help?"

"Absolutely," he said. "Drivers, mechanics, financiers—they're the voices of trust. Build relationships. Respect your brokers. Pay on time. And remember—ethics first. One lie can undo a brand."

Bikash chimed in, "Sir, in this digital age, do brokers still matter as much?"

"Excellent point," Mr. Chetri nodded. "Digital tools are growing fast, but traditional influencers still dominate in rural and small-town markets. The trick is to balance both—use digital outreach without ignoring human relationships."

The AC let out a soft click, prompting a few distracted glances. Unfazed, Mr. Chetri stepped forward, his smile widening.

"Let me simplify it. Sales is like being a hawker. I know what you're thinking—'Sir, we sell trucks, not vegetables!'"

Laughter rippled across the room. Bikash elbowed Prakash. "We'll need a pushcart for Turbo Cheetahs!"

Mr. Chetri chuckled. "Exactly. Hawkers don't wait for customers. They call out, move around, make themselves visible. Their livelihood depends on daily sales. We may not sell daily, but our effort must be daily. Leads are our lifeline."

Rahman nodded thoughtfully. "So we need to keep moving, keep pushing?"

"Exactly!" he clapped. "Sales isn't about luck—it's about consistency."

Walking to the whiteboard, he picked up a marker. "Think of it like this: if you want to close deals at the month's end, you must keep your enquiry flow strong throughout. If that flow stops, your sales stop. Picture a fisherman—can he catch fish if the river dries up?"

Raju replied, "No, sir, no water, no fish."

"Exactly. The river brings the fish; the net catches them. If the river dries, the fisherman returns empty-handed. Leads are your river. Keep it flowing."

Partha wiped his forehead. "So, inquiries are the river; sales are the fish?"

"Right on. You stop enquiries, your pipeline dries up."

Prakash grinned. "Sir, you've got so many analogies. What's next, election campaigns?"

Mr. Chetri laughed. "You guessed it! Think of political candidates—do they stay home and hope for votes? No. They go out, connect with people, and build visibility. Similarly, in market activation, we must show up, be seen, and make an impression."

The AC gave a tired wheeze.

Mr. Chetri smirked. "See? Even the AC knows we're heating things up!"

The room chuckled, but the message had landed. Sales was not about waiting—it was about showing up, again and again, until you win.

As the session drew toward its end, Mr. Chetri's voice softened, carrying the calm of someone speaking from years of scars and success.

"In my experience," he said, "there are two kinds of salespeople—hunters and cultivators. Hunters chase quick deals. Cultivators build relationships. Hunters rise fast and fall faster. Cultivators grow slowly, but their roots hold strong. The best ones? They do both."

The room was heavy with post-lunch fatigue. Partha sat half-slumped, eyes dull from the heat, until the words hunter and cultivator pulled him upright.

"Sir," he asked, rubbing his eyes, "what exactly does that mean?"

A faint smile crossed Mr. Chetri's face. "Good question—and fitting. You're a born hunter."

The room stirred with quiet amusement. Partha tried to smile back, but the comment stung.

I leaned forward. "Sir, could you explain a bit more?"

"When your sales depend on brokers and middlemen," Mr. Chetri said, "that's hunting. You chase deals, rely on others, and sprint from one lead to the next. Some months you fly; others, you crash. That's Partha's pattern—five trucks one month, none the next. Hunters live off the thrill, not the soil."

He clicked to the next slide. "Hunters cold-call, attend expos, push discounts. Always running, never planting. They taste quick success but lose their footing when the tide turns."

Partha's eyes fell to the table. His pride, I sensed, was bruised but thinking.

"Now take Raju," Mr. Chetri continued, turning softer again. "He sells an average of seven vehicles a month—sometimes three, sometimes ten, but never zero. Why? Because he cultivates. He builds trust, revisits old customers, and keeps the ground fertile. Cultivation is slower, but it lasts."

He paused, letting the silence stretch. "The best salespeople hunt to start—but cultivate to endure. If you only hunt, one dry season can ruin you. But if you also cultivate, you'll never run dry. That's not just sales—it's survival."

Something about that line stayed with me. Not just sales—it's survival. The word carried a weight that reached beyond the showroom, into every corner of my own struggle.

Partha nodded faintly, as if the lesson had finally taken root.

By the time Mr. Chetri wrapped up the final slides on lead generation, the light had changed. The sun was low; the air was still heavy. Papers rustled, chairs scraped, yet no one spoke.

He looked toward Mr. Vikram Singh and Mr. Aggarwal. "Shall we start the next session?"

Vikram checked his watch. "Let them go. We'll continue on the business plan."

Mr. Aggarwal didn't look up, already buried in numbers.

"Alright, team," said Mr. Chetri, smiling again. "We'll stop here. Tomorrow, sharp at nine."

Then, with a pointed glance at Prakash: "And no excuses."

The room loosened. I gathered my notepad, still thinking of that single line echoing in my mind—

Hunt to begin. Cultivate to endure.

CHAPTER 8

# When She Walked Beside Me

My colleagues slowly drifted out of the room. Just then, a familiar, lilting voice cut through the fading buzz.

"Arjun!"

I turned instantly. It was Isha.

She was hurrying toward me, the soft evening light casting a golden hue on her face. Dressed in a light office shirt and black trousers, her black-and-brown hair swayed with her movement. Her presence stopped me in my tracks. The dealership's heartthrob—admired by everyone from the office boys to senior managers—was walking straight to me. My pulse quickened.

"Hey, Isha," I said, smiling.

Slightly breathless, she adjusted the strap of her bag. A faint scent of jasmine lingered in the air between us.

I chuckled. "You know, the bus won't wait for me."

She tilted her head playfully. "You've been so serious all day, Arjun. Relax a little. Life's not a sales review."

Falling into step beside me, she asked, "So—how was your training?"

"It was excellent," I replied. "I never expected someone as strict as Mr. Aggarwal to explain auto basics so well."

She laughed. "And Mr. Chetri?"

"That was something else—storytelling, analogies... he made complex ideas seem easy."

She raised an eyebrow, smirking. "Okay, okay, I get it. You *loved* the training."

I laughed. "Maybe I did."

After a pause, she said softly, "Let's walk to the bus stand together. I'll keep you company."

I hesitated for a second—surprised, unsure. Was this a coincidence, or something more? Still, I nodded. Her presence felt effortless, natural.

As we walked, she asked, "What do your parents do?"

"My father passed away. My mother is a homemaker."

"I'm sorry," she said gently.

"Do you have siblings?"

"I'm an only child."

She nodded, thoughtful. "So, you carry your family's full responsibility."

"Yes."

Just then, my bus pulled into view. I turned to her. "My ride's here. See you tomorrow at 9."

"Bye, Arjun," she said, with a smile that lingered longer than her words.

As I climbed aboard, something inside me stirred. Was this just friendly small talk… or the beginning of something different?

Whatever it was, the evening felt changed—and my heart hadn't quite settled.

CHAPTER 9

# Where the Mission Began

The next morning, we reached the training room at nine sharp. Prakash was already there, unusually early. Raju's hair was still damp from his bath, neatly parted. Bikash looked a little swollen around the eyes—either from a restless night or one that went on too long.

Mr. Vikram stood near the screen, arranging his slides with quiet focus. Chetri was on the phone, already managing the day's chaos. Heeru Da moved between desks, his tray of tea and biscuits gliding like clockwork.

Aggarwal Sir hadn't arrived. Punctual to a fault, he was likely still in his chamber, reading through reports as part of his pre-session ritual. The air was cool, even without the AC—filled with the scent of polished wood and new leather. Rana Motors always smelled of ambition.

Then Isha walked in. Calm, self-assured, carrying a hint of jasmine that softened the room. She smiled and took her seat as though the chair had been waiting for her.

At 9:10, Aggarwal entered, and the session began.

"Good morning, team," said Vikram, his voice crisp and measured. "I hope yesterday helped clear some doubts."

"Yes, sir," said Bikash, sitting straighter. "GM Sir's way of explaining marketing through stories—it stayed with me."

Rahman added, "Even in engineering, I didn't learn the basics this clearly. Aggarwal Sir made it easy."

Vikram smiled. "That's why we didn't hire outsiders. Who better than Mr. Chetri and Mr. Aggarwal—men who built this business from the ground up?"

Isha raised her hand slightly. "Sir, one thing—I've been wondering. What exactly is Mission 51%?"

Vikram's eyes lit up. "Good question. Let's begin with that."

Rahman leaned forward. "Does it mean selling fifty-one trucks a month?"

Vikram chuckled. "Not quite."

Partha jumped in, grinning. "Maybe if we hit fifty-one percent of the target, we get full salary?"

Aggarwal snapped, "Yes, Partha. Do fifty-one percent of your job, and I'll give you fifty-one percent of your salary."

Laughter rippled through the room.

Chetri raised a hand, smiling. "Alright, team. Keep the spirit, but let's get serious."

Then Raju spoke, his voice calm and steady. "Sir, is it about converting fifty-one percent of enquiries into sales?"

"Close," said Vikram, reaching for a marker. "But before we reach Mission 51%, you must know one thing—what is TIV?"

Partha frowned, adjusting his spectacles. "Sir... Test-drive Is Vital?"

The room fell silent. Chetri stepped in kindly. "TIV stands for Total Industry Volume." He saved the moment, sparing the team from further embarrassment.

"Thanks, Rakesh," said Vikram. On the board, he drew a large circle and divided it into five parts.

"This is the market," he said. "Each slice represents a competitor's monthly average."

He turned to Aggarwal. "Sir, what's the Turbo Cheetah's monthly average?"

Aggarwal hesitated, fingers fumbling on his laptop. Vikram smiled lightly. "No issue, sir. I have it here—thirty units a month."

He paused, scanning the room. "And our competitors?"

No one spoke. The silence was heavy, awkward.

Aggarwal, sensing it, turned on the team—scolding them sharply, trying to hide his own lapse. The act was too transparent.

Chetri watched quietly, the truth plain to him: when a manager stops watching the market, the team stops seeing it too.

Vikram didn't intervene. He simply turned back to his laptop, calm and unbothered. A moment later, he rose, uncapped his marker, and began sketching quick figures on the whiteboard.

"Here's the latest road tax data for small trucks in your territory," he began. "Total Industry Volume—TIV—is 150 vehicles a month."

He underlined the number and went on,

"Tejas Automotive leads with 83 units—55% share. Turbo Cheetah follows with 30 units, 20%. Load Max sells 18, that's 12%. Raftar Motors 11, and StormX 8—together making up the rest."

He stepped back. The silence felt heavier than the math. Only pens scratching, a few deep breaths.

Chetri leaned forward, face tight. Aggarwal looked tense, knowing the storm to come. Heeru Da entered softly with tea. The faint aroma of Darjeeling floated through the air—comfort trying to enter a room that refused it.

When the cups were cleared, Vikram spoke again.

"Now, the real question—what is Mission 51%?"

"Yes, sir, we're waiting," Isha said, leaning forward. We all were.

"Tejas holds 55% of this market—83 vehicles a month," Vikram said. "Strong bottom line, strong brand."

Bikash raised a hand. "Sir, what does bottom line mean?"

"Net profit," Vikram said simply. "What remains after every expense."

He turned to Chetri. "If Tejas earns from 83, what are we earning from 30?"

Chetri hesitated, then answered quietly, "Vikram, we haven't broken even yet."

I asked, "Sir, what is break-even?"

Chetri smiled. "It's the point where our revenue equals our cost. No gain, no loss."

Just then, the door opened. Mr. Sanjay Mittal, Managing Director of Darjeeling Auto Works, entered. We stood. His presence changed the air.

"Mission 51%, is it?" he asked.

"Yes, sir," Vikram replied. "If we capture 51% of the small truck segment, your dealership turns profitable."

Mittal leaned back. "Go on."

"Right now, as Rakesh said, you're below break-even. That must change fast."

Mittal interrupted, voice sharp. "Vikram, I checked the books yesterday. Turbo Cheetah is bleeding us. Thirty units can't sustain the dealership. Add service complaints and customer payouts—it's a drain."

Chetri stayed silent. The truth didn't need a defense.

Vikram stepped in. "I understand, sir. But this mission will turn that around."

Mittal nodded. "Proceed."

Vikram pointed at the board. "To reach 51%, we'll phase it—45 per month in Quarter 1, 60 per month in Quarter 2, and 77 per month by year-end. That's our goal—Mission 51%."

He capped the marker. The sound clicked through the silence.

Aggarwal spoke, hesitant but defiant. "Sir, that's too high. With our manpower and product issues—it's impossible."

Mittal snapped, "No excuses, Aggarwal. We sell—and make profit."

Vikram's tone stayed calm. "We must respect the product we represent. The company invests crores and gives us its best. Flaws will come—that's why service exists. That's how we stand by what we sell."

Mittal leaned forward. "Exactly. Once a product launches, there's no retreat. We sell, and service closes the gaps."

Vikram met his gaze. "A salesman doesn't choose his battlefield. Even if it's selling refrigerators in Antarctica—we find a way."

Mittal's palm hit the table. "Exactly!"

The sound cracked through the room. Heads turned. All eyes fell on Aggarwal.

A bead of sweat slid down his temple. His jaw tightened, his eyes restless. The humiliation was sharp and public—his doubts about the product laid bare before his own team.

"What's the current productivity per sales executive?" Vikram asked.

Aggarwal hesitated.

Rakesh replied, "About five units per person per month."

"Thank you." Vikram wrote on the board:

Productivity = 5

"To reach 77 units, you'll need 15 sales executives."

Mittal leaned forward, uneasy. "No new hiring, please. We're already in losses—and new recruits aren't a guarantee."

Aggarwal added, "Finding good manpower is tough in this trade."

Chetri, ever the bridge between calm and crisis, offered a middle path.

"If Rana Motors shares the cost—say fifty-fifty—we can consider hiring."

Vikram smiled. "Fair enough, Rakesh. I'll try to get that support."

Mittal nodded. "If Rana agrees, we'll move ahead."

"Then," Vikram said, "I'd request ten new sales executives within ten days."

Rakesh, cautious as always, asked, "Will they become productive fast enough?"

Vikram paused, then met his gaze.

"They'll work under each senior sales executive. Their numbers will count toward the seniors' targets."

Rakesh frowned slightly. "So they'll mainly help seniors with lead generation?"

"Exactly," Vikram said, smiling. "They'll fuel the engine—and the seniors will drive it."

The room fell silent. Then Rahman, the most grounded among us, voiced what we all felt.

"Sir… even after all our effort, we sell only thirty units. Where will we find seventy-seven customers?"

Mr. Vikram Singh stepped forward, closer to the team in the conference room. With a knowing smile, he said,

"To achieve our target, you'll have to play a bit of hide and seek—with the customers."

Partha, holding a cup of tea from Heeru Da, looked up.

"Hide and seek? That's a kids' game, Sir. How can we play that with customers?"

Vikram chuckled.

"Every month, around 150 buyers are out there—ready with money to buy their dream vehicle. They're not invisible, just hidden in plain sight. Some eye the Turbo Cheetah, some other brands. Your job is to find them before the competition does."

He paused, sipped water, then went on.

"These customers won't come on their own. You must uncover them—through conversations, community links, and smart outreach."

Raju, our star performer, frowned.

"Sir, we already do that every month. Still, we sell only 30 vehicles. What more can we do?"

"Good question," Vikram said warmly. "That's where marketing bridges the gap. Rakesh has shown you—events, campaigns, cold calls, influencer ties—none of these are random. Each is a tool to find those hidden customers."

Sanjay Mittal, our Managing Director, had been listening quietly. Time was money for him.

"Aggarwal," he said, turning to our manager, "I like the analogy. But what's the plan to actually find those 150 buyers?"

Mr. Aggarwal straightened.

"Sir, we're using targeted strategies—data-driven segmentation, events, influencer outreach, digital campaigns, and referral programs. Each taps a different pool."

Still not convinced, Mr. Mittal looked at Rakesh Chetri.

"Is that enough?"

Rakesh, ever the bridge between office and field, nodded.

"Strong fundamentals, Sir. I'd just add more personal cold calls and a system to track conversions."

Vikram smiled.

"Exactly. Personal outreach is the heart of modern selling."

I raised my hand.

"Sir, what exactly is personal outreach? Is it just a follow-up?"

Vikram moved closer, his gaze steady.

"Follow-up is a reminder. Outreach is being remembered. It's a connection, not conversion."

Bikash leaned forward.

"So we stay in touch beyond the sale?"

"Exactly," Vikram said. "If a father buys a Turbo Cheetah for his daughter's new business, don't just deliver it—call a week later, ask how she's doing. That's outreach."

Partha grinned.

"Like birthdays or anniversaries?"

"Yes. But not auto-texts. A note, a call—something real."

Raju asked softly,

"And in tough times? If a customer suffers a loss?"

Vikram's voice gentled.

"That's where real relationships begin. If a loyal customer passes away, attending the funeral or sending a condolence shows we care."

I found myself asking,

"Is that sympathy—or empathy?"

Vikram smiled.

"Sympathy is feeling sorry. Empathy is feeling with. It says, ' I can't imagine what you're going through—but I'm here.' "

Bikash nodded.

"So sympathy sees pain, empathy walks with it?"

"Well said," Vikram replied. "When customers feel that, they never forget. That's how bonds last."

Partha's eyes lit up.

"So we're not just selling vehicles—we're joining their stories."

Raju laughed.

"And when that happens, why would they buy elsewhere?"

"Exactly," Vikram said. "That's The Drive Beyond the Funnel. It's not about closing deals—it's about opening relationships."

From his seat, Mr. Mittal clapped softly.

"Excellent, Vikram. If we live this, Mission 51% won't be a target—it'll be a reality. By the way… what's a funnel?"

Before Vikram could answer, Rakesh smiled.

"Sir, let's take that after lunch? It's already 1:30."

Mr. Mittal nodded.

"Fair. I'll stay for the next session. This is worth my time."

We broke for lunch—fish curry with rice. The room was quiet. Everyone seemed lost, not in the meal, but in what waited ahead.

By 2:30 p.m., we were back. Rakesh and Aggarwal had come early, setting things up. Soon, Mr. Mittal entered with Mr. Atunu Chakrabarty and Service Manager Selim Khan from Rana Motors.

"Alright, team," Vikram began, "let's talk funnels. Does anyone know what a sales funnel is?"

Prakash—our informal teammate with a paan-stained moustache—grinned.

"Like pouring diesel into a tank, sir—lots go in, only a little reaches without spilling!"

Laughter rippled through the room. Everyone except Aggarwal, Rakesh, and the MD.

Vikram smiled. "Not bad, Prakash. Many leads go in at the top, only a few become buyers. That's the funnel."

He drew three stages on the board—Awareness, Consideration, Conversion.

"At the Awareness stage, we make ourselves visible," he said.

Bikash added, "Ads, events, social media."

Partha joined in, "Transport unions, local mechanics."

"Exactly. Highlight strengths—mileage, power, price. No pushing."

Mittal turned to Aggarwal. "Have you ever explained this to your team?"

Aggarwal hesitated. "Sir, not everything fits neatly into a funnel."

Rakesh stepped in smoothly. "We follow it, sir. Rana has a strong SOP."

Mittal nodded. Vikram continued.

"Stage two—Consideration. That's where customers compare brands. Prove why Turbo Cheetah stands out. Stage three—Conversion. Test drives, follow-ups, closing the deal."

The room was quiet, attentive.

Partha asked, "After they buy, do we just move on?"

Vikram smiled. “No, that’s when loyalty begins. Birthdays, service reminders, family gestures—small things that make them return.”

I said, “So we don’t just sell trucks; we build relationships?”

Mittal nodded. “Exactly. We build trust. One happy buyer brings ten more.”

Bikash added, “So conversion isn’t the end—it’s the start.”

“Right,” Vikram said. “That’s The Drive Beyond the Funnel. The best don’t stop at sales—they build loyalty and advocacy.”

I said, “Like maintaining a good truck—if we care for it, it runs for years.”

“Well said,” Vikram replied. “Sales is about people, not numbers. Make that birthday call, send that note—those moments stay.”

Mittal leaned forward. “And if a customer meets with an accident, we should call first, check their safety, and help with repairs.”

Rakesh added, “Even a toy car for their child builds a bond.”

Vikram nodded. “That’s how we become partners, not just salesmen. People can buy anything—but trust is rare.”

Mittal smiled. “Remember—trucks don’t build businesses. People do.”

I raised my hand. “Sir, what’s personal branding?”

Rakesh answered, “It’s the image people have of you—your reliability, your tone, your care. Products are forgotten, people remembered.”

Vikram stood, smiling. “Then let’s hit the road—and make Mission 51% real.”

Mittal applauded. “Excellent. Implement this fully. The Drive Beyond the Funnel will take us there.”

As he spoke, Aggarwal stayed silent, eyes distant. “In ten minutes,” he said, “Rana Motors will start the product session. Take a short break.”

At the urinals, Partha joked, “Our urinary system’s like a funnel—so much in, only a trickle out!”

Laughter broke the tension.

Raju muttered, “Theories sound fine, but the market’s tougher.”

I said, “Still, it made sense to me.”

Bikash flicked his cigarette. “I’ll try them.”

Rahman nodded, packing his khaini. “My plan—51% or nothing.”

Prakash stubbed his smoke and said quietly, “Hmm.”

CHAPTER 10

# The 20–20–60 Rule

After the break, we filed back into the conference room.

Mr. Selim Khan stood at the front—medium height, clean-shaven above a Lincoln beard, his white shirt crisp against the soft hum of the projector. Calm, but with a gravity that commanded silence. Beside him stood Mr. Atunu from the service team, waiting with a laptop open like a quiet witness.

"Alright, team," Selim began, his voice even. "What problems are you facing in the field?"

Prakash spoke first. His tone carried years of bottled frustration.

"Sir, how can we reach Mission 51% when our own trucks fight against us?"

Selim tilted his head. "Explain."

"In Jalpaiguri, twenty Turbo Cheetah Trucks have cracked chassis. We've followed up again and again—no replacements, no answers."

Raju joined in. "Sir, our tyres wear out too fast. Customers are furious. They say we sell promises, not machines."

Rahman spoke softly, almost to himself. "In Malda, mileage complaints are spreading. We're losing the trust we built."

The room went still. These weren't complaints—they were confessions.

All the technical points I had prepared had already been voiced. But something deeper pressed on my chest—ethics.

I stood and spoke before I could stop myself.

"Sir, some of our executives have overcharged customers and misled them during finance deals. Those customers feel cheated. They'll never return."

The silence after was heavy.

Before anyone could speak, Mr. S. P. Aggarwal cut in sharply. "Arjun, we'll take that matter separately."

I saw a flicker cross Vikram's face. Mittal avoided his eyes. Aggarwal looked to Rakesh Chetri for rescue.

"Thank you, Arjun," Chetri said smoothly, his tone a mix of grace and caution. "Such issues must come to us directly. We'll act. And anyone guilty of misconduct will face termination."

Diplomacy, polished and practiced. But the truth hung in the air, stubborn and unsaid.

Mittal checked his watch, eager to move on. Vikram stepped forward and drew two columns on the board: Turbo Cheetah Truck | Tejas Maxx.

"Let's return to product training," he said. "What are our advantages? And theirs?"

I listed Turbo Cheetah's strengths.

Vikram nodded, then asked the room for Tejas Maxx.

Bikash spoke first. Then Prakash—ten flaws in our own truck.

When it came to Tejas Maxx, silence. Rahman added five points. Aggarwal and Vikram filled in the rest.

Vikram stepped back. "See this? Each has 20% strengths, 20% weaknesses, 60% common ground. That's how you train your pitch—focus on our strengths, own our gaps, fix them. But never badmouth the competition."

Partha smirked. "Sir, if we expose Tejas Maxx's weak spots, customers will choose us easily."

Vikram's tone sharpened. "No, Partha. That's not selling—it's slander. You win trust through truth."

Chetri nodded, his voice calm again. "Integrity is our only lasting advantage."

Then Selim rose, turning the page of the meeting.

"We know Turbo Cheetah's issues," he said. "And we're ready to act."

Atunu switched on the projector. Slides glowed to life.

"In six months," Selim continued, "we'll replace every cracked chassis, every faulty tyre, every seized engine under warranty."

"At the same time," added Atunu, "we'll hold weekly service camps, mileage rallies, and driver training sessions. We'll host family gatherings for customers—to remind them we're still here."

Selim looked straight at Mittal. "And Rana Motors will bear every cost."

Mittal's expression softened—profit and relief finding common ground.

Something shifted in the room then. The air lightened. Shoulders straightened. For the first time in months, hope didn't feel naïve.

It was already six. Mittal glanced again at his watch, ready to close. But Vikram wasn't done.

"Team," he said, his voice steady, "this isn't just training—it's the foundation of Mission 51%. We've spoken of strategy, service, and ethics. Now it's your turn. Go into the market. Rebuild what's broken. It'll take time—but trust always returns to those who earn it."

There was a pause—a quiet recognition of something real.

Then Mittal stood and clapped. "Well said, Vikram. Team, you're lucky to have a leader who believes in you. Now go make Mission 51% happen."

Applause rose—not out of duty, but belief.

As we stepped out into the evening, the mood had changed.

The same men who'd entered weary and doubtful now spoke in sharper tones, their laughter lighter, their eyes steadier.

Something had shifted—not in the numbers, but in us.

CHAPTER 11

# The Eagle's Push

On 10 May 2013, my phone beeped with a message — my salary had been credited.

I stared at the screen in disbelief. In April, I had not sold a single vehicle, and Mr. S. K. Aggarwal had already warned me that he would block my pay. This felt like a drop of water to a thirsty man in the middle of summer. How had it slipped past his approval?

At 11 a.m., Isha called.

"Hi Arjun, how are you?" she asked warmly.

"I'm fine, thank you. And you?"

"Great, Arjun. Excited to be working on Mission 51%," she said, her tone mixing professionalism and friendliness. "By the way, did you get your salary?"

"Yes," I said slowly. "But I didn't sell last month. Aggarwal wasn't supposed to approve it."

"You should thank Prakash," she explained. "He transferred one of his sales to you. That's why Aggarwal passed your salary."

I was speechless for a moment. "I'm really grateful to him."

"Then tell him that!" She laughed and hung up.

I called Prakash immediately to thank him.

That same month, Darjeeling Auto Works ran a recruitment drive, hiring many new salespeople for both rural and urban coverage. I worked hard, but May ended with another zero. Aggarwal was furious. My salary was held back again, and this time, he warned me directly about termination.

On 5 June, during the monthly business meeting, Aggarwal and Mr. Rakesh Chetri criticised me harshly in front of everyone. Humiliation burned in my chest.

Later, Mr. Vikram Singh called me into a small adjoining room.

"What's going on, Arjun? If you don't bring in sales this month, they'll terminate you. I know you're capable. I want to keep you here."

"Sir, I'm doing everything you taught me, but nothing is working," I admitted.

He leaned forward, looking me straight in the eye.

"Arjun, we've trained you well. We've mentored you so you can stand strong in this industry. We've given you enough time to prove yourself. Now, it's your turn to show what you're capable of.

There are gaps in your work. Find them. Fix them.

Listen—" his voice softened, but his words carried weight—

"An eagle builds its nest high in the tallest tree. When the chicks hatch, the eagle pushes them out. The ones who flap their wings and fly survive. The ones who don't… fall.

Arjun, it's your time to fly. You have the strength to soar high, and I don't want to lose you."

His words stayed with me long after he left the room.

CHAPTER 12

# Three Days Without Food

The next morning, I woke up before sunrise. I told myself, "I can do this." I will not eat until I make a sale. I didn't tell my mother.

"Won't you have breakfast?" she asked.

"No, Ma. I'm in a hurry. I'll eat outside," I lied.

That day, I approached fifty prospects. All rejected me. I came home tired, but told Ma I had eaten at the company's expense. She smiled and said, "Then bring me something next time."

The second day was the same. No sales. No food.

By the third morning, my legs felt heavy and my head light. I left early to avoid Ma's questions and sat at a tea shop without ordering. I called customers, financiers, brokers—anyone who could give me a lead. Nothing.

I went from one customer to another, joined every marketing event, and tried every trick my bosses and trainers had taught me. But nothing worked. It felt like I was begging in the market for just one Turbo Cheetah Truck sale.

The sole of my cheap shoes was worn out. My dark skin, broken shoes, and tired face showed how hard I was working to get even one deal. This was a different kind of fight for survival, in a field I barely knew.

By the third afternoon, I was finished. My head was spinning from three days of hunger, and my throat was dry. Frustrated, I felt my love for automobiles disappearing. I decided to quit.

I wrote my resignation on my notepad and was about to send it to my bosses. Just then, a phone call popped up on my screen and stopped me.

At exactly 2:10 p.m., I received the call.

"Are you Arjun?" a voice asked.

"Yes. Who's this?"

"I'm Biren Roy from Lataguri. We need two trucks."

His words were like rain after a long drought. "Turbo Cheetah Trucks?"

"Yes, yes!" he confirmed.

I caught the next bus to Lataguri. After understanding his needs, I gave my presentation, handled objections, and booked two trucks.

It was the victory I had been starving for. I called Vikram Singh immediately.

"Sir, your eaglet has started to fly."

He laughed. "Good job, Arjun. You'll soar high."

I told Rakesh, Prakash, and Isha. They were happy for me. Aggarwal's response, however, was cold:

"Two sales after two months of salary? That's nothing. I need five from you."

I stayed silent.

When I reached home, I was weak but smiling.

"Ma, can you give me dinner?"

"So, today your office didn't feed you?" she teased. "Good. I've cooked something special."

I hugged her and told her about my two bookings, but she only said, "Go take a bath; you smell of sweat."

From that day, I didn't stop. Selling became easier. I used both hunting and cultivation methods to build a strong base in the market.

CHAPTER 13

# Before They're Born

Darjeeling Autoworks didn't rest. The air buzzed with urgency, just like in our training days. More people joined, all chasing one goal—Mission 51%. Every sales trick was thrown into the wind, hoping some would stick. New recruits teamed with seniors, turning every street into a battlefield. Leads poured in as we marched ahead like soldiers, pushing Mission 51% forward.

To reclaim the market, we hit the streets. Service camps popped up like repair festivals—cracked chassis replaced, worn tires rolled away, dead engines revived. In towns and villages, mileage contests drew crowds, our Turbo Cheetah gleaming under the sun, proving its strength. Old dues were cleared; trust slowly returned. Like new shoots after rain, the market began to respond.

But my work wasn't only about machines. I stepped into my customers' lives—sharing sweets on birthdays, standing with them in hospitals, or at funerals heavy with silence. Their children called me "gift uncle," not for what I gave, but because I always showed up. When a truck broke down or crashed, I was there before the dust settled.

This was my quiet strategy—to add value not just to sales, but to people. My honesty and word became my identity. Gradually, my name carried weight—and with it, the Turbo Cheetah's name too. Buyers came not only for me, but also for others who followed the same path.

Four months after training, the numbers proved what we already felt—the tide was turning.

On 4th October 2013, Darjeeling Autoworks held its half-yearly review. The room buzzed with energy. Mr. Aggarwal and Mr. Rakesh Chetri led the meeting. Mr. Aggarwal looked cheerful, ordering a good lunch and even bringing a cake.

"Team, we've closed H1 with 40% growth," he announced. "That's higher than any other Rana Motors product. Great job, everyone!"

Then, smiling, he added, "Best performer of H1 is Raju Roy. Big hand for him!"

After the celebration, Rakesh spoke up, serious again. "Forty percent growth is good, but our market share hasn't moved. Mission 51% is still ahead. The whole industry grew 50%, so we're still at the same level. We need to convert more customers from other brands."

Isha asked, "So we grew, but didn't gain share?"

"Exactly," he said. "Now we must grow faster than the market."

We discussed strategies late into the afternoon, ready for the next battle.

The market felt charged again—like fresh batteries in an old machine.

No one showed that energy more than Raju Roy.

Mr. Aggarwal's praise had lit a fire in him. Strategy wasn't his strength, but persistence was. He tore through the market like a bull, chasing customers everywhere. With the service team fixing old trucks and marketing pushing hard, Raju stayed ahead of everyone. But his weakness was his temper—it burned fast and often left behind hurt customers and uneasy colleagues.

Rahman was the opposite—calm, steady, determined. In three months, he doubled his sales. Bikash rose quietly too, his smart planning making him a favourite across the hills of Darjeeling and Sikkim.

Partha, though, kept slipping. Late, careless, and unreliable—in sales, that's enough to sink you.

That's when Mr. Rakesh brought in a new name—Sahil Kumar.

He was thirty-two, dark-skinned, with a fox-like face and a bright smile. He carried himself like a man already winning. Gold chains flashed, his phone buzzed nonstop, and sometimes a premium car rolled up outside the office. For our salary level, it didn't add up.

But the numbers did. Within months, he was selling ten trucks a month. The bosses clapped, customers liked him, and no one questioned the whispers about his "other ways" of making money.

Sahil's rise soon collided with Raju's pride—one jealous, the other arrogant. Their rivalry became part of the office air.

I kept to my own lane. No flashy rings, no race to outshine anyone. My goal was simple—build trust. I visited customers at home, stood by them in trouble, celebrated their happy moments, and showed up when their trucks broke down at night. Slowly, they stopped seeing me as a salesman and started calling me their man.

Sales came slower—seven or eight trucks a month—but my footing grew stronger. I wasn't just selling Turbo Cheetahs. I was selling trust.

By the end of 2014, Darjeeling Autoworks had nearly doubled its growth. The company celebrated numbers; I celebrated roots.

On April 10, we gathered for the annual meeting at a resort in Malbazar. The automatic gate slid open; cool air carried the scent of polished wood and fresh flowers. For a moment, I just stood there, taking it in.

Inside, round tables filled the hall—over a hundred employees waiting for the evening gala. The AC made it feel like December in April.

I spotted Isha—crisp, confident, radiant. "Arjun, sit here," she said, smiling and pointing to the chair beside her.

Bikash and Rahman were already there. Then Sahil walked in, taking the seat next to Isha, leaning too close. His gold chain glinted, his smile lingered a moment too long.

Isha shifted, then stood. "Excuse me," she said.

"What happened, Isha?" he asked, smile fading.

She gave a polite nod and walked away.

I stepped in. "Hi, Sahil. All good?"

He gave me a quick, dismissive look. "Fine," he said, and walked off.

The MD, Mr. Sanjay Mittal, called the room to order.

"Thanks to Mr. Mittal's leadership," Rakesh began, "our Turbo Cheetah Truck sales grew over 100% this year." Applause followed.

"What's our F14 exit market share?" Mr. Mittal asked.

"Fifteen percent growth, sir. We now hold thirty-five," Rakesh replied proudly. More applause. I caught Isha's eye across the hall—she was clapping, pride shining in her face.

"Excellent," said Mr. Mittal. "You've beaten the competition and strengthened our base."

Mr. Aggarwal smiled too, though his eyes stayed distant.

After the speeches came the review—what went right, what went wrong.

Since this was a dealership meet, the Rana Motors team wasn't present in person. But a video call was arranged. On the big screen appeared Mr. Vikram Singh and his boss, Mr. Raj Kapoor—a man known for military discipline, ethics, and zero tolerance for unresolved complaints.

Vikram spoke first.

"Hello, everyone. I hope you're celebrating today. Double growth in Turbo Cheetah sales and a 15% market share gain is no small feat. It shows your hard work and commitment. Great job, team—kudos to all!"

Applause filled the room. Then he introduced his boss.

"Now Mr. Raj Kapoor will address the team."

At first, the connection lagged, but soon Mr. Kapoor's voice came through—firm and clear.

"Good evening, team. I'm proud to see such energy, even through a screen. A 100% growth and 15% market gain don't happen by luck—they come from discipline, focus, and responsibility.

We're not just selling trucks. We're here to serve, solve problems, and keep every promise we make. Discipline, ethics, and customer-first thinking are non-negotiable."

Numbers looked strong, but for Regional Manager Raj Kapoor, real success meant winning hearts.

"Now," he said, his tone steady but charged, "I want all of you to aim higher—51% market share by mid-year. No stone unturned. No chance missed. Make Mission 51% a reality!"

Thunderous applause shook the hall. It felt like Kapoor had plugged the team into a live wire of purpose. His eyes scanned the screen, searching for fire in every face.

Then, after a pause, his voice deepened:

"Crush the competition before they're born in the market."

The air crackled. The team felt unstoppable—driven to claim every deal, every inch of the market, until Mission 51% was theirs.

The prize ceremony followed. As expected, Raju Roy won Best Sales Executive of the Year in the small truck segment, with Sahil Kumar second. I was recognized as a promising newcomer. Watching Raju hold the trophy, I promised myself—next year, it would be mine.

After the conference, the team worked with full energy. Every month, our share was tracked. Some months we surged; some months the industry outpaced us. Each review pushed us harder.

But in my area, the mission wasn't smooth. Customer issues kept surfacing. Still, we managed, kept them satisfied, and kept chasing Mission 51%.

Then came the incident that changed everything—one that tarnished both Darjeeling Auto Works and Rana Motors. Competitors seized the chance. And since the case came through me, I became the main culprit—in the customer's eyes, the dealership's, and the company's.

Over a year of hard work and trust collapsed overnight. My mission stalled. Instead of racing toward 51%, I now faced my biggest test—to win back my name and rebuild everything I'd worked for.

CHAPTER 14

# Case No. 15/2014: Truth in Question

The sharp, acrid scent of burnt tobacco clung to my fingers as I stubbed the cigarette against the cold cement. I patted my pockets for coins—desperate for one more drag of nicotine to numb my nerves. But there were none. Only three crumpled hundred-rupee notes and two coins jingled faintly—barely enough to stretch through the next few days.

It was 4:30 PM on July 22nd, 2014. Eleven days left until salary day. Eleven long, hungry days. I was already rationing lunch, skipping dinner. The math was brutal. Every coin counted. Those few rupees were sacred—kept aside for groceries my mother needed.

To add insult to injury, Mr. Aggarwal had marked me absent for being late—never mind the reason. My empathy, my effort, my risk... all rewarded with a salary deduction. Just one more cut on a body already wounded by the weight of survival.

My phone buzzed, jolting me. It was Ma.

“Arjun, where are you, beta? What time will you be back?” Her voice held that soft concern only mothers have—half worry, half hope.

“I’ll be back by eight, Ma. “Don’t worry,” I replied, forcing steadiness into my tone. “And yes, I’ll bring the groceries.”

There was silence on her end—trust, resignation. Maybe both.

By 5 PM, I had returned to the showroom. The mechanical clatter of spanners and hushed mutters from customers formed a dull backdrop. I spotted the works manager, Mr. Debashis, who gestured curtly.

"Boss wants to see you," he said.

I already knew which boss he meant.

Mr. S. K. Aggarwal—the man whose pride outweighed empathy, whose cigarettes outlasted conversations. His chamber reeked of stale smoke and power.

I stepped in. He didn't look up. Just exhaled smoke and said, "You damaged the demo vehicle. The workshop says repairs will cost fifty thousand rupees. Who's going to pay?"

I swallowed my frustration.

"Sir, I took the vehicle to rescue a fleet customer—Mr. Pintu Haldar. He was stranded during the storm. I was thinking of our long-term business—"

"Spare me the drama," he cut in with a sneer. "You damaged our vehicle. That's your responsibility."

"I risked my life out there," I said, my voice tightening. "Would the company compensate my family if I didn't return?"

He laughed. Sarcastic. Cruel.

"I'll speak to the bosses... But you'll pay half. Rs 25,000."

"That's not fair," I replied, standing my ground. "This was a service act for a customer. An investment. We'll win loyalty, future sales."

"You've got strange ideas about business," he scoffed. "You're not a social worker, Arjun. This customer service nonsense is a waste of time."

Then, without warning, he turned to the accounts manager and said, "Deduct Rs 3,000 from his salary each month till he repays."

I stood frozen for a second—anger, helplessness, and humiliation flooding my chest. Then I turned and left without another word, the tension crackling in my bones. Outside, the world seemed unchanged, but inside me, something had cracked.

The next morning, at precisely 9 AM, the shrill ring of my phone broke the silence.

"Mr. Arjun?" A harsh voice called; an official voice spoke. "Sub Inspector Sanjeev Singh from Maynaguri Police Station. We have a complaint filed against you."

I straightened up. "What kind of complaint?"

"A customer, Mr. Hamid Alam, has accused you of cheating. He claims you tricked him and withheld his vehicle."

The words hit like a slap.

I sat down, stunned. Mr. Hamid? A customer I personally served?

"No, sir. There must be a misunderstanding. I handled his delivery properly. All paperwork was cleared. It was approved by Mr. Aggarwal himself."

But the inspector was unmoved. "The vehicle was financed. He claims he cleared all the dues, but the dealership forcefully withheld his truck. You're required to come to the station."

After the call, I sat still—numb. The ceiling fan whirred above me, the tick of the wall clock suddenly louder than usual. Outside, traffic buzzed faintly. Inside, the air thickened with anxiety.

My breath caught in my throat. A police case? Jail time? Cheating charges? My name, which I'd built on trust and long hours, was now threatened to be tarnished—shattered by a deal gone wrong and a manager who wouldn't back me.

Just then, Ma walked in with a cup of tea. She placed it on the table and looked at me.

"You seem worried. What's happened?"

I looked up at her. That soft face, weathered but always composed.

"Ma… this job is killing me."

She sat beside me and placed her hand on my arm. "We've seen harder days, Arjun. You've never lied or wronged anyone. The truth will speak for itself."

For a moment, her words grounded me. But the storm outside was nothing compared to the one brewing within.

An hour later, my phone rang again.

It was Harun—Mr. Hamid Alam's son. The moment I saw his name on the screen, a knot formed in my stomach. I remembered what his father had confided during our earlier meetings—about Harun's aggression and his problems with trouble.

"Hello, Arjun!" he barked through the receiver.

"Yes, Arjun here," I replied cautiously, my voice low, alert to the hostility radiating from the other end.

"I'm calling about my father's truck," he said, voice rising like a gathering storm.

"Yes, Harun Bhai. Tell me. How can I help you?" I tried to remain calm and create intimacy by saying "Bhai," which means "brother."

But his response came sharp, fast, and furious: "You don't have to help us. Just return the truck. You're a fraud. A cheat! If you don't, you'll pay."

I took a breath, choosing my words with care. "I understand you're upset. I'm trying to get the matter resolved. Please believe me—I'm doing everything I can."

"If the truck isn't returned soon," he interrupted, voice dripping with threat, "you won't sell a single vehicle in our area. If you step foot here, we'll make sure you regret it."

I felt a bead of sweat trickle down my back. "Harun Bhai, I hear you. Trust me, I'm working on a solution. Please give me a little time."

But he cut the line before I could say more.

The silence in the room suddenly felt deafening. His final words echoed in my ears: *You'll pay for this, Arjun.*

I stood there, clutching the phone like it still held the heat of the threat.

With dread settling into my bones, I called Mr. Aggarwal. He picked up after a few rings.

"Why was Mr. Hamid Alam's truck held back, Sir?" I asked, trying to keep my tone respectful, though frustration bubbled beneath the surface.

He replied coolly, "Who said it was held?"

"Sir, the delivery team informed me that the instruction came from you. The customer's finance was approved, and documents were cleared. Why was it stopped?"

"That's your mistake, Arjun. You picked a customer with a weak credit profile," he said, brushing off my concern as if it were nothing more than an inconvenience.

My chest tightened. "Then why approve the delivery in the first place, Sir? If there were issues, why wasn't I told earlier?"

He paused. Then said curtly, "Come to the office. We'll talk."

The line went dead.

I stared at the phone. The fear was real now—deep. I was expected at the police station later that day, where Mr. Hamid Alam and Harun would be present. And now, my manager had disowned all responsibility.

If I were arrested, everything I'd worked for would collapse—my job, my name, my future. And worse, I would be branded a fraud.

The documents were in order. The vehicle had been delivered with full authorization. I had followed every procedure. Yet, here I was—hunted by a customer's rage and hung out to dry by my boss.

My breath grew shallow. My thoughts raced.

I needed help.

I called Anup Roy, a friend and trusted lawyer who handled both civil and criminal matters.

"Hey, Arjun," he answered cheerfully. "What's going on?"

"Anup, I need to know—what happens if someone files a fraud case against me?"

He chuckled, sensing my seriousness. "Who did you cheat now, Mister Ethical?"

"No jokes today. This is serious. The police called. There's a case against me."

His tone shifted immediately. "Tell me everything."

I quickly explained. The truck, the threats, the police call.

"Arjun, listen carefully. Cheating under IPC Section 420 is a non-bailable offense. It carries up to seven years in prison and a fine. Don't go to the station right now. If they arrest you, you won't get bail easily."

Panic surged inside me. "What should I do then? I have to show up."

"No, stay low for now. Let me speak to them. I'll handle the situation. You trust me, right?"

"With my life," I replied. My voice trembled, but I meant it.

"You've always been honest, Arjun. I know that. This isn't your fault, and I won't let this ruin you," he reassured me.

"Thanks, Anup," I said quietly. "I've spent several months building trust with every customer. I've walked miles, fought storms. And now—this."

"That's exactly why you'll come through it," he said. "Hold on. Let me do what I do best."

As I ended the call, I leaned back against the wall. Outside, the world went on—cars passing, people talking, a child laughing. But inside, everything had changed.

The accusation had entered my life like a crack through glass—quiet, swift, and dangerous. And now, I had to find a way not to shatter.

CHAPTER 15

# The Planned Escape

Anup and I spoke early that morning. His advice was clear: disappear for a while—stay low. Let him manage the mess with the police. I packed my bag quietly, stuffing just enough to make the lie feel like a plan.

Ma noticed, of course. She stood by the doorway, arms folded, eyes sharper than usual.

"Where are you going, Arjun?" she asked, her voice even but alert.

"Bhutan," I said casually. "There's a deal in progress. A company wants to buy ten of our Turbo Cheetah Trucks."

She didn't respond right away. Just nodded, as if bracing for something she'd already imagined.

"When will you be back?" she asked, softer now.

"A week," I said, trying to sound confident.

She sighed. "Call me. Three times a day."

I smiled to ease her worry, but the bags on the table, the creaking ceiling fan, and the crows arguing outside made the house feel like it was holding its breath.

At **9:00 a.m.**, my phone buzzed.
**Sub Inspector Sanjeev Singh.**

"Where are you, Mr. Arjun?" His tone was curt. "Mr. Hamid Alam is waiting at the Maynaguri police station."

I paused before replying. "I'm near the Bhutan border, Sir. In Jaigaon. There's an important client meeting. I'll handle the matter with Mr. Hamid soon."

"You should've informed me," he snapped. "This looks sloppy. Irresponsible."

"I understand. Please give me some time, sir."

"You have fifteen days," he said firmly. "If this doesn't get resolved, I'll have to proceed legally."

"I'll fix it, Sir. As always—our customers come first."

"Assure Mr. Hamid. I don't want to be forced, Arjun."

The line went dead. I put the phone down, heart thudding, knowing full well that "fifteen days" meant little when tempers ran hot.

The truth? The Bhutan deal wasn't urgent. The client had asked me to visit ten days later. But with the police tightening their grip and Harun showing up at stations, I needed space—time to think, breathe, and regroup.

This trip wasn't just about selling trucks. It was a way out of a trap I hadn't set but was stuck inside.

I still couldn't shake off the call from Mr. S. K. Aggarwal the day before. His voice lingered like a burn.

No greeting, no context—just orders. "We need to repossess Hamid Alam's vehicle."

I was stunned. "Why, Sir? He's paid six EMIs. He's on track as per records."

His tone grew colder. "You won't understand. Just follow instructions."

"But, Sir, he's my client. I've assured him everything's in place. He's not in default."

"Don't cross your line, Arjun. Ask him to bring the vehicle in for servicing next Monday."

That was it. No room for questions. Just power, pressed flat into words.

"Okay, Sir," I said, defeated. "But please consider the impact. He's a loyal customer."

He had already disconnected.

It wasn't just a disagreement. It was something deeper—**a conflict between authority and conscience**. I had followed every protocol. Yet I was the one facing cops, threats, and betrayal.

At **10:15 a.m.**, just as I zipped my bag, the phone buzzed again. **Isha Sharma.**

Her voice came through light and warm. "Hi Arjun, how are you? All good?"

I stepped outside to avoid Ma's stare. The street was waking up—stray dogs yawning, birds filling gaps in the silence.

"I'm fine. You?"

"I'm good too. So, what's the plan today?" she asked.

I smiled at the sky. "Who should I report to first—Miss Isha or Mr. Aggarwal?"

She laughed. That soft, honest kind of laugh that doesn't hide anything.

"I'm available all day, Arjun. Morning to night."

"I wouldn't mind that," I said. "In fact, I want to make you my full-time boss."

Her voice turned playful. "Really? You sure?"

"Absolutely."

Then her tone shifted. More formal. "Okay, okay, I need to submit a report too. So—your plan?"

"I'm heading out of the country today."

"Out of the country?" she said, surprised. "Where?"

"To a neighboring one."

"Bangladesh?"

"No," I chuckled. "Bhutan. Phuentsholing."

A pause. Then laughter. "You're going near my home! I'm from Jaigaon, near the Bhutan gate."

Before I could say more, someone near her scolded her for chatting too long. The line went quiet.

But her laughter stayed with me—light as the morning breeze, trailing behind as I tied my torn shoe tighter, zipped up my bag, and stepped into the uncertain road ahead.

Returning to my mom, I bid her goodbye as I prepared for my journey to Bhutan, a smile tugging at my lips—grateful for the unexpected connection.

The sultry weather wrapped around me, the mix of petrichor and sunlight thick in the air, creating a mood both intimate and intense. Despite the heat, I settled into my Turbo Cheetah Truck, the cabin warm and already making me restless.

Wearing my sunglasses—a cheap souvenir from Siliguri's Bidhan Market—I caught my reflection in the side mirror. Surprisingly, I looked composed in my formal shirt and sunglasses. From my shirt pocket, I pulled out a cigarette, lit it, and watched the smoke curl as I adjusted my hair, stealing glances in the mirror.

I started humming a romantic Hindi song, letting its melody drift me away from the stress of the day. For a fleeting moment, I imagined myself as Isha's ideal partner. A strange confidence flooded me, as if I had momentarily stepped into a Bollywood romance.

Then—HONK!—a loud blast broke my reverie. I snapped out of my three-minute daydream and turned the ignition. My Rana

Turbo Cheetah truck roared to life like a beast awakening from slumber.

Reversing out of the parking space, I glanced both ways before easing the truck onto the highway. Shifting gears, I pointed east and began accelerating.

First gear—steady crawl. Second—20 km/h. Third—momentum rising, but traffic thickened. The narrow road swarmed with rickshaws, cycles, buses, and wandering pedestrians. Overtaking felt like threading a needle with greasy hands.

Each motion—clutch, gear, accelerator—was a battle against chaos. Yet somehow, I was in control, commanding the Turbo Cheetah like a seasoned warrior.

Inside, though, it was a storm. The Hamid Alam case loomed large. Why would a properly financed, company-approved vehicle be repossessed? Mr. Alam had done everything right—EMIs paid, paperwork clear, Aggarwal's nod secured. Now he was a defaulter? It didn't add up.

Part of me wanted answers, but police pressure and Harun's threats kept me low.

The wind tangled in my thoughts as I drove faster. A strand of hair kept falling across my sunglasses, grounding me in the moment. In the mirror, I looked confident—fair-skinned, composed—but inside, doubt coiled like smoke.

Whenever things grew heavy, thoughts of Isha returned—her laughter, her warmth. They softened the sharp edges of my mind, like a song you didn't know you needed.

Approaching Dhupguri, I slowed. The junction buzzed like a living organism. One road veered to Cooch Behar, another to Daukimari. I kept northeast, toward Jaigaon.

Jaigaon wasn't just a border town—it was a gateway. On this side, India's bustle; beyond the Bhutan Gate, Phuentsholing's calm. Trade flowed between them like breath.

Here, every road mattered. Every person was part of a web—supply chains, politics, and survival. And for me, this mission with the Turbo Cheetah wasn't just sales—it was redemption, maybe even a way out.

CHAPTER 16

# *The Stand-Off at the Stand*

After that special training, Mission 51% stopped being a slogan. It became a shared obsession. Rana Motors pushed Darjeeling Auto Works hard, and that pressure flowed down to every one of us—quietly, constantly.

No matter our role or rank, everyone pushed harder. Results weren't even, but the spirit was. Sales went up across the board. At our dealership, the monthly average of Turbo Cheetah Trucks doubled—sometimes even more.

Yet the joy didn't last.

The numbers looked better, but the market share still told another story. We had grown, yes, but nowhere close to 51%. My own sales touched ten trucks a month—good, but not enough for Jalpaiguri. To reach the top, effort wasn't enough. We needed trust.

And that's where my real trouble began—the Hamid Alam case.

It had turned into a shadow following me everywhere. One allegation, one false story, and everything I'd built in two years could crumble. If the police complaint spread, competitors would twist it, customers would doubt me, and referrals would vanish.

Before chasing Mission 51%, I had to save the one thing no training could bring back—trust.

As I neared Jaigaon, the gateway to Bhutan, the noise of the Dhupguri crossroads swallowed me whole. Horns blared, buses stood idle, rickshaws zigzagged, and people moved like restless tides. Trucks groaned in every direction, caught in a slow dance of confusion.

When I finally broke free and turned onto the Jaigaon road, I allowed myself a breath. Parked trucks stretched on one side, heavy vehicles thundered past the other.

Then I saw it—the fleet in my rearview mirror.

A line of vehicles was closing in fast. At the front, a battered Veer Motors SUV lunged forward like a hunter leading its pack. My chest tightened.

I hit the brakes and swerved left. The truck skidded, kicking up a storm of dust. Tires screamed behind me. When it cleared, I was surrounded. Twenty vehicles circled me, engines humming, faces unreadable.

At the center stood Harun's SUV, dented but unmistakable. In Dhupguri, it was a symbol—rough, loud, feared. Harun used it like a crown.

He stepped out. Six feet tall, brown-skinned, clean-shaven, wearing a black t-shirt and grease-stained jeans. A cigarette dangled from his lips, smoke curling around his words before he spoke.

He spat khaini onto the road and walked toward me as if the outcome was already decided.

I rolled down my window. Sweat gathered at my temples. Around me, his men watched—some rubbing khaini into their palms, others smirking, waiting for the scene to unfold.

"You, Arjun!" Harun barked. "Get down. Today, you settle all your accounts."

The words cut through the noise.

But I wasn't alone—not completely. Many of these men had once stood by me. They weren't just customers; they were people I'd helped when no one else showed up. I'd listened, fixed their problems, and kept my word. They knew me as someone who delivered, not just promised.

That's how I had built my name—not with tactics, but with loyalty.

Every truck I sold came with my own word. Every complaint, every breakdown—I faced them myself. That's how I earned a name among them—

The Mushkil Aashaan.

The one who made hard times easier.

And today, I hoped that name still meant something.

As I stepped down from the truck, Ravi, one of the drivers, came forward.

"ArjunDa, we trusted you," he said, voice trembling. "Why did you hijack Hamid Alam's truck?"

The accusation hit like a blow. Faces turned. Paresh shouted from his van, "We thought you were different. But you cheated Harun and his father."

I stood in the middle of the crowd—once their ally, now the accused.

Questions flew like stones.

From the back, Moksedul said bitterly, "Salesmen are all the same. Can't trust any of them."

Then Harun's voice rose over the noise.

"From today, no one from Darjeeling Auto Works steps into our stands. And no one goes to Arjun for a vehicle."

The crowd murmured in agreement. Around me, engines idled, dust swirled, and the name I'd worked for years to build hung in the balance.

A voice in the crowd sneered, “Look at that—‘Mushkil Ashan’ just made things harder for Harun.”

Laughter erupted. Mocking. Loud. Cruel.

Harun flinched. Their mockery stung him more than the betrayal. He spat his khaini onto the ground and crushed the cigarette under his heel. The rage in his eyes turned feral. Then—without warning—he lunged.

The air thickened. The crowd stiffened. I didn’t move. I knew what was coming.

Harun’s eyes blazed. His body tensed like a spring as he advanced. His fists clenched. Muscles flexed under his black t-shirt. There was no reasoning in his face—just raw fury.

“You lied. You played us,” he growled. His voice cracked, not from weakness, but from restraint about to be broken.

The first punch caught me square on the jaw.

I staggered.

Then came the second—into my ribs. The third—my nose.

Pain exploded across my face. My knees buckled. I dropped to the ground, blood already trickling into my mouth. The crowd gasped—then closed in.

Someone shouted, “Hit him harder, Harun Bhai! He has to learn what betrayal costs!”

Another echoed, “This is for cheating our people. Teach him a lesson!”

The voices swirled, blending with the honking of distant trucks and the acrid scent of diesel. I tried to speak, to defend myself—but no one was listening. All they saw was a villain in a story someone else had written.

Harun didn't stop. His blows were fast, merciless, and fueled by humiliation. My face throbbed. My back burned. The world tilted sideways.

More kicks. More punches.

I felt hands push me, drag me, and spin me. The mob had surrounded me—predators in a circle, snapping jaws. A boot landed on my side. Another on my shoulder. I curled inward, protecting my face.

The nickname they once gave me—'Mushkil Ashan'—was now a punchline. I heard it in their taunts. Their laughter. Their spit.

The world blurred. My thoughts, once sharp and strategic, now scrambled for air. For dignity. For escape.

The ground beneath me spun. The only thing I could think of—how did I go from being their hero to this?

And somewhere, amidst the haze of fists and fury, I realized—this wasn't just a beating. It was a verdict.

The situation spiraled out of control. The stand drivers and vehicle owners, once watching with anticipation, turned into a raging crowd. Their frustration rose like a tidal wave—and I was its target.

In our two-day Mission 51% training, they taught us how to prospect, pitch, and close. But no one prepared us for this—for when a customer's anger turns into assault. Thanks to my careless manager, Mr. Aggarwal, I was out here dodging fists instead of objections.

This wasn't sales anymore. It was survival.

The mob wanted revenge. And I was the villain they'd chosen. No theory, no manual could save me now. My only instinct was to run. Mission 51%, market share, customer outreach—none of it mattered if I didn't make it out alive.

A blow hit my back. Another struck my jaw. I stumbled, breathless, the world spinning. One thought kept me going—my truck. My trusted Rana Turbo Cheetah. It wasn't just a vehicle; it was an escape.

I pushed through the crowd—dodging curses, fists, and accusations. I reached the cabin, yanked the door open, and slammed it shut. Their fists pounded the metal as I locked it, my breath ragged, my face bloodied. But I was safe—for a moment.

I turned the key. The engine roared like a guardian awakened. As the gears caught, the truck lunged forward, parting the mob like a ship cutting through stormy water. A drop of blood fell onto the steering wheel—a sharp reminder of my mother's warnings.

She never wanted this life for me. "Find a government job," she'd said. "Stability matters." But I needed to earn, not wait for exams and promises. That choice had led me here—to this bloodstained steering wheel, this road of no return.

"God, just get me home," I whispered. "I'll listen to her this time. I'll prepare. Just let me live."

Outside, the mob howled. They banged on the truck and screamed my name. I didn't wait. My foot slammed the accelerator. The Turbo Cheetah leapt forward, a beast in full flight. The crowd scattered.

But it wasn't over.

In the mirror, twenty vehicles followed—pickups, autos, and light trucks. A convoy of fury. At the front, Harun's battered SUV surged ahead, its dents glowing with pride and rage. Tires screeched. The air vibrated with pursuit.

I gripped the wheel tighter. My shirt clung to me, soaked in sweat and blood. My hands shook, but the truck surged ahead. Its 190 Nm torque kicked in, the RPM climbing like a racing heartbeat. The speedometer hit 120 km/h.

In the mirror, my face looked back—bruised, bloodied, but unbroken.

One lie had turned my world upside down. Hamid Alam's case had made me enemy number one. I couldn't plead or explain—not to twenty furious men. All I had were my wits, my skill, and the steel beneath me.

My Turbo Cheetah was now my shield, my sword, my only chance at redemption. Every gear shift was a heartbeat. Every turn, a lifeline.

The road ahead was madness—buses, cycles, pedestrians blurring past. From Gairkata to Birpara, the highway boiled with chaos. But I knew these roads. I trusted my truck. I trusted myself.

So did they.

They were veterans—road kings in their own right—driving with deadly precision. Honking furiously, they weaved closer. Some even drove Turbo Cheetahs—the very trucks I had sold. My own product is now chasing me like wolves.

But I wasn't done. Not yet.

Sweat in my eyes, blood in my mouth, fear in my lungs—I told myself one thing:

If I survive this, I'll rewrite everything. Starting with the truth.

CHAPTER 17

# Judgment at Suktikhola

An idea struck—I swerved off the main road toward the dry riverbed near Birpara. Taking the Bandapani trail, I aimed for the Suktikhola crossing. Most days it lay dormant and dusty, but in the monsoon it turned wild—water, sand, and sudden dips. Dangerous, yes, but crossable if you had nerve and the right machine.

I had both.

My 4WD demo truck wasn't just for display—it was built for this terrain. And I knew these parts better than my pursuers. On the main road, they'd trap me. Off-road? That was my ground.

As the concrete turned to forest trail, the town's noise faded. Sal trees whispered above, and the jungle thickened. Bandapani was infamous—for elephants, silence, and mystery. I chose nature's uncertainty over human fury.

In the mirror, their numbers thinned—twenty had become six. But Harun stayed on, his battered Veer Motors SUV still leading the pack.

The trail spat me out onto the Suktikhola riverbed. The setting sun threw molten light across the stones. The river whispered through the shallows, and the far bank—wild and free—seemed to call me closer.

I pressed down hard. The Turbo Cheetah roared.

The riverbed came alive under my wheels. Mud, rock, and water twisted into a treacherous path. My tires kicked up spray as I skidded through shallows and slick sand, but the truck held firm—its suspension dancing, its engine growling in defiance.

Harun's men followed seconds later. The riverbed turned into a battleground—splashes, horns, and engines clashing with nature.

But this wasn't a chase anymore. It was judgment.

To them, I was guilty—accused of withholding Hamid Alam's truck. No hearing, no facts. Only rage.

Harun's SUV lost control and spun into a shallow ditch. He screamed, but I couldn't hear the words—only his fury.

Then, without warning, my front tyres dug in.

The Cheetah jolted.

I downshifted, then slammed into reverse—nothing. Forward—nothing.

I was stuck.

Panic rose in my throat. I slammed the steering wheel. 'Move!' I shouted.

Warning lights flashed across the dashboard. The temperature gauge ticked upward. The engine strained. I could feel the heat under the hood, like the truck was sweating with me.

And then—I heard them.

Footsteps.

Water splashing. Boots crunching on gravel. Tools clanking together like iron teeth.

They were coming.

Rods, crowbars, and service wrenches turned into weapons. I saw them approaching in the side mirror. The mob, once my customers, now transformed into judges and executioners.

I was locked in a metallic coffin.

The Turbo Cheetah had carried me across three districts—Darjeeling, Jalpaiguri, Coochbehar—through storms, tea gardens, and industrial yards. It had been my office, my shelter, my badge of honour. Now, it was just a cage.

I thought of my mother. Her voice echoed from long ago, full of worry: *"Leave this private job. Sit for government exams."*

She hadn't wanted this life for me.

But I had bills to pay. Dreams to chase. And no time to wait for Sarkari lists.

I whispered a prayer, voice trembling. "If I get out of this alive, I'll listen to her. I promise. But first—save me, God. Just this once."

Outside, the six vehicles surrounded me. Harun's men climbed down, their faces hard. Their silence was louder than their accusations.

They weren't here to talk.

And I, trapped and bloodied, with my steering wheel slick with sweat and blood, waited for what would come next—not a punchline, not a redemption.

A verdict.

As their words rang out, each insult cut through my resolve like a blade. The thick, wet air of the riverbed mingled with the stench of mud as my tires spun helplessly in the ditch. Harun's voice cracked across the riverbank like a thunderclap.

"You scoundrel! Come out of that truck. Today, I'll teach you what betrayal costs. No one can save you now."

Beside him, Shyamal's rage flared.
"Don't spare him, Harun Bhai. Drag him out. Finish him."

Their fury made the atmosphere electric. My heart pounded. I floored the accelerator. The wheels screamed, spraying mud in all directions—but the vehicle remained stuck, trapped in the river's grip.

I leaned out of the window, my voice straining over the roar of the engine.

"Harun, this is madness! I don't have your father's truck. You're chasing the wrong man."

He stepped closer, holding a rod, his eyes wild.

"Then tell me—who withheld it?"

"Give me a month!" I shouted. "I'll find the culprit."

"Why didn't you show up at the police station?" He barked.

I hesitated. "I was scared of harassment. I swear, I'm innocent. Just give me time."

Harun scoffed, "Your running doesn't inspire trust."

The tires groaned. Suddenly, they caught traction. The truck jerked upward, lurching from the ditch in a spray of mud and fury. I slammed the brakes in front of Harun, our eyes locking. He stood drenched, iron rod in hand, unsure whether to strike.

"Give me one month," I pleaded, voice cracking. "I'll fix this, I promise. Please, Harun Bhai."

"How can we trust you?" he shouted, anguish twisting his face. "For six months, my father begged for answers! You people gave him none. No explanation, no decency!"

I hesitated, blood hammering in my ears.

"I know he's not a defaulter. He's a good man. But something went wrong—we just don't know what. Let me find out."

Their grips on the rods loosened. The hostility receded, just slightly. But the air still pulsed with danger.

Then—my phone rang. My mother.

Her voice filled the cabin, soft and unsuspecting.
"Arjun, where are you, son?"

I hurriedly rolled up the windows to muffle the chaos.

"Just 60 kilometers away from Jaigaon, Ma," I said, forcing calm.

"You should've reached hours ago," she said, concern heavy in her voice. "Is everything alright?"

I glanced at the circling drivers, Harun's SUV idling nearby.

"Yes, Ma. I visited a customer. Took longer than expected. I'm back on the road."

She paused, unconvinced. "Call me as soon as you reach. And be careful."

"I will. I promise."

The call ended, but her voice lingered. The only thread keeping my mind together in a night falling apart

The sun dipped low, casting golden fire over the riverbed. Dark clouds loomed. The Suktikhola, usually calm, glistened with rising rainwater from Bhutan, ready to flood.

The Rana Turbo Cheetah Truck roared, tires gripping the monsoon-slicked ground. Sweat and blood mixed on my brow as I held the wheel. Behind me, Harun's SUV struggled, stuck in the muddy riverbed, his friends trying in vain to free it.

The riverbed had become a battlefield of mud and knee-deep currents. But my truck—born for this—surged forward, powered by high clearance and relentless torque.

The sky opened. Rain slammed jungle and tin alike. Water filled the ruts beneath my tires. Wheels churned harder, flinging mud behind me like a war cry. The scent of soaked jungle, diesel, and fear closed in. Evening fell. The forest whispered. The river turned violent beneath the wheels.

I looked back. Harun's team wasn't giving up. Their SUV groaned, tilting as wheels spun uselessly. That day, they weren't just chasing me—they were chasing retribution.

I picked up speed, trusting the truck. The rain began in earnest. I tightened the 4-wheel drive, pressed the gearstick, bouncing through water as the vehicle obeyed. I entered Bhutanese territory briefly but couldn't go far without clearance. Turning back toward India, the riverbed fought me—mud clinging to wheels, each shift a lifeline.

Harun's SUV was trapped, wheels spinning. He pressed the pedal, shouting, but it was useless. My truck tore through the riverbed like a wild animal, carrying me forward, one muddy splash at a time.

They struggled in a waterlogged patch. Mud-caked hands grasped ropes, trying to free the SUV. From a hundred meters away, I shouted, "Harun Bhai, don't worry! I'll help you get your vehicle back. Just give me a few days—I'm going now, but the rescue team will come."

Ignoring the stones and curses he hurled, I climbed back into my truck, reassured him once more, and drove toward Jaigaon—the entry point to Bhutan.

Exhausted, aching, and with blood dried on my face, I glanced in the rearview mirror. A man who had barely survived a violent chase stared back. I called the dealership's support team to arrange help for Harun's SUV, still stuck in the riverbed.

CHAPTER 18

# Bleeding Isn't in the KPI

After about 45 minutes of driving, I pulled into a small roadside motel to catch my breath. I quickly washed my face, scrubbing off the dried blood.

Inside the motel's dining area, I ordered a tea. Lighting a cigarette, I called Mr. S. K. Aggarwal.

"Hello, Sir, it's Arjun," I said.

He replied in his usual rude tone, "Where have you been all day?"

"I told you this morning, Sir. I was heading to Jaigaon."

"Oh, really? Have you reached yet?" he asked sarcastically.

"Not yet, Sir," I answered.

"Why not?"

"I was attacked by Harun's team," I explained, hoping he would show some concern. But instead, he asked, "Who is Harun?"

"He's the son of Mr. Hamid Alam," I said.

"What did you do to them?"

His question stung. I could feel my anger rising, but I held it in and replied calmly.

"Sir, I have never wronged any customer. I try my best to make sure they're satisfied. But I still don't know why Hamid Alam's truck was taken back. There's been no clear explanation."

He cut me off. "You need to watch your tone. I don't have to answer all your questions."

"But, Sir," I insisted, "Harun and his men attacked me because of that truck. They chased me for kilometers. I'm injured; my nose and mouth are bleeding. I escaped with great difficulty."

He just laughed coldly. "This is nothing new. Sales guys get attacked all the time. It's part of the job."

"I don't accept that," I shot back. "This shouldn't be normal."

Trying to change the subject, he asked, "How many vehicles have you sold this month? You've only sold three out of ten. Will you reach your target? All your key performance indicators (KPI) are down this month."

His question irritated me further. I replied, "I'll update you at the end of the month, Sir."

He tried to shut me down with his authority. "We'll talk in the performance review next month."

That was his only real weapon—his position as my boss. And he used it like a shield to avoid my questions.

My head throbbed, my face hurt, and the traffic noise outside felt like it was stabbing into my ears. His words had left a bitter taste.

Sensing my irritation, Mr. Aggarwal changed his tone.

"By the way, Arjun, Vikram Singh is coming to Siliguri tomorrow. You're supposed to meet him for that Bhutan bulk order deal. He'll meet you at Jaigaon tomorrow evening."

Hearing Vikram Singh's name lifted my spirits. He was our Territory Manager and someone I respected deeply. I couldn't hide my excitement.

"Will you be joining him, sir?" I asked.

"No, I won't. You handle everything. But be careful—he's from the manufacturer. Don't mention any internal dealership issues. It could backfire."

"Don't worry, Sir. I'll take care of it," I said.

He ended the call. I finished my tea and snacks and got back on the road, heading to Jaigaon.

# CHAPTER 19

# *After the Storm, Her Voice*

At 6:55 p.m., I turned left from Hasimara toward Jaigaon—just twenty kilometers away. The narrow road wound through tea gardens, my headlights brushing across rows of bushes shimmering in the night.

The phone rang. Isha's voice filled the cabin through the receiver.

"Hey Arjun, where are you?"

"Almost at Jaigaon," I said.

"Are you okay? Mr. Aggarwal said Harun's men attacked you in Birpara—you were hurt!"

Even in my exhaustion, I smiled faintly. "I'm fine, Isha. Just another day in sales. Nothing I can't handle."

After a pause, she said softly, "I'm coming to Jaigaon tomorrow to meet you."

"Tomorrow?" I asked, a wave of relief washing over me.

"Yes. I asked for leave—Aggarwal grumbled, but gave me three days off," she said, laughing lightly.

"So, you managed to win that battle too," I said, steering carefully through the dark bends.

"Yes—and he also gave me a task dur—"

Her voice broke. The signal dropped.

"Isha? Can you hear me?"

Static. Then faintly: "Hello, Arjun? Hello…?"

The line cleared.

"Yes, Isha. Got you now," I said.

"Good. You're clear, too."

"So, what task did he assign you?"

"He wants me to help you close the Bhutan bulk deal," she said, with a smile I could almost hear.

"That's good news," I said.

"And maybe," she added playfully, "we'll get to spend some time together too."

"You're right. Come early tomorrow. I need to prepare for the deal."

"Okay, Arjun. I'll head home now and start early," she said, before the call faded into the hum of the night road.

CHAPTER 20

# Room No. 206: Where Business Blurs

While talking to Isha on the phone, I heard a faint beep—someone else was calling. But I was so lost in her voice that I ignored it. When the call ended, I glanced at the screen—ten missed calls. That couldn't be good.

I stepped out of the truck, turned on the parking lights, and walked a few steps into the dark. I really needed to pee. After that, I lit a cigarette and stood quietly, letting the smoke and silence ease the day's stress.

Then I checked my phone again. All ten missed calls were from Sonu Kumar—the broker from Jaigaon who often passed me key updates about the Bhutan market. I called him back right away.

After a few rings, he picked up. He sounded annoyed.

"Arjun Da! I've been calling for ten minutes! Where were you?"

I laughed. "Sorry, Sonu. I had to take another call."

"You should've picked up mine first. You know I don't call without a reason," he said, half serious, half joking.

"My mistake, bhai. I'll make sure to answer faster next time." I called him. "Bhai"—brother—a simple word of kinship, offered to ease his heart.

"So, when will you reach Jaigaon?"

"I'm almost there. Just 5 kilometers away. Should reach by 8:30 p.m. Can you book a room for me?"

"No problem. I've arranged everything—hotel, food, and even some fun," he teased.

Laughing, I said, "I just need a clean room and your company. That's enough for me."

"Great! I'll come meet you at the hotel around 9:30," he replied cheerfully.

At 9 p.m., I reached Imperial Lodge, tired after a long, rough day. I checked into my favorite room, 206, took a quick shower, and asked the room service guy to send me a cup of tea.

Then I called my mom. As soon as she answered, her worried voice came through.

"Arjun! Why didn't you call after reaching? " Ma's voice shook on the line.

"I was dying with worry."

Her words pierced me. I closed my eyes for a moment, guilt pressing heavily on my chest.

"Ever since your father left us… You're all I have."

My grip tightened on the phone.

Her voice cracked.

"Please, come back home."

A pause hung in the air. She was almost whispering now.

"Find a steady government job. This risky field job of yours…"

Her breath hitched.

"Every day it feels like I might lose you, too."

I swallowed hard, the weight of her words sinking deep into me.

I could hear her holding back tears. I felt a wave of guilt wash over me. I tried to calm her down.

"Ma, please don't worry. I'm fine now. Just give me three more days—I'll be home soon. I've started preparing for my MBA exam. One day, I'll get a good office job. Picture this—your son in a cabin, AC blowing cool air, working with a team, travelling on flights, and staying in star hotels."

I knew I was trying to make it sound better than it really was. But I wanted her to feel proud and happy.

Even though I didn't tell her about today's attack, somehow she sensed something.

"Are you okay? Did anything happen today?" she asked softly.

I looked at myself in the mirror. My face was clean, but the cuts from Harun's attack were still visible—one on my cheek, one near my lip.

"I'm fine, Ma," I lied gently. "You always worry too much. There's nothing wrong."

She didn't sound convinced. "Just take care of yourself. Have you eaten anything?"

"Not yet. I was about to order dinner," I replied.

"Please eat well, and call me early tomorrow morning," she said before hanging up.

After my mother hung up, I heard two short beeps from my phone. I glanced at the screen—two unread messages. The first was from Mr. Vikram Singh of Rana Motors.

"Hey Arjun, I'll be there tomorrow for the Bhutan deal. Let me know where I'm needed."

I typed back immediately:

"Good evening, Sir. I'm already in Jaigaon and making preparations."

Another message popped up within seconds:

"Great to hear. You're always ahead, Arjun. Let's catch up tomorrow. Good night!"

I replied with a simple:

"Good night, Sir."

The room was quiet. The low hum of the ceiling fan stirred the air. Just then, the doorbell rang—two quick chimes.

"Come in," I called out, expecting room service.

Instead, it was Sonu Kumar. He stepped inside with his usual bold stride. Slim, sharp-eyed, and slightly hunched, his tobacco-stained smile lit up as if he owned the place.

"Arjun Da! Long time, huh?" he said, reaching out for a handshake.

I stood up and shook his hand, motioning toward the sofa. He pushed the glass table a bit and dropped into the seat, as he belonged there.

"How's everyone at home?" I asked out of courtesy.

"Same as always," he said vaguely, already scanning the room, as if looking for something more interesting than small talk.

He wore faded jeans and a loose shirt with overstuffed pockets. Settling in, he crossed one leg over the other and tapped his foot nonstop. He reached into his pocket, pulled out a cigarette, and lit it without asking. Smoke rings floated into the air as his restless eyes wandered.

In a sudden move, he stood up again. From one of his oversized pockets, he pulled out two small bottles of whisky and placed them on the table like prized possessions.

His grin widened. "Arjun Da, tonight we drink!"

Sonu ran a used car showroom in Jaigaon. His reach extended across Darjeeling, Alipurduar, and into Bhutan. He had brokered the current Bhutan truck deal—twenty vehicles—thanks to his local influence.

On paper, he was a business ally. In practice, he was unpredictable. His days were spent chasing leads; his nights chasing liquor and women. That duality made him both useful and dangerous.

I smiled politely but didn't reach for the bottle. Drinking with Sonu was always risky. He didn't know when to stop. I'd seen him lose control too many times to pretend tonight would be different.

"Come on, Arjun Da, just one drink! It's a gift from me!" He laughed, his reddish teeth showing through the smoke.

"I'm not in the mood tonight," I said, keeping my tone light.

Unbothered, he waved his hand and said, "Then just order some chakna for me, at least."

I called room service. "One plate of French fries and one peanut masala, please."

Sonu leaned in and snatched the phone from my hand.

"Add a crispy chicken and two fish fingers," he said, grinning like a kid in a candy store.

He kicked off his shoes, threw his legs on the sofa, and kept smoking. Ash spilled onto the floor. I sat back, watching the bill climb in my mind. His appetite would land me in trouble again with the accounts team. Mr. Aggarwal would have something to say for sure.

But Sonu wasn't just anyone. His referrals brought real business. Customers trusted his word more than any of our ads or brochures. That influence came at a price.

To keep him close, I had worked out a commission deal. For every lead that converted into a sale, he got a cut. It wasn't ideal, but in our world, it was how things worked.

He looked at me again, still grinning.

"So, ArjunDa… what's the plan for tonight? You're awfully quiet."

I didn't answer right away.

I just leaned back and listened to the fan spin above us, counting the seconds between each whir.

The room started to smell awful—Sonu's sweaty socks and cigarette smoke made the air heavy. I felt lightheaded and restless. I got up, opened all the windows and doors, and stepped out to the balcony for some fresh air.

When I returned and sat on the bed, I asked, "So, Sonu, what's the update on that 20-truck deal in Bhutan? We really hope to close it soon."

Sonu crushed his cigarette into the ashtray and leaned forward. "Don't worry, Arjun Da. I've got it under control."

"You know Mr. Vikram Singh is coming tomorrow—from Rana Motors. Is the customer really serious about buying 20 Turbo Cheetahs?"

Sonu grinned. "Of course. They trust me. I've already delivered 10 trucks. These are big construction firms—they don't waste time once they decide."

Sonu wasn't just a broker; he had strong local influence, especially in Bhutan. Still, when I asked for the company's name, he refused.

"First, confirm my commission, Arjun Da. You keep chasing me, but you haven't fixed my payment."

I nodded. "Relax, Sonu. I'll speak to Mr. Aggarwal tomorrow and confirm everything."

He frowned. "No friendship in money matters, Arjun Da. This is business."

I took a breath and asked, "What exactly are you expecting?"

"Twenty thousand per vehicle. That's four lakhs for the whole deal."

His directness made me pause. I lit a cigarette from his packet and took a slow puff, watching him pace the room again, leaving muddy footprints on the clean floor.

"Let me check with my boss first," I said calmly.

He sat down again. "Fine, but I won't take you to the customer until it's confirmed."

Just then, the doorbell rang. I called out, "Come in."

It was Ashis, the room service boy. He walked in carrying trays of food. "Hello, Sir, how are you? Today's food is extra tasty," he said with a smile.

Ashis was a young man, barely twenty, with a dark face and thin mustache. Another boy followed, bringing chicken crispy and fish fingers. The warm smell filled the room. After a long day, I realized how hungry I was.

Sonu turned to them. "Where's the soda and water bottles? Go bring two sodas and four mineral waters."

"Yes, Sir!" Ashis replied quickly.

Before he left, I gave him a ₹100 tip. He smiled and thanked me. I always tipped hotel staff—it made future service easier.

Sonu, now in a full party mood, looked at me eagerly. "Come on, Arjun Da. Just one drink with me."

I hesitated but said yes to keep him happy. "Fine. One drink."

Sonu lit up like a kid. "Yes! I've got company!"

He knocked on the whisky bottle three times, then opened it with a smile. As he poured himself a drink, he grumbled, "This hotel's service is so slow."

Soon, Ashis returned with cold soda and water bottles. The bottles were frosted, tiny water drops forming on their sides. Sonu added soda to his whisky and handed me a glass.

I took a small sip, picked up a fish finger, and bit into it.

Sonu, true to his style, gulped his first drink down in one go. He leaned back, looking satisfied. I, on the other hand, took it slow, the weight of the day still resting heavily on my shoulders.

As Sonu lit another cigarette and filled the room with smoke, he changed the topic without warning.

"Arjun Da," he said in a low voice, "feel like meeting someone special tonight?"

I looked at him, surprised. "What do you mean?"

"There are two new girls staying at a nearby hotel," he said with a grin. "Young, about nineteen or twenty. The manager said they're fresh faces. If you want to join, just say the word."

He poured himself another drink and nudged my glass, urging me to finish mine. Though Sonu was helpful in getting business from Jaigaon and Bhutan, his habits — heavy drinking and late-night activities — always made me uncomfortable. His lifestyle didn't match my values. Still, I kept calm. The business mattered.

"Not tonight, Sonu. I'm really not in the mood," I said firmly.

"Are you sure? They looked pretty good. Your night could turn interesting," he chuckled.

His suggestion made me uneasy. I didn't know how serious he was or how much he cared about his own reputation, but I had my own image to think of. Still, I knew people like him held influence—and that couldn't be ignored.

Sonu was good at his work, no doubt. He brought in valuable deals for our company. So, I smiled and politely turned him down.

"I'm not feeling well, Sonu. You go ahead if you want to," I said, trying to end the conversation.

He looked at me for a moment. "Yeah, I noticed those bruises on your face. Forgot to ask. What happened, Arjun Da?"

"Had a bit of an accident today," I said. "But nothing major. I'm okay now."

"Take care of yourself, okay?" he replied, pouring himself another drink.

"Want to order dinner?" I offered.

"No need," he mumbled. "The snacks were enough."

By now, Sonu was fully drunk—his words were slow and his eyes heavy. Around 10:20 pm, he got a call. I heard him speak into the phone, "Pradhan! Everything ready tonight?"

Then his tone turned into bargaining mode. "No, no… seven thousand is too much. You know I don't go beyond five for a fresh face."

His phone conversation dragged on for a while. He was clearly lost in his own world now, giving in to whatever desire was leading him.

His eyes had changed—no longer lively, just glazed over. He walked clumsily to the door, nearly stumbling.

"I'm off to enjoy my night, Arjun Da," he whispered.

"You're too drunk, Sonu. Go home and rest," I said, trying to get him out safely.

He called for the bill. I told him, "Let it be, Sonu. I'll pay for tonight."

But he pulled out a bunch of Rs. 2000 notes, the smell of alcohol and food still heavy on his clothes. "That Pradhan lies all the time," he mumbled. "Says she's fresh—but I know better."

Room service came with the final bill. I tried to take it, but Sonu grabbed it first and paid for it all.

While staggering toward the door, he turned and said, "See you tomorrow, Arjun Da. But don't forget — I want that commission sorted before Bhutan."

He was drunk, messy, and difficult—but when it came to money, Sonu never joked.

CHAPTER 21

# Chasing the Yes

The next morning, I woke around seven. The air was cool, the world fresh and quiet. After a quick stretch and shower, I sat with a cup of tea and the morning paper. The sun had already turned sharp, hinting at the monsoon heat.

Following my mother's advice, I called her. I told her about my plans for the day; she reminded me, as always, to eat well and stay careful. I promised I would—and reminded her to take her medicines too.

Just after I hung up, my phone rang again. It was Isha.

"Hey Arjun, good morning! Still in bed? I'm already at Dhupguri," she laughed over the traffic noise.

"No, I'm up. Just planning my Bhutan visit," I said.

"Oh, nice! Vikram Sir's going to Jaigaon today too. We might all meet there!"

I smiled. Vikram Singh had that effect—everyone liked him.

"When will you reach Jaigaon?"

"Around noon."

"Perfect. Drop by my place," I said, though my mind was elsewhere—on the Bhutan deal that refused to leave me in peace.

Sonu had asked me to reach his office by eleven to sort the Bhutan permit and paperwork. It added more weight to an already loaded morning.

At nine, the phone rang again. The ringtone cut through the air like a warning. It was Mr. Sanjeev Singh—the police inspector.

I took a breath and answered.

"Hello Arjun, where are you? This is Sanjeev Singh from Maynaguri police," he said, his tone firm.

"Good morning, Sir. I'm in Jaigaon for some urgent work."

"What's going on with Hamid Alam's case? He keeps calling. You seem decent, no record—maybe it's just a gap in the process."

"Yes, Sir, we're fixing it," I said quietly.

"Listen, legally you can't repossess a vehicle unless there's a default. The complaint is against you—not your company. You're the face here."

"I understand, Sir. I'll resolve it soon."

"You have one week. After that, I'll have to act," he said flatly.

"Yes, Sir," I replied, heart sinking.

As the call ended, I looked up. The ceiling fan spun fast, but it didn't help. Two drops of sweat rolled down my forehead. The pressure was building.

Just then, the doorbell rang. Room service brought breakfast, but I couldn't focus. My mind was stuck on the Hamid Alam case.

Everything looked fine on paper—the customer had signed, the finance company had approved, and Mr. S. K. Aggarwal himself had handed over the vehicle. Then why did he repossess it without telling me?

His silence was ruining everything. It was driving me crazy. I felt trapped.

As I ate the puri, sabji, and curd, my thoughts wouldn't stop. It felt like I was eating stress. I had never gone over my boss's head before. But this was serious—maybe even dangerous.

I had to speak to Mr. Rakesh Chetri, our General Manager. I had no choice now.

After finishing breakfast, I washed my hands and dialed Mr. Rakesh Chetri.

"Hello, Sir. It's Arjun."

"Arjun! Good to hear from you. How are things? And how's your mother?" His tone was warm and professional.

"I'm doing well, Sir. She's okay, too," I replied.

There was a pause. Then came the real talk.

"So, what's your target status this month? We're falling behind on Mission 51%. You've always been one of our strongest performers—we're counting on you."

"My monthly target is 12. I've sold 5 so far. I'm confident I can close the rest before month-end," I said, steadying my tone.

"Confident, huh? Any big opportunities?"

"Yes, Sir. I'm heading to Bhutan today. A construction company is showing interest in 20 Rana Turbo Cheetah Trucks. If it works out, they'll issue a work order for 10 this month itself."

"That's big. If you pull it off, we'll be able to increase our market share significantly in your territory. Go all in. And remember—Mission 51% is our top priority now. If you need help, reach out. Mr. Vikram is joining you at Jaigaon today. Coordinate with him."

I hesitated for a second, then spoke.

"Sir… I need to share something. There's an issue with a customer—Mr. Hamid Alam."

"What kind of issue?"

"Sir, his paperwork and payments were all clear. But somehow, our dealership repossessed his vehicle. I wasn't informed. Now there's a police case against me. They've given me seven days to fix it."

"Have you spoken to Mr. Aggarwal about this?"

"Yes, Sir. He said he's working on it, but nothing's been resolved yet."

"Alright. I'll speak to him directly."

"Thank you, Sir. This has become a serious issue. If it stays unresolved, the competition will use it to damage our reputation. I really need your support."

"Understood. I'll handle it," he said. Then the call ended.

I exhaled deeply. It felt good to be heard. But I knew the toughest conversation was still waiting.

Five missed calls were already stacked on my screen. One was from Mr. S. K. Aggarwal. My immediate boss.

I took a deep breath, tapped his name, and held the phone to my ear.

"Good morning, Sir," I said, trying to stay calm.

"Morning," he replied dryly, like the word was bitter.

"So, enjoying yourself in Jaigaon?" he asked, heavy with sarcasm.

I clenched my jaw. "Sir, I'm not here for leisure. I'm chasing a major bulk deal."

"Oh, a deal. "How exciting," he snapped. "It's the 24th of July, and you've sold five vehicles out of twelve. Should I close your sheet at five?"

"Sir, today, BKBC Finance is confirming the delivery order for two more. Plus, I have ten hot prospects that could close by month-end," I said confidently.

"And how do you plan to deliver those? You're lounging in Bhutan."

"I'm not lounging, Sir. I'm working in the field. Building trust, warming up leads. These customers will walk into the showroom ready to sign."

"I'm not your delivery boy, Arjun. You want sales? You manage deliveries."

"I know that, Sir. I've been leading sales every month. I arrange finance, handle objections, and bring in retail cases—and I hand over ready deals. All I ask is a little backup when things heat up."

He scoffed. "Save the speech. Just give me your list of potential cases. And by the way—I need a minimum of 15 TCT sales from you this month. We're under massive pressure from Rana Motors to secure 40% share."

He continued without waiting. "The regional manager wants us to hit Mission 51% by September. Half-year closing. This isn't a joke."

"I understand, Sir," I said. "That's why I'm pushing for the Bhutan bulk deal. If we close it, that alone will lift our numbers."

He paused for a beat. "This deal better happen this month. I want those 20 vehicles booked now."

I knew closing a bulk deal in a few days was like chasing clouds. But I gave him the only thing that might cool his anger.

"Yes, Sir. I'll try my best to close it within the month."

Mr. Aggarwal's voice barked through the phone. "Tell me the status of each of your cases—right now. I need to go through everything."

I glanced at my watch. It was already 10:30 a.m. I had a meeting with Sonu at 11. Time was running tight.

Still, I pulled out my diary from the bag and sat down on the sofa. There was no skipping this.

For the next 45 minutes, Mr. S. K. Aggarwal went over every single customer name and deal. He picked apart each case, questioning the details, the follow-ups, and the odds of closure. His tone was sharp, clinical—like he was dissecting a body, not reviewing sales.

I answered patiently, flipping through notes, giving him numbers and timelines. One by one, we moved down the list.

Finally, after nearly an hour, he paused. Then, in his usual cold tone, he said, "Is there anything else you need from me to help reach your target?"

I forced a steady voice. "No, Sir. Nothing as of now. If I need any support, I'll reach out."

What I really wanted to mention was the Hamid Alam case. That was the real pain point—the one thing weighing down everything else. But I knew him too well. Instead of helping, he'd twist the knife further. His support always came wrapped in sarcasm and blame.

And just like that, without another word, he hung up.

After Mr. S. K. Aggarwal called, I quickly left my hotel room and handed the key to the receptionist. Sonu's office was just a kilometer away, so I rushed there on foot.

Sonu seemed a little off that morning. He greeted me with a serious "Good morning" and asked me to sit down. As always, he offered tea. I asked for green tea—it helps me stay sharp.

"Arjun Da, just chill for a bit," Sonu said. "Let me finish this morning rush. Then I'll take care of your Bhutan entry permit. Keep your vehicle documents, government ID, and company ID ready."

I nodded. "Also, Sonu, please arrange permits for Mr. Vikram Singh—he's the Territory Manager—and our receptionist, Isha."

He already knew Vikram. But when I mentioned Isha Sharma, his eyes lit up with a trace of mischief. Still, he kept his tone professional.

"Alright," he said. "Share their ID proofs."

"No worries," I replied. "I've already sent them over messaging."

He opened his phone and scrolled through the documents. Then, with a half-smile, he said, "Isha Sharma, 23 years old. What's she up to in Bhutan?"

I answered calmly, "Mr. Aggarwal wants her there to help close the deal."

Sonu closed his phone and slipped it into his pocket. With a knowing smile, he said, "This Bhutan trip might turn out interesting."

I didn't react. Instead, I opened my diary and got to work. I had to call fifty potential customers that day. Most had shown interest in buying a vehicle within three months, but were facing one issue or another. My job was to follow up, solve their problems, and move them closer to booking.

I began my calls for the day.

The first number was Mr. Anil Ray from Shalbari in Jalpaiguri. He cared more about discounts than the truck itself. Our July offer was ₹20,000 off, but he wanted ₹30,000. I had approval for ₹25,000, but thought I'd try my luck.

I dialed. After a few rings, he picked up.

"Hello? Who's this?"

"Hello, Mr. Ray. This is Arjun from Darjeeling Auto Works, Rana Motors. How are you today?"

"Oh, hey, Arjun! I'm fine. What's going on?"

"I just wanted to follow up on our last discussion about an extra ₹5,000 off. Maybe I can do a little better."

He paused. "Hmm… I appreciate that. But things are tight. I'll need a bigger discount to move forward."

"I understand. How about ₹30,000 off? That's ₹10,000 more than the base offer."

His tone shifted—a flicker of interest. "That does sound tempting. But I'll still have to check my budget."

"Of course. The Rana Turbo Cheetah fits your needs perfectly. At this price, you're getting real value."

He chuckled. "You make a good case. Let me think about it."

"Sure. But the offer's valid only till July 28. I wouldn't want you to miss it."

"Got it. I'll work out the numbers and let you know by day's end."

"Great, Mr. Ray. I'll wait for your call."

I noted his status in my diary. Just then, Bappa—Sonu's office boy—brought in green tea and biscuits.

"Thanks, Bappa," I said, taking a sip. The tea was hot and strong. After a few bites, I felt fresher—ready for the next call.

Next up was Mr. Shibu Ghosh, a small tea garden owner.

Phone rings.

"Hello? Who's this?" His voice carried fatigue.

"Good afternoon, Mr. Shibu. This is Arjun from Darjeeling Auto Works. How's everything in Malbazar?"

"Oh, Mr. Arjun. I'm alright, just a bit tied up. What's up?"

I pictured him in his garden—workers scattered across rows of green, the season at its peak.

"I know you're busy, sir. Just wanted to follow up on our earlier talk about the Rana Turbo Cheetah Truck. It could really help this season."

In the background, I heard workers loading freshly plucked tea leaves.

"How exactly would it help me?"

"Speed matters in your business," I explained. "The fresher the leaves, the better the price. The Turbo Cheetah gets them to the factory faster, keeping quality intact."

He hesitated. "That engine you mentioned—it sounded good. But I still need to check more."

"Of course. It's a 2400 cc, 4-cylinder engine—powerful yet smooth. Quick pickup, strong brakes, excellent control. Built for terrain like yours."

"But other trucks also offer similar features. How is yours better?"

"A fair question," I said. "On paper, many trucks look the same. But the Turbo Cheetah pulls ahead—better torque on hill climbs, stronger suspension, a build that lasts. Take a test drive and see."

He gave instructions to someone nearby, then said, "It does sound solid. But I've got another issue—cash. I don't have enough for the down payment. Can you manage with just 5% upfront?"

That caught me off guard. Most banks went up to 90% financing. Ninety-five was rare.

"I understand, sir. Luckily, we work closely with BKBC Retail Finance. They've helped customers in similar situations. I'll check if we can stretch beyond 90%."

He called out to weigh tea leaves, then returned.

"Okay, that sounds better. But I won't go ahead unless the interest stays below 10%. Can you make that happen?"

I winced silently. BKBC's best was 12%. Still, I couldn't let the deal slip.

"I'll speak to them today and try my best. If we find middle ground, can we book it now? We even have online booking."

He was firm. "Not until I get clear answers on down payment and interest. Take your time, but get back to me within a week."

He hung up.

I stared at my screen. A solid deal—slipping away, but not lost. I needed a plan. Fast.

I dialed the next number.

"Hello? Who's this?" came a weary voice.

"Hello, is this Mr. Ferdous Alam? This is Arjun from Darjeeling Auto Works, Rana Motors' authorized dealer."

"Yeah, Ferdous here. What's up?" His voice was heavy, like someone carrying a long day.

I knew he was busy with his fertilizer shop. I tried to ease the tone.

"Hope I'm not catching you at a bad time. Just wanted to talk about our Rana Turbo Cheetah Truck. We've got a special offer this month that could help your deliveries."

He wasn't enthusiastic. "Special offer? Not in the mood. Business has been slow."

"I understand," I said gently. "The monsoon's hit everyone hard. But this truck can ease some pressure—faster deliveries, better mileage. Plus, we're offering ₹20,000 off this month."

I heard the bustle of traffic outside his shop, followed by his long sigh.

"Look, Arjun, I appreciate the call. But money's tight. I can't afford risks right now."

"I get that, Ferdous. Times are uncertain. But this isn't just a purchase—it's something that will save you money in the long run."

He hesitated. "Maybe. But right now, even small risks feel big."

Just then, Isha walked into the office and took a seat. I gave her a quick nod, then turned back to the call. Ferdous needed full attention.

"I hear you," I said. "Let's see if we can work out something that fits your situation—maybe a financing plan that keeps your cash flow safe."

He went quiet, then spoke more softly.

"It's not just the money. The market's unpredictable. And I've got debts."

I leaned in. "Then let's take it step by step. We'll explore a loan plan that works. And with better logistics, your business might recover faster."

Another pause. This time, he didn't sound as guarded.

"Alright, Arjun. I'm open to hearing what you've got—just nothing that drains my wallet."

Relief flickered inside me. The door wasn't closed.

"Fair enough. Give me three days—I'll speak with my boss and our finance team. I'll come back with something practical."

"Okay," he said at last. "I'll wait for your call."

CHAPTER 22

# *Margins on Fire*

After ending the call with Mr. Ferdous Alam, I looked at Isha. She was scribbling in her diary, a light breeze playing with her hair. A stray strand rested gently on her forehead, adding to her calm charm.

She noticed me staring and smiled. “So, how’s it going with the deliveries? Still on track for this month?”

“Not really,” I sighed. “Five vehicles delivered so far. Two more might go tomorrow—BKBC Finance is issuing the orders.”

“But your target was twelve, right? How do you plan to close the gap?”

“I’m following up hard today. Maybe two more deals. That’ll take me to nine,” I said, trying to sound hopeful.

She nodded. “Don’t forget the Bhutan deal. If that clicks, it could take you past target.”

“You’re right. It’s big—but tough too. It’s for a construction company. Hard to please.”

I turned to the window, thinking aloud.

Just then, Bappa, the office boy, walked in with sweets and cold drinks—clearly Sonu’s treat for Isha.

As Bappa set the tray down, I smiled. “Looks like Sonu’s spoiling you today. Go ahead, Miss Beautiqueen. But keep an eye on him!”

Isha smirked. “Sonu knows better. We’re both from Jaigaon—he won’t try anything funny.”

“Good. Then enjoy the treat,” I said, trying to lighten the mood.

She offered me a sweet. I refused at first, but then took a spoonful and smiled.

She popped one into her mouth. "So, what's making this Bhutan deal so tricky?"

"We're up against four other companies," I replied.

Isha leaned back on the sofa, curious. "You ready for the challenge?"

"Yeah. I've prepared for most of their technical questions. But still…" I paused.

She placed the cold drink down. "But what's bothering you?"

I took a sip of water. "You know the names—Raftar Motors, StormX Automotive, Tejas Automotive. All in the game."

"They're strong players," she said, adjusting her glasses.

I nodded. "Raftar's new, offering huge discounts. StormX skips all formalities—just drops vehicles at customers' homes. And Tejas? ₹50,000 cheaper, 3.99% interest."

I sighed. "And both Raftar and StormX give 2 km/l better mileage than our Cheetah. That's a big factor."

Isha listened carefully. "Sounds tough. But don't worry—Mr. Aggarwal's backing you on discounts."

I chuckled. "If I lose, he'll blame me. If it works, he'll take credit."

She smiled. "Come on, Arjun. You've got Rakesh Chetri and Vikram Singh helping too, right?"

"Yeah. If they step in, we might pull this off."

Just then, Sonu walked in—files in hand, chewing betel nut, cigarette in the other. He sat beside Isha, who shifted slightly.

He looked straight at me. "So, Arjun Da, what's happening with my commission?"

I hadn't spoken to Mr. Aggarwal about Sonu's cut yet. The heat outside and traffic noise made the air feel heavier.

Our dealer margin was only ₹50,000 per truck. But Sonu wanted ₹20,000—leaving hardly anything for discounts or costs.

I said calmly, "Sonu, we can't go above ₹5,000. We need the rest for customer offers. The margins are tight."

Sonu frowned. "No problem. If your dealership won't pay, others will."

"I'll talk to my seniors," I said evenly. "Give me some time."

Sonu leaned in, voice cold. "Arjun Da, talk to your bosses. Finalize my commission—twenty thousand, not a rupee less."

He stood up slowly, letting his words sink in.

"You'll have your permit in half an hour. But I'm not sharing the client details till I get confirmation. I'll be back in thirty minutes."

He paused. "If you can't match my terms, I'll hand this case to someone else."

And with that, he walked off—leaving behind silence and a rising pulse.

Outside, he went to the display area to check refurbished cars—old hatchbacks to luxury models, all neatly lined and polished, each with a six-month warranty.

He noticed the tires looked dusty and told his office boy, "Polish the tires again. They need to shine. Customers notice these things."

This showroom was his main source of leads. He sold 10–15 used cars a month. For vehicles he couldn't sell, he passed the leads to other dealerships—and always earned a commission.

Brokers like him ruled the market. They knew local buyers well and had earned their trust over the years. Sometimes, customers trusted these brokers more than the authorized dealers.

Many buyers didn't fully understand how authorized dealerships worked or what benefits they offered. Brokers took advantage, convincing people that buying through them was safe. In reality, customers often lost out on discounts, warranties, or better finance options—while brokers earned high commissions from dealerships.

To maintain sales, dealers and even manufacturers gave in. The market had accepted this flawed system, and until customers became more aware, the unfair game would continue.

CHAPTER 23

# Sweet Visits and Bitter Truths

This passage is strong, cinematic, and emotionally grounded — it doesn't need major trimming. However, it can be made around 20% tighter while keeping the tone, rhythm, and emotional flow intact. The trimming mainly removes minor repetitions or slow spots without losing depth or charm.

Here's a refined version with the same tone and content:

After Sonu left, I turned to Isha. "Lunch at a hotel?"

She smiled. "Let's eat at home. It's just a kilometer away. My parents already know about you."

"I don't know… what if they don't like me showing up?"

"They won't mind," she said, laughing. "We can also discuss Sonu's commission there."

I hesitated, but she took my hand. "Come on."

A little shy, I followed. On the way, I stopped at a sweet shop. "You really don't have to," she said.

"Still," I smiled, buying sweets—and chocolates for her sister Nisha, who she'd mentioned was in class eleven.

We walked through the busy lanes of Jaigaon. Her long hair flowed in the breeze, her perfume lingering in the air. The way she walked—confident and effortless—was almost like music.

Soon, she stopped before a gate. "We're here."

Her mother, a woman in her forties with a kind smile, opened the door. Beside her stood a teenage girl—Nisha. They greeted me warmly.

The living room was tastefully done—elegant furniture, a flat-screen TV, and an aquarium glowing in one corner. I sat quietly, feeling slightly out of place. Isha came from comfort; I didn't. I reminded myself not to dream too far.

Her mother turned on the AC. "I know who you are," she said warmly. "Isha talks about you a lot. How's your mother?"

"She's better now, Aunty," I replied.

Isha returned, changed, and brought me sweets and water.

"I can't finish all this," I said, embarrassed.

"Oh, stop being formal," she teased. "You've got a sweet tooth."

Nisha walked in, munching on the chocolates. "Your chocolate is amazing, Arjun!"

"Nisha," her mother said, smiling, "call him Arjun Da."

"Okay, Arjun Da," she giggled. "Isha says your truck flies like lightning. Will you take me on a ride?"

I laughed. "Of course. Next month."

"But in the hills!" she added eagerly.

While chatting, Isha nudged me. "Eat quickly—we've got work."

After two sweets, I gave in.

Then she turned to her mom. "Ma, can lunch be ready soon? We have office work after."

Her mom nodded. "Give me 45 minutes."

As she left for the kitchen, Isha adjusted the AC. "By the way, Arjun," she said, her tone firm, "could you call Mr. Aggarwal about Sonu's commission? We need that 20-truck deal closed."

Her words snapped me out of guest mode—it was business again. I dialed Mr. Aggarwal.

"Hello," he answered, his tone sharp.

"Good afternoon, Sir."

"What made you call at lunchtime? Have you eaten?"

"Not yet, Sir."

"You're at 42% of your target. If you can't sell, at least eat. Don't roam Phuntsholing like a tourist."

His words stung. I steadied my voice. "Sir, the issue is Sonu's commission. He's asking for ₹20,000. I offered ₹5,000."

"You what?" he snapped. "We're not running a charity. Think about profits. Closing deals is fine—but do it responsibly."

"I understand, Sir. But this deal could lift our numbers and strengthen the brand. Please think it over and let me know by evening."

He sighed. "You complicate everything. I'll check with the GM and MD." Click.

Even in the cool air, I was sweating. Isha noticed but said nothing.

At lunch, her family treated me with warmth, but I felt distant. Their comfort reminded me of what I didn't have. They lived in abundance; I lived counting coins. The contrast made me feel small.

The smell of fish curry filled the room, but my appetite was gone. I couldn't stop thinking—how could I ever match this lifestyle? I felt guilty for even dreaming of being part of it. Guilty for feeling so strongly for Isha, knowing I couldn't offer her what she already had.

Taking a bite of the fish, my guilt only grew. It wasn't just about money. It felt like I was crossing a line—aspiring to something I didn't deserve.

Isha's voice broke my thoughts. She reminded me about the upcoming meeting with Mr. Vikram Singh. Business didn't wait for feelings. No room for doubt.

As I forced myself to eat, Nisha made a light joke about age and shyness. It hit a nerve. But I let it go. I couldn't afford to be sensitive. I had to prove myself—to them and to myself.

In that moment, surrounded by comfort and expectations, I made a quiet promise: I would rise. No matter the odds, I'd earn my place here.

Just as we finished lunch, my phone buzzed. I dried my hands and checked—it was Mr. S. K. Aggarwal. I hurried to the drawing room. Isha followed.

I answered the call.

"Arjun," he said, "we've discussed Sonu's commission with Mr. Rakesh and Rana Motors. We can go up to Rs. 12,000."

"Thanks for the update, sir. But Sonu's holding firm at Rs. 20,000. Can we settle at Rs. 15,000?"

"Arjun, improve your negotiation skills," he said firmly. "Rs. 12,000 is the final offer."

"Understood, sir. I'll do my best to convince him."

"Good. Sit with him and close it today. Also, did Isha meet you in Jaigaon? She'll help with the financial paperwork. But first, focus on getting this done."

He hung up.

I looked at Isha. "Let's go to Sonu's office now. We have to get him to agree to Rs. 12,000. This deal is too important. We can't afford to lose it."

CHAPTER 24

# Everything But the Name

We hurried through the busy street and reached Sonu's office around 4:15 PM.

Inside the small showroom, two ceiling fans and a table fan spun loudly, fighting the heat. Sonu sat at his desk, talking to three customers. The place felt worn out from the long day.

He noticed us and pointed to the chairs. We sat quietly, waiting.

As he spoke with his customers, I kept thinking of how to convince him. Even though our company discouraged using brokers, people like Sonu still ruled the market.

A few minutes later, he came over. Sweat on his forehead, voice low, he asked, "Did you both eat anything?"

"Yes, Sonu," I said. "We had lunch."

"And you?"

He shook his head. "No, Arjun Da. But I'll order some snacks for us." He called for the office boy. Then got straight to the point. "So, what's the final word on my commission?"

I looked at Isha, then said, "Sonu, we spent the last three hours fighting for ₹20,000 for you. But the dealership can't manage that after all the discounts. Still, we've got approval for a fair amount."

He raised an eyebrow. "And what's this 'fair' amount?"

"₹12,000," I said. "That's the best we can offer without hurting the dealership. But closing this deal will really boost our presence in Bhutan."

Sonu frowned. "Arjun Da, I waited for you because we go way back. Otherwise, I could've given this deal to someone else. The managing director trusts me—they'll only go through me."

Before I could reply, Isha spoke gently, "Sonu Da, I know how strong your connections are in Jaigaon and Bhutan. As your neighbor, I'm asking you—let's make this work together."

Sonu looked surprised. "Sister Isha? No one calls me Da except my real sisters. But… you've touched something in me. I'll consider it."

Isha smiled. "To me, you're like a brother. And brothers look out for each other."

Sonu nodded. "Of course, Sister Isha."

I was stunned. Sonu—known for his flirtatious ways—had just accepted Isha as a sister.

The office boy returned with tea and snacks—sandwiches, pakoras, and crunchy corn.

Sonu took a bite and said, "These are just for my sister and me. But if you're hungry, join us."

I smiled. "Alright, Sonu. But first—₹12,000, agreed?"

He munched on a pakora. "I'm losing ₹8,000 per vehicle, but I'm agreeing because of Sister Isha—and our bond. Prepare for tomorrow. The customer will have many questions. For now, let's enjoy the snacks."

For fifteen minutes, we sipped tea and chatted casually, finally feeling like a team.

Around 4:55 PM, my phone rang. It was Mr. Vikram Singh.

"Hey Arjun, I'm about 30 kilometers from Jaigaon. Where are you?"

"Good evening, Sir! I'm already here. We're looking forward to seeing you," I said.

"Before anything else, book me a clean hotel with good food," he said. "I don't want to land in some shady place."

"Don't worry, Sir. I'll handle it. Are you coming alone?"

"Yes, alone. Mr. S. K. Aggarwal arranged an SUV for me."

Then his tone sharpened. "Are you ready for tomorrow's deal? The customer won't go easy on us."

"Yes, Sir. I've prepared thoroughly. The deal won't slip through."

"Good. And about finance—lower interest rates, down payments?"

"Isha is taking care of that, Sir."

"Perfect. I'll be there in an hour. Let's have dinner together."

"Absolutely, Sir."

After the call, I told Isha, "Let's wrap up everything before Vikram Sir gets here. Tomorrow's going to be big."

"Where is he now? Is Mr. Aggarwal with him?"

"No, he's coming alone," I said. "And he mentioned dinner tonight."

Isha grinned. "Great! More fun without Mr. Aggarwal."

I walked over to Sonu. "Please book a good hotel for Mr. Vikram Singh."

"Don't worry," he said. "I'll book Capitol International. Best nearby—clean rooms, good food."

"Perfect. He'll want to freshen up before dinner."

Sonu chuckled. "I'll come too. If Vikram Sir wants company, I can help."

I warned, "He's from the principal company. Be respectful."

Sonu laughed. "Don't worry. Just a couple of drinks. No drama."

I didn't argue. I knew how Sonu got after a drink. I left to join Isha in preparing for tomorrow's Bhutan deal.

A few minutes later, Sonu sent me the hotel details. I forwarded everything to Mr. Vikram Singh.

Around 6 PM, he called. "Arjun, I've checked into the hotel. The room's fine. Don't be late. I'll be ready in 20 minutes—we'll meet in the lobby to discuss this month's updates. Only official people."

"Of course, Sir. Only Isha and I will be there."

"Good," he said in his usual corporate tone.

Feeling a bit anxious, I asked Isha to finish up the prep. Once everything was packed, we got ready to leave for Capitol International.

Just as we were stepping out, Sonu called, "Arjun Da, Isha—you're ignoring me!"

I smiled. "No, Sonu. We're meeting Vikram Sir for business. I'll call you later."

Sonu laughed. "Don't forget to take me along for the party tonight!"

"Sure, Sonu," I said.

At Capitol International, the polished marble floors and soft lighting made me pause. My inner voice whispered, Someday you'll stay here—not as a guest, but as someone who belongs. Keep working. You're close.

As we approached, the glass doors slid open automatically.

**"These sensor doors are impressive," Isha said, smiling.**

I nodded. Cool air brushed past us, and the scent of freshener lifted my mood.

A waiter offered water. “We’re here to meet Mr. Vikram Singh,” I said.

“Certainly, Sir.”

Ten minutes later, Mr. Vikram Singh appeared—mid-thirties, fair, with a neatly trimmed beard, confident.

He extended his hand. “Hey Arjun, Isha—how are you both?”

“We’re good, Sir.”

He noticed the cut on my face. “What happened, Arjun?”

“Minor accident yesterday, Sir. Nothing serious.”

“Be careful,” he said, then glanced down at my torn, stained shoes—survivors of the Pintu Haldar rescue. His expression changed.

“Arjun, why are your shoes in such bad shape? Replace them.”

I smiled faintly. “Next month, Sir.”

“No. Immediately. You represent the company. Customers notice.”

He wasn’t wrong. The words stung, but I nodded.

He offered tea; we declined. “We just had some at Sonu’s showroom,” I said.

He turned to business. “Isha, how’s the showroom?”

“Better than last year, Sir, but slower than last month—heavy monsoon.”

He nodded. “Arjun, what about your targets?”

“Twelve vehicles this month. Seven done. Five to go.”

“Confirmed customers?”

I hesitated. “We’re expecting the Bhutan bulk deal soon.”

“What’s the customer’s name?”

I froze. “Sir, the broker hasn’t shared it yet.”

“That’s not acceptable, Arjun. Never count a sale without basic info.”

“Yes, Sir. I’ll collect details tonight.”

“Good. Don’t depend only on that deal. If it slips, you’ll have nothing. Find fresh leads.”

“You’re right, Sir. I’ll start again.”

His tone softened. “After Bhutan, we’ll explore the market together.”

I nodded, grateful.

Then he leaned forward. “Arjun, what’s your plan for Mission 51%? Raju and Rahman are already past 40%. You must aim for 60%.”

“Yes, Sir. I’m on it.”

“Tomorrow morning, conference call at 9 AM sharp. After that, we’ll head for Phuentsholing. Understood?”

“Absolutely, Sir.”

As we wrapped up, he asked if Isha would join us in the evening.

She smiled politely. “Sorry, Sir. I have personal work tonight.”

I was relieved. “She just got back after two months, Sir. Wants to spend time with family. I’ll drop her home and join you. By the way, Sonu wants to come along—should I bring him?”

Vikram Singh nodded. “Yes, that’s fine.”

CHAPTER 25

# Negotiating Over Bottles

I dropped Isha at her place and headed to Sonu's showroom. It was already 7 PM. He greeted me with his usual energy.

"So, where are we taking Vikram Singh tonight?" he asked eagerly.

"I haven't finalized it yet," I said. "By the way, can you share the Bhutan customer's details?"

Sonu's smile faded. "I'll send it tomorrow."

"Sonu, I need it now. Mr. Vikram Singh asked for it personally."

Without a word, he stepped outside, spat his betel into a dustbin, and pulled out his phone. Moments later, a message arrived:

Himalayan Construction Company

223A, P.O. Box #1964

Chang Gedaphu, 11001 Phuntsholing, Bhutan.

He grinned. "Happy now? Let's not waste time—party time!"

I smiled, relieved to have the details.

Just then, my phone rang. I assumed it was Mr. Vikram Singh—but it was Mr. Rajesh Gupta, a longtime customer.

"Hello, Arjun Da. Where are you?" he asked warmly.

"Gupta ji! How are you?"

"All good. But it's been three months since you last visited. What happened?"

"Apologies, Gupta ji. Been hectic. How's everything at your end? Trucks running fine?"

"All three Rana Turbo Cheetahs are performing beautifully," he said. "Your company's service has been excellent."

He added, "You said you're in Jaigaon, right?"

"Yes."

"Perfect! My Dhaba's just 30 km away in Madarihat. Come over—we'll have a great night!"

Instantly, I thought—it could be the perfect spot for dinner with Mr. Vikram Singh. Rajkamal Dhaba was a famous stop on NH31—great food, clean restrooms, family crowd, and loyal customers.

I said, "Gupta ji, I'll bring one of my bosses there tonight."

"It'll be my pleasure. I'll get the best food ready!"

Sonu asked, "So, where are we going?"

"Rajkamal Dhaba in Madarihat."

He smirked. "Rajkamal Dhaba?"

"Yes," I said. "They have your favorite drinks. And the owner's our loyal customer—bought three Turbo Cheetahs."

Sonu raised an eyebrow. "Let's see how good their hospitality is."

"Behave tonight," I warned. "Don't drink too much. Vikram Singh is our guest—and Gupta ji is a valued customer."

"Don't worry, Arjun Da. I'll behave," he said—but I wasn't so sure.

At the hotel, I introduced Sonu to Mr. Vikram Singh.

"So, where are we heading, Arjun?" he asked.

"To Rajkamal Dhaba, Sir. About 30 km from here."

He looked unsure. "Rajkamal Dhaba? Is the food any good?"

"Absolutely, Sir. It's one of NH31's most popular spots—authentic Punjabi food. The owner is one of our best customers."

His expression softened. "Alright then. Send me the location. I'll follow you."

"Yes, Sir."

And with that, the night's plan was set.

I took Sonu in the demo truck, and we headed out. In our sales job, there's rarely any time to think. You just keep moving, chasing targets, forgetting everything else. But even as I drove, I couldn't stop thinking about the Hamid Alam case. The warning from Sub-Inspector Sanjeev Singh echoed in my mind.

I had a feeling Mr. S. K. Aggarwal was hiding something. His team had seized Hamid's vehicle wrongly, and he stayed silent. I was sure of it. As I pressed the accelerator, I made a promise: I'll uncover the truth. His mistake won't destroy my career.

The truck hit a speed bump hard. Bright headlights from an oncoming truck blinded me for a second. I steadied the wheel. Sonu stayed quiet, eyes on the road.

"Sonu," I asked, "the customer's in Bhutan. Have you arranged everything for the border?"

"Don't worry, Arjun Da," he said, finishing his cigarette. "Everything's arranged. Just focus on driving—and tonight's fun."

"I really need this deal," I said quietly.

"I'm with you," Sonu replied. "But tomorrow, be ready. Our competitors will be there too."

Flashing lights appeared in the rearview mirror. A car behind us honked and pulled up beside us—it was Mr. Vikram Singh.

"Hurry up, guys! We're already late!" he called, then sped ahead.

Sonu grinned. "You're too slow, Arjun Da. Step on it!"

I pressed the pedal—speed climbing to 80.

When we reached Rajkamal Dhaba, Mr. Vikram Singh was already there, standing beside his car, smoking. I parked next to him and stepped out.

The Dhaba was large and full of life. On the right, cooks worked fast in an open kitchen; on the left, the owner managed the reception and cash counter, with a small bar behind him. A big dining area was packed with people, and five hut-style seating zones plus AC rooms served families. At the back, twenty clean washrooms stood ready for truck drivers, and outside, cots were laid out for them to rest.

The place buzzed—people eating, sipping tea, chatting. Families had their space. Five guards watched quietly.

Mr. Vikram Singh offered us cigarettes, and the three of us stood outside smoking and observing.

At the counter, Mr. Rajesh Gupta smiled as he handled bills. About fifty-five, with a neat white shirt, round belly, and red paan-stained lips, he looked calm and content. A gold watch gleamed on his wrist.

He stepped out to greet us warmly when I introduced him to Mr. Vikram Singh and Sonu.

"It's a hot night," he said. "Please sit in the AC room. I'll join you soon."

Inside, the air was cool and pleasant. A waiter brought chilled water.

"Tea, please," said Mr. Singh. Sonu and I ordered the same with some snacks.

Mr. Singh smiled. "Your customer seems well-known. How many vehicles has he bought?"

"Three, sir," I said proudly.

"Good. Think he'll buy more?"

"Not now, but I keep in touch."

He nodded, satisfied. Even here, away from office walls, the chase continued. Mission 51%.

Sonu sat fidgeting, tapping his foot, craving a smoke but restraining himself before the boss.

Breaking the silence, Vikram asked, "Sonu, tell me about yourself. You've been quiet."

"I'm just listening, sir," he said quickly.

"How many used cars do you sell a month?"

"Ten to fifteen, sometimes twenty," Sonu replied confidently.

"Good. What about other brands?"

"I pass leads to my dealer friends," he said.

"And small trucks?"

"Four to five a month," he added, exaggerating.

Vikram turned to me. "How many leads do you get from him?"

"Two to three a month," I said, covering for him.

Vikram stayed silent, expression unreadable.

Then he asked, "How did you get the Himalayan Construction deal in Bhutan?"

Sonu brightened. "Sir, I've built good market trust. Even international clients come to me. Their manager visited my showroom looking for a double-cabin truck. I told him about our pride—the Rana Turbo Cheetah. Then I passed the lead to Arjun Da."

Vikram gave a half-smile. "Impressive network, Sonu."

Sonu sat taller, pleased, but soon picked up the AC remote and began pressing buttons at random. The temperature kept changing.

Vikram said nothing, but his irritation showed.

After a moment, Sonu stood up. "Excuse me, Sir. Need a smoke."

"Go ahead," Vikram said politely.

Sonu stepped out, restless as ever.

Soon, Mr. Rajesh Gupta entered, cheerful as always.

"You haven't ordered food yet?" he asked. "Try something from my Dhaba—it's famous among travelers."

Vikram chuckled. "Yes, I can smell the flavors from here. Makes me hungrier."

"Thank you, Sir!" Rajesh beamed. Then he looked at me. "Why so quiet, Arjun Da? Usually, you're after me to buy more trucks—that's how I ended up buying three!"

I smiled. "Thank you, Dada."

Turning to Vikram, he added warmly, "He's one of the best sales executives I've met—honest and reliable. Never had any trouble with service or support."

Vikram nodded appreciatively. "What do you use the trucks for?"

"I run a hundred-acre tea garden," Rajesh said. "Your Turbo Cheetah Trucks help transport green leaves fast, keeping the flavor fresh."

"That's great to hear," Vikram smiled.

Rajesh rang the bell for the waiter. Just then, Sonu returned—smelling of cigarettes and whisky. My body tensed. He must've been drinking at the dhaba bar.

Rajesh noticed. "Feel free to smoke and drink here, Sonu," he said casually.

Sonu's face lit up. "Tonight, the party's on me!" Rajesh announced. "It's been a while—we'll celebrate Arjun Da!"

Vikram smiled. I nodded, though I was worried. Sonu drinking more could mean trouble—and in front of my customer and boss, that was risky.

The waiter came. Rajesh ordered starters and top-shelf whisky. Vikram stayed alert, reading Rajesh's signals.

Over snacks, Rajesh said warmly, "Your trucks have boosted my business."

I knew he'd soon need two more trucks, but stayed quiet—Sonu was nearby, and I didn't want my lead leaking.

"Business looks good," Vikram said. "Any plans to expand?"

"Definitely. The tea season's coming," Rajesh replied, excited.

Vikram glanced at me—he'd caught the signal. A sale was closed.

Still, I could sense his anxiety. Month-end was near. Every lead mattered.

"If there's anything else we can help with, just say so," Vikram said.

Rajesh hesitated. "I urgently need two more Turbo Cheetah Trucks," he said. "But I'm short on funds. Can I get delivery now and pay the down payment in three months?"

"Sir, without registration and insurance, we can't release the trucks," I said gently. "The finance company needs at least 10%—about Rs. 4 lakh."

Vikram asked, "What's his repayment record like?"

"He has an ETR, sir."

"Excellent!" Vikram said.

"What's ETR?" Rajesh asked, curious.

"It means Excellent Track Record," Vikram explained. "You've never missed a payment."

Rajesh laughed. "Ha! Then give me the trucks now!"

Vikram called someone—probably Shibu from the bank. "Customer runs a big tea garden, perfect record. Try for 100% funding, including insurance and registration."

Rajesh beamed at the praise.

When the call ended, Vikram offered cigarettes. Everyone smoked except me. The room soon filled with smoke.

Two waiters entered with snacks—fish fingers, paneer tikka, peanuts—and two bottles of premium whisky.

"Let the party begin!" Rajesh said cheerfully.

Sonu's eyes gleamed. Vikram and Rajesh took doubles; I skipped mine. I needed a clear head.

Vikram was pushing hard—for both our targets.

Rajesh was just being generous, unaware that every smile, every sip, was part of a bigger race—Mission 51%.

Vikram downed his drink and leaned forward.

"Mr. Gupta, I have an excellent offer for you," he said.

Rajesh grinned. "What does Mr. Singh offer?"

"I'll arrange on-road funding for you—as our valued customer."

Rajesh sat up. "On-road funding?"

I was surprised. Was this real? Or just the whisky talking?

I stayed silent, watching.

Rajesh asked, "And what's the interest rate?"

I replied, "Sir, 11%."

Rajesh shook his head. "Too high. I can't pay more than 8%."

He set his glass down firmly. He meant it.

Sonu, now drunk and greasy-fingered, leaned toward me.

"I can get 8% finance for him," he whispered.

His breath stank of whisky. "Stay quiet," I hissed.

The waiter refilled our glasses. The air was thick with whisky, smoke, and fried food. Sonu was now freely pouring drinks from the bottle.

Vikram, on his second glass, said calmly,

"Mr. Gupta, two options—take a ₹30,000 discount per truck, or 9% finance for two years."

Rajesh called his manager to check the deal.

"Give me a few minutes," he said.

While waiting, he looked at Sonu.

"What will you have for dinner—chilli chicken, kebab, or mutton kossa?"

"Mutton kossa and roti," Sonu said quickly.

Rajesh laughed. "Only two items, Mr. Sonu?"

Sonu grinned, slurring. "This whisky and your food—perfect!"

Rajesh turned to Vikram. "And you, Mr. Singh?"

"Tandoori Roti and Paneer Butter Masala," Vikram said.

"Oh, vegetarian!" Rajesh smiled.

"I'll have the same," I added.

Rajesh nodded. "Sonu and I are the non-veg guys tonight." He placed the order and told the waiter to add it to his bill.

Vikram offered politely, "Please let me pay tonight."

Rajesh frowned. "No, no, it's my treat. Just make sure I get the best deal."

The air felt heavier—not from food, but pressure. Vikram and I were thinking of targets. Sonu looked too relaxed. I worried he might leak the deal to someone else.

Soon, the waiters returned with trays of hot food—Mutton Kossa, Paneer Butter Masala, and fresh rotis. The smell filled the room.

Sonu, now drunk, played with his food. Rajesh looked happy.

Finally, he said warmly, "Arjun, Sonu—start eating! Mr. Singh, help yourself. This dinner is my way of saying thank you. Your trucks have helped me a lot."

Vikram stretched, smiling.

"Mr. Gupta, we're glad our Rana Turbo Cheetah Trucks serve you well. We'll always support you."

Rajesh smiled. "Good! Now eat."

Vikram ate lightly. Rajesh enjoyed his mutton, praising his dhaba's food.

Sonu, half-drunk, mumbled, "Gupta Ji, your mutton's amazing. Where do you buy it from?"

Rajesh laughed. "That's a business secret, Sonu Ji."

We all laughed. The tension finally melted away.

As we ate, Rajesh's phone rang. He stepped out, spoke briefly, then returned.

"My manager, Rizwan, is smart with numbers. He says I should go with the 9% offer," Rajesh said, smiling.

"So, Arjun, when will you deliver my vehicles?"

I swallowed a bite of roti. "Sir, we need to complete the paperwork first. 100% finance isn't easy."

But Mr. Gupta didn't care about rules. "I want three Rana Turbo Cheetah Trucks—with minimum down payment. You two sort it out."

Vikram asked, "How much can you pay upfront?"

Gupta replied, "Three lakh for three trucks."

"Too low," Vikram said calmly.

I added, "If you give six lakh, the process will be faster."

Vikram suggested smartly, "Make it four lakh, and we'll deliver in two days."

Mr. Gupta frowned. "Sorry, I can't arrange more than three lakhs now. I'll delay the purchase."

He finished his drink, looking disappointed.

Sonu quietly poured another peg, filled his plate, and leaned toward me.

"Arjun Da, you won't close this deal. Let me handle Gupta—I'll convince him."

I snapped, "Shut up."

Vikram leaned back, smoking silently, lost in thought.

Then Gupta smiled again. "Forget business. Let's enjoy dinner!" He called for dessert.

When it arrived, we ate quietly. But both Vikram and I were still thinking about the deal.

I said, "Sir, if you don't buy this month, you'll lose ₹20,000 per truck—₹60,000 total."

Gupta froze. "₹60,000 loss?"

Vikram added, "If you buy now, I'll add ₹20,000 more per truck—₹1.2 lakhs total benefit. Miss this month, and it's gone."

Gupta looked thoughtful. "It's peak season, and funds are tight—but I don't want to lose this offer."

He called Rizwan and asked him to bring the checkbook. Relief washed over me.

Soon, Rizwan arrived. Gupta said warmly, "I respect how you and Arjun handled this. You asked for four lakh—but I'm giving five."

He wrote the cheque to Darjeeling Auto Works and told Rizwan to send the finance papers.

We sat for another hour before leaving. Gupta thanked us and refused to let us pay the bill.

We were slightly tipsy but composed—except Sonu, who got loud.

"Gupta Ji, great party! Drinks, mutton—and next time in Jaigaon, I'll host—with music, drinks, maybe even girls—"

I cut him off with a sharp look and changed the topic.

Outside, we stopped for Paan. Gupta went to settle his dhaba's accounts.

Vikram leaned toward me. "Arjun, Gupta may bargain, but he's rich. Stay close. Handle the delivery carefully."

I nodded. "Don't worry, sir. I'll take care of it."

He asked, "And Sonu?"

I looked around. Sonu was wandering near the dhaba, looking dazed.

"Not sure, sir—maybe another drink."

"Keep an eye on him," Vikram said quietly. "He's unpredictable."

Just then, my phone rang. It was my mother.

"Hello, Ma," I said, stepping aside.

"Where are you, Arjun? You didn't call all day. Are you back at your hotel?"

"No, Mom. I'm still with Mr. Vikram Singh. We were at a customer's place. A big deal was closed for three Turbo Cheetah Trucks. I'm very happy."

But she didn't sound happy. Her voice turned serious.

"Arjun, what kind of job is this? You work odd hours—sometimes you leave at 3 AM, sometimes return at 2 AM. I'm worried all the time. This sales job gives us no peace."

I knew how she felt. This job had poor pay, endless travel, and lots of stress—but I had no choice.

"Ma, I understand. I'll prepare for a government job. But right now, I have to continue this. I'm the only one earning."

She sighed.

"Okay. At least take care of your health. Call me once you reach your hotel."

After I hung up, Vikram asked,

"Everything okay?"

I smiled and said,

"That was Mom. She wants me to reach the hotel soon."

"Alright," he nodded. "Let's go to Jaigaon. Call Sonu and start the vehicle."

I called Sonu, and we started the journey back to Jaigaon.

CHAPTER 26

# Ambush on the Highway

Mr. Vikram Singh followed behind as I started the Turbo Cheetah Truck. The engine roared, headlights cutting through the dark. Sonu kept saying he wanted to drive.

"You're too slow, Arjun Da," he complained.

I ignored him. He was drunk, and I wasn't letting him touch the wheel.

Just as I was about to move, six trucks came and blocked us from every side. Engines growled, and men jumped out.

Harun was leading them.

"Arjun, you cheat!" he shouted. "You escaped from Bandapani last time, but not tonight!"

We were only a hundred meters from Rajkamal Dhaba, but no one could see or hear us. The men hit the truck, yelling,

"Come out! Return the truck!"

Sonu looked shocked. "What's going on? Did you really cheat them?"

"It's a finance issue," I said quietly.

He smiled faintly. "Then I guess I'll have to help you."

Behind us, Mr. Vikram's SUV waited, unaware of what was happening.

I stepped out and said, "Harun Bhai, please listen. I didn't keep your father's truck. There's a finance issue, but it'll be fixed soon."

But Harun wouldn't listen.

"We paid you directly!" he shouted. "You took our money and never gave us the truck!"

Before I could speak, someone punched me from behind. Another man slapped me hard. Harun grabbed my collar.

Then Sonu jumped out—holding a small gun.

"This is not a fake gun. It's real. And I'm not calm like Arjun. If you don't stop, I will shoot."

"Back off!" he shouted. "If you've got a problem, go to the showroom. Don't hit him!"

Everyone froze. The gun silenced the night.

"Arjun, get in the passenger seat," Sonu said. Still aiming, he stepped back into the truck, started the engine, and drove off fast.

The Turbo Cheetah roared ahead. My heart pounded. Mr. Vikram's SUV followed close behind.

Sonu drove fast through the highway, overtaking heavy trucks.

"Slow down," I said.

"Trust me," he replied, grinning. "I can still drive fine."

The speed climbed to 80, then 90. Thc truck moved like a tiger through elephants.

Then, flashing lights appeared in the mirror—Harun's men were chasing us again.

Sonu pressed the accelerator harder. The chase had begun.

As Sonu changed gears, he muttered, "Arjun Da, they've got more men this time. Some are armed. We can't fight them—especially if they're drunk."

"You're right," I said. "Last time I escaped with off-road driving. But tonight, they're angrier."

He glanced in the mirror. "What's the deal with Harun? Did you cheat them?"

The headlights lit his tense face. “No. I’ve always treated customers fairly. That’s why I still survive in this job.”

He lit a cigarette. “I know you’re honest. Then what went wrong?”

“Six months ago, I sold a Turbo Cheetah to Harun’s father, Hamid Alam. They paid three EMIs. One day, our manager, Mr. S. P. Aggarwal, told me to call them in for ‘urgent servicing.’”

Two trucks tried to overtake us, but Sonu cut ahead with sharp precision.

“When Hamid brought it,” I said, “Aggarwal kept the truck—said there was a problem. Three months now. No sign of return.”

The Turbo Cheetah growled as its 2400cc engine surged. Sonu handled the machine like instinct—gear smooth, torque steady, headlights slicing the dark.

But ten of Harun’s trucks were closing in, their lights flashing wild and angry.

“Can you manage?” I asked.

“Trust me,” Sonu said. “I’ll get us out.”

He swerved past a lorry; my heart slammed against my ribs. The smell of diesel filled the cabin. I’d faced pressure before—but never like this.

“We’re in for a long night,” he muttered.

A bump appeared before the bridge. He braked hard; the tires screeched but held. The chase trucks slowed. Then Sonu veered suddenly toward the Jaldapara forest. Branches lashed against the truck as we entered the narrow trail.

“Hold tight,” he warned. “An open field’s ahead—we can lose them there.”

The headlights revealed a wide, wet clearing. The truck bounced through mud and grass; the others followed.

"They're still behind us!" I shouted.

"Trust me," he said again.

He shifted to four-wheel drive, guiding the truck through the slush. One by one, Harun's trucks sank into the mud. When Sonu spotted a paved road, he swung the wheel sharply. The Turbo Cheetah roared back onto solid ground.

Minutes later, the highway opened before us. Sonu slowed, breathing hard, a faint smile on his face.

"We did it," he said.

"Yeah," I replied, feeling the fear fade. But inside, I knew it wasn't over. Hamid's anger would only grow—and Aggarwal's silence was digging me deeper.

My phone rang. It was Vikram Singh.

"Where are you, Arjun? What's going on?" he snapped.

"The customer's upset, sir. Something unexpected happened."

"Upset? They chased you! Meet me at my hotel—now."

The line went dead. Sonu grinned, eyes still on the road.

"You're in trouble now," he said, half amused, half proud.

After an hour's drive, we reached the hotel. It was quiet outside. Just a few streetlights lit the road. A couple of stray dogs were digging through garbage across the street. A lone security guard stood at the hotel entrance, and the receptionist was busy on the phone.

Mr. Vikram Singh stepped out of the lobby and walked straight towards us.

"What's going on, Arjun? Why did the customer attack you?" he asked angrily.

Sonu wandered off to the side, probably to buy cigarettes.

I stood in front of Mr. Singh and began explaining. "Sir, the customer is Mr. Hamid Alam. He bought a vehicle from me a few months ago. At the time of delivery, everything was clear—no dues, no documents pending."

Mr. Singh interrupted, "What happened after that?"

"Three months later, Mr. Aggarwal asked me to call Mr. Alam for servicing. I followed his instructions. Mr. Alam came in, trusting us. Then Mr. Aggarwal told him the vehicle needed a special service. Since then, the vehicle hasn't been returned. Three months have passed."

Vikram lit a cigarette and said, "Then?"

"Now, Mr. Alam's son, Harun, has become aggressive. He doesn't understand the company's processes. He only knows I sold them a vehicle, and now we've kept it. He's threatened to attack me if they don't get it back."

"And Aggarwal?" Vikram asked.

"He avoids my calls and refuses to speak with the customer," I replied.

"Did you tell Rakesh?" Vikram asked.

"Yes, sir. I informed him yesterday. He said he'd look into it."

"Has anything changed since then?" Vikram asked again.

"No, sir. Nothing's changed. I'm hoping for a meeting when we return to Siliguri."

Vikram sighed and pulled his phone from his pocket. He dialed Rakesh's number. After a few rings, Rakesh answered.

"Hello, Rakesh. Sorry to call so late," Vikram said. "Arjun and I closed a deal today for three vehicles."

Rakesh replied warmly, "That's great news, Vikram. Well done."

But Vikram didn't react to the praise. "Are you aware of the Hamid Alam issue?"

"Yes, Arjun told me about it yesterday. What happened now?" Rakesh asked.

"You're asking me?" Vikram snapped. "You should already know! This issue is damaging our reputation in the market."

There was silence on the line.

"I told Arjun the matter would be resolved once I spoke to Mr. Aggarwal," Rakesh said hesitantly.

"Mr. Aggarwal is the problem!" Vikram shouted. "He has no sense of business. He's done nothing but create trouble. Tell him to solve this by tomorrow or remove him. I won't tolerate anything that harms our company's image. Do you understand?"

"Yes, Vikram. I'll handle it by tomorrow," Rakesh replied.

"I'll be back the day after tomorrow. I want this issue closed by then," Vikram said firmly and ended the call.

CHAPTER 27

# When Sleep Won't Come

After speaking with Mr. Vikram Singh, I returned to my hotel room. The long day—filled with work, a late-night party, whisky, and stress—left me feeling strangely uneasy. I took a bath at 1 a.m., hoping the cold water would calm me down. My body felt lighter, but my mind was still heavy with worry.

I lay on the bed, staring at the ceiling fan. The soft glow from the night lamp filled the room, but sleep wouldn't come. My head was spinning with thoughts—about the Hamid Alam case, and the corporate deal I had to close in Phuentsholing, Bhutan.

At 2 a.m., still wide awake, I called Isha. She answered in a sleepy voice.

"Arjun? Why are you calling so late? Hold on..." she whispered. After a short pause, she continued, even softer now, "I'm in the bathroom. Nisha is sleeping beside me. If she hears this call, she'll tell my mother. Please be quick—what's wrong?"

Her voice was gentle but cautious.

"I wasn't feeling okay. That's why I called," I said, trying to sound calm.

"Are you back at your hotel?" she asked.

"Yes. But I can't sleep," I replied.

"What happened? Tell me quickly."

"It's a long story," I said. "Let's talk tomorrow."

"Alright. You have a long day ahead. Sleep now. I'll see you at 9:30 a.m.," she said, mixing care with urgency. "Goodnight."

After the call, I lay still, watching the fan spin, just like my thoughts.

The next morning, my phone rang at 8:15 a.m., waking me up. Sunlight was pouring into the room, making it hotter. The fan was spinning fast, but the heat and sweat clung to me.

I checked the caller ID and felt a jolt—Sub Inspector Sanjeev Singh.

I answered slowly, “Good morning, Sir.”

“Good morning, Arjun. Where are you?”

“I’m in Jaigaon, Sir.”

“I’ve received another complaint from Hamid Alam,” he said. “This time, it’s serious. They’re saying you attacked his son, Harun, with a weapon. I may have to arrest you.”

My heart pounded, but I couldn’t let fear take over. I had to speak up.

“Sir, Harun has been chasing and threatening me for days. Yes, the dealership may have made mistakes, but that doesn’t give them the right to harass me. Last night, they even tried to kill me.”

There was a pause. Mr. Singh’s voice softened slightly.

“They attacked you?”

“Yes, Sir. Last night at Rajkamal Dhaba in Madarihat, around 11 p.m. A group of drivers surrounded me. It was scary.”

“Hmm,” he muttered, listening closely.

“When things got out of hand, my friend Sonu took out his licensed revolver to protect me.”

“Licensed?” Mr. Singh asked, clearly suspicious.

“Yes, Sir. Fully licensed.”

Mr. Singh sighed. "Arjun, I know you. You're a hardworking sales guy. But this case is becoming serious. You need to fix this, and fast."

"I've already told senior management. They promised to take action soon."

"Arjun, I've given you time. But if this continues, I'll have to take legal steps," he warned.

"I understand, Sir. I'll close this matter by next week."

After a pause, he said, "Alright. I'll speak to Hamid Alam and warn him about his son's behavior. But don't delay anymore." Then he hung up.

Two drops of sweat fell on the white bedsheet. The room felt hotter now. I got up, opened the windows, and went straight to the bathroom.

After a quick shower, I called room service for breakfast. Just as I sat down, Isha called to say she'd reach Sonu's showroom by 9:30 a.m. I checked the clock—it was already 9:00.

As I hurried to get dressed, my phone rang again. It was Ma.

Her voice sounded tired, and she said she was having pain in the left side of her chest. My stomach turned.

Balancing my job and her care was getting harder each day. I had no siblings. No neighbors who'd help. Relatives? They had their own lives. And I was always on the move for work.

I called a pharmacist friend and asked him to check on her. I told him to arrange a doctor if needed. But even after that, I was worried. Was this enough?

Then I called my aunt and begged her to stay with Ma for a few days. At first, she hesitated. After a long conversation, she finally said:

"Okay, Arjun. I'll come. But only for two days."

"Thanks, Aunty. I'll be back by then."

But inside, I knew two days wouldn't be enough. I had to finish everything in Bhutan quickly and return. The pressure was crushing—my job, my mother, my promises. Everything is pulling me in different directions.

I stood still for a moment, trying to breathe, trying to focus. But the worry never left—it just sat quietly beside me, refusing to go away.

CHAPTER 28

# The Shirt That Spoke

After breakfast, I walked to Sonu's showroom. Last night, I'd asked him to keep my demo vehicle ready for today's presentation in Phuentsholing. I arrived at 9:30 a.m. sharp.

Sonu smiled. "Good morning!" he called. He offered breakfast, but we politely declined.

Isha was already there, standing near the car, looking every bit the professional—light shirt, dark trousers, black heels gleaming under the showroom lights. Her hair was tied back neatly, laptop bag on her shoulder. She looked sharp, focused—ready to win the day.

"You're looking gorgeous," I said. "The customers will be impressed."

She laughed. "Only the customers? Aren't you?"

"I always am," I replied, smiling.

She glanced at my shoes. "Still muddy. And you didn't shave."

Then she adjusted my collar—one small gesture that made me feel both comforted and exposed.

"I'll be back in fifteen minutes," I said. "You get ready for the meeting."

Vikram Singh called just then—he'd arrive in ten minutes. I asked Sonu and Isha to receive him while I freshened up.

At a salon near the Bhutan gate, I got a shave. The heat of Jaigaon was harsh; sweat trickled down my back. Outside, trucks rumbled, and autos honked. A cobbler sat nearby. I handed him twenty rupees and asked him to hurry. Within minutes, my shoes shone.

When I returned, Vikram hadn't arrived. Isha smiled. "Now you look handsome! Just need an ironed shirt."

Her perfume drifted between us—soft yet assured. Beside her polished grace, I felt rough-edged, my shirt sticking to my skin. The light fabric tried to hide its wear, but it felt cheap against the heat. My five-hundred-rupee shoes gleamed, yet whispered the truth—I couldn't afford better. Even my thin, frayed socks had a story to tell.

And there she was—branded, elegant, distant. A world apart. I admired her, but also wanted to be good enough to stand beside her.

"When's Mr. Vikram expected?" she asked.

"Soon," I said.

Then, quieter, "Why did you call me so late last night?"

I hesitated, then told her everything—the pressure, the fear.

She listened, eyes full of concern. "Arjun, your job's becoming tougher. You can't carry this alone."

"I'm trying," I said.

"And your MBA exams? Final year?"

"Yeah. I'm so behind, I don't know how I'll pass."

She leaned closer. "You have everything it takes to be a great manager. But you must manage yourself too."

Her words stayed with me. For the first time, I felt someone truly believed in me.

"I will," I said quietly. "I promise."

Mr. Vikram Singh arrived half an hour late, his SUV gliding to a stop before the showroom. He stepped out in a crisp shirt, hair still damp from a quick shower, the faint scent of cologne mixing with the air of diesel and polish.

"Good morning, everyone," he said, his voice calm but charged with energy.

"Good morning, sir," we replied together.

"Apologies for the delay—the boss called an early meeting," he said with a quick smile.

"No problem, sir. It gave us more time to prepare," I replied.

"Good," he nodded. "That's how success works—turn delay into advantage."

He turned to Sonu. "Everything ready? Spoke to the customer?"

"Yes, sir. Karma Tshering from Himalayan Construction confirmed. They want us there by two. The deal happens after lunch," Sonu replied.

"How far is it?"

"Ten kilometers from the Bhutan gate. It's already eleven, so we should leave soon. There's paperwork at the border."

"I'll hold a short team meeting—forty-five minutes," Vikram said. "Can you manage that?"

"Of course, sir. The client starts after three," Sonu said confidently.

Vikram looked at Isha and me. "I'm sending you the meeting link. Call the team and join in ten minutes. I'll have Mr. Aggarwal and Rakesh with me."

At 11:15, the meeting began. The faint hum of the showroom fans mixed with the static of login pings. Mr. Aggarwal appeared first on screen, his tone clipped as always; Rakesh joined last.

"Team," Vikram began, "this is a quick review before the next deal. The dealership's doing well toward Mission 51%. Rana Turbo Cheetah has hit 35% market share in the Darjeeling Auto Works region. Credit to everyone—especially Arjun, Raju, and Rahman."

He shared a slide. "Arjun leads at 45%, Raju at 42%, Rahman 40%."

Aggarwal's voice cut in, sharp as a blade. "Does that include new recruits?"

"Yes," Vikram said calmly. "But their share's small."

Aggarwal went on, "Arjun doesn't always follow the training process. He spends too much time solving customer issues."

I felt my chest tighten. The words landed like a quiet slap.

Vikram smiled slightly. "That's what makes him stand out—customer trust. Others should learn from that."

Rakesh nodded. "True. Arjun's closing deals while others still chase leads. But he must keep applying our 360-degree method."

"Yes, sir," I said. My voice sounded steadier than I felt.

"Good," Vikram continued. "Raju balances new leads and follow-ups well. Rahman's local promotions helped us win back territory."

Aggarwal unmuted again. "And Bikash deserves credit too—he's thriving in the tough hills. His kindness wins hearts."

A brief round of applause followed. I smiled, but my palms were damp. Praise never came without pressure.

Vikram's tone softened. "We've done well, but 35% isn't 51%. This month, aim for forty. By September, we cross it. Mission 51%—that's the goal."

Rakesh added, "No time to waste. Reach out if you need help—from Mr. Aggarwal, Vikram, or me."

The meeting ended. The air felt lighter, though my mind was still racing. Isha and I got ready to leave for the Himalayan Construction visit in the Turbo Cheetah demo truck. Sonu rode with Vikram.

As I stepped outside, the heat hit hard. The smell of diesel and sun-warmed metal filled the air. Another deal, another day to prove myself.

CHAPTER 29

# The Pitch

After two long hours at the entry permit office, we finally entered Phuntsholing at noon. Often called Bhutan's gateway, the town felt like another world. The moment we crossed the Bhutan Gate, the noise of Jaigaon vanished. Everything here moved more slowly and calmly.

Phuntsholing was a mix of tradition and modern life. The buildings had sloping roofs, bright colors, and intricate designs showing Bhutanese art. Roads were spotless, lined with trees and prayer flags gently swaying in the breeze, adding peace to the air.

As we drove through town, it felt like breathing calm itself. By the time we reached Himalayan Construction at 1 p.m., our pace had slowed to match the town. I gave my card to the guard and asked him to inform Mr. Karma Tshering about our 2 p.m. meeting. Then we waited, sinking into the stillness.

Time moved slowly. The Managing Director's meeting was after 2, but the minutes dragged on. Sonu, restless, smoked in the garden. The place was quiet, broken only by the footsteps of staff carrying files or trays of tea. Vikram struggled with his Indian SIM, frustrated until Sonu shared his hotspot—his Bhutanese SIM kept him connected even here.

Through tall glass windows, we could see distant mountains. Their calm presence filled the neat, professional office. At 2:30, the receptionist approached.

"Who is Mr. Sonu Kumar? Mr. Karma Tshering is calling you all to the conference room."

Finally, the wait ended. I signaled Sonu, and the four of us walked in. Mr. Karma Tshering greeted us with a polite smile and sharp eyes, asking us to sit.

Sonu introduced everyone to Mr. Tshering and the Managing Director, Mr. Suraj Parikh. Calm and confident, Mr. Parikh sat at the head of the table. On the desk lay brochures from Raftar Motors, Tejas Automotive, and Load Max Motors.

As he flipped through them, I began nervously, "Good afternoon, Mr. Parikh, Mr. Tshering. Thank you for meeting us. I hope our Rana Turbo Cheetah Truck proves the performance and reliability you expect—"

Mr. Parikh cut in. "Mr. Arjun, we need twenty pickups for construction. Show the presentation first. Then we'll decide."

"Of course, sir," I said, heart pounding. I looked at Isha and Vikram, hoping for support, but both stayed silent. Then Isha spoke up. "Sir, may I use your projector for the presentation?"

"Sure," said Mr. Tshering, handing it to her.

Isha connected it quickly. The first slide lit the wall. "Arjun, it's ready," she said softly.

I had hoped she'd present, but it was clearly my turn. Taking a deep breath, I began. My palms were sweaty, my voice unsteady. Facing top businessmen wasn't easy. I glanced at Vikram—his calm look steadied me.

I followed my training, moving into the product details—the Turbo Cheetah's strong engine, best-in-class mileage, and safety. Isha's slides showed the truck in real construction sites, dusty but dependable.

"The Turbo Cheetah is trusted across India and abroad," I said with growing confidence. "It's tough yet comfortable, powered by a 2400cc turbo engine that performs even under full load."

Halfway through, I felt a rhythm. Mr. Vikram watched silently, tracking every word. I wanted to make him proud—and win this deal.

Then Mr. Parikh leaned back, ready with questions. He interrupted often, testing me. I did my best, but when things got tough, Vikram stepped in smoothly, handling the harder ones from Mr. Parikh and Mr. Tshering.

Mr. Parikh asked sharply, "Mr. Arjun, everything looks good, but I'm worried about mileage. Will your truck really give 16–17 km per litre when fully loaded? And what about uphill roads?"

I took a sip of water and replied, "Sir, the mileage is based on certified tests with standard load. In hilly or overloaded conditions, it may drop slightly. Still, our Turbo Cheetah gives the best mileage in its class."

Mr. Karma Tshering, silent till then, looked up. "Raftar Motors, Tejas, and Load Max are also in talks with us. They offer similar mileage and safety. Our trucks must perform well on plains and hills. How does yours compare?"

I straightened and replied confidently, "Sir, safety is our strength. The truck has front disc and rear drum brakes for all terrains, ABS to prevent wheel lock, and ELR seat belts with roll bars for protection."

Mr. Parikh scanned the slide. "Mr. Arjun, what does an engine immobilizer do?"

"It prevents the vehicle from starting without the right key," I explained. "It's an anti-theft feature."

Mr. Karma kept typing but asked again, "These are basic features. What about safety for hilly terrain? We're also reviewing other brands. Can you share something unique?"

"Certainly, sir," I said. "Our truck has advanced systems rarely seen in this category."

Vikram stepped in. "Sir, our safety engineering leads the market. Mr. Arjun will explain the details."

"Thank you, sir," I said, continuing. "Our truck includes Traction Control, Electronic Stability Control, Hill Descent, and Hill Start Assist—features built for all terrains."

Mr. Suraj Singh leaned forward. "Can you explain them?"

"Of course, sir," I said. "Traction Control keeps grip on slippery surfaces. It senses wheel slip and reduces engine power while applying brakes to that wheel until control returns."

Karma asked, "How does it know when to do that?"

"It activates automatically when a tyre slips—on mud or wet roads. It balances power and brake pressure to regain control," I explained.

Mr. Suraj nodded. "Useful in monsoons. But what about sharp turns?"

Isha switched to the next slide on Electronic Stability Control.

"That's where ESC helps," I said. "It tracks movement. If the truck oversteers or understeers, it brakes individual wheels and cuts power to keep it steady, even in near-roll situations."

Karma still looked serious. "And downhill driving with heavy loads? That's risky."

Vikram stepped in smoothly. "Sir, Hill Descent Control manages that. It applies brakes automatically to maintain a steady speed and control on steep slopes."

Both Mr. Suraj and Mr. Karma seemed impressed, but Karma had one more question.

"How does it handle starting on a slope? Drivers struggle with that."

Isha moved to the final slide. Vikram continued, "That's where Hill Start Assist helps. It holds the brakes for a few seconds after the driver lifts his foot, giving time to accelerate without rolling back. It makes steep starts safer."

Just then, Mr. Suraj's phone rang. He picked it up, spoke briefly, and placed it back on the table.

"Vikram," he said, "I have to leave now for another meeting. I liked the presentation, and the vehicle looks promising. But Karma will handle the final decision. You'll need to offer a good discount and a strong finance plan."

Then he looked at Karma and added, "Before finalising anything, test the mileage."

"Sure, sir," Karma replied.

As Mr. Suraj left the room, I felt a small wave of relief—but I knew it wasn't over yet.

Karma looked at us and smiled. "Please, sit down. Would you like some tea?"

"Sure, sir. A cup would be nice," said Mr. Vikram politely.

Karma signalled his assistant for tea, then turned to us again. "So, where are you from? How long have you been with Rana Motors?"

We chatted for a few minutes—nothing about the deal, just light conversation. But I could feel it—Karma hadn't made up his mind yet. There was more work to do.

CHAPTER 30

# Technically not zero, psychologically yes

Sonu wasn't around during my presentation—he'd gone to meet a client in Phuentsholing. Just as we were wrapping up, he walked in without knocking, a strong smell of smoke trailing him.

Karma Tshering smiled. "Please, have a seat."

Sonu wiped his forehead. "It's so hot. Can I get some cold water?"

Karma turned to the assistant. "Bring him cold water."

Then Sonu faced me. "So, Arjun, what's the update? Has Karma finalised the deal? What did Suraj Singh say about our vehicle?"

Before I could answer, Karma said, "We liked the presentation. But my boss wants a better discount, a solid finance offer, and a mileage test. It's up to you now."

Sonu turned to me. "Arjun, why haven't you shared the finance scheme yet?"

It felt like a public scolding, but I stayed calm. "We're discussing that now."

I turned to Karma. "Sir, we're offering ₹20,000 off. For bulk, we can extend another ₹10,000. Isha will explain the financial details."

Isha stepped in, confident and clear. "Sir, will the vehicles be registered in India or Bhutan? Finance schemes differ."

Karma replied, "In West Bengal."

"Perfect," she smiled. "We have strong retail finance options."

Karma leaned forward. "Can you explain the plans?"

"Sure, sir. What down payment and tenure do you prefer?"

After a few queries, Karma made a tough ask: "We want ten vehicles for a year—no down payment, no interest, no processing charge."

I looked at Isha. She didn't blink. "Then your EMI will be higher."

"That's fine," Karma smiled.

The office boy entered with water and tea. I watched Isha—focused, calculating. Karma checked his screen; Sonu, bored, turned on the TV to Hindi songs, then quickly muted it after realising the mood.

Isha opened the EMI sheet again, frowning. "Arjun, what's the discount now?" she whispered.

"₹20,000. They'll push for more."

"What's the max we can go?"

"₹30,000. Mr. Aggarwal's limit."

She sighed. "I can't offer zero interest without at least ₹50,000 off."

"Should we ask for a break?"

Without replying, she stood. "Mr. Karma, may we take a short internal break?"

"Of course," Karma smiled. "Let's reconnect after lunch."

Outside, Sonu headed for the washroom, then lit a cigarette near the gate. I joined him briefly.

Soon, Vikram Singh approached. "Tough nut to crack, Arjun?"

Isha arrived, tense. "Sir, how much discount can we offer?"

"What's he asking?" Vikram asked.

"Zero interest, zero down payment."

"That's risky," Vikram said. "He's sharp."

Isha smiled. "Don't worry, sir. I have a plan—it'll look like 0% without hurting us."

Curious, I asked, "What plan?"

"The vehicle's ₹15 lakh," she said. "At 10.5% interest, the customer pays about ₹86,000 extra in a year."

Vikram frowned. "So how do we make that 0%?"

Before she could answer, Sonu said, "Let's go eat."

"Good idea," Vikram nodded. "We'll continue at the restaurant."

After a five-minute walk, we entered a nice, cool restaurant. We sat down, and Sonu quickly placed the order.

Without wasting time, Isha leaned forward again. "Sir, here's the solution. If we give a ₹50,000 subvention from the dealership, we can reduce the interest burden."

I asked, "So how much would the customer pay after that?"

"Only vehicle price," she replied confidently

Vikram thought about it. "Good. But how does that become zero?"

Sonu jumped in, still confused. "Just don't lose the customer, okay?"

Isha smiled. "Don't worry. The key is that the customer is paying 5 EMIs in advance. That reduces the loan amount upfront. So, with the ₹50,000 subvention and 5 EMIs paid early, the customer feels like there's no extra interest. It's technically not zero, but psychologically it is."

I looked at Isha. "Can you break it down for me?"

Isha opened her diary and scribbled quickly, showing us the numbers. "Look, the vehicle costs ₹15 lakh. Normally, at 10.5% interest for one year, the customer would pay around ₹86,675 extra. But here's the trick:

We give a ₹50,000 subvention from the dealership.

The customer pays the first 5 EMIs in advance, which immediately reduces the principal.

With these adjustments, the remaining loan amount and interest balance out, and the total outflow for the customer is almost exactly the vehicle price. So technically, there's still some interest, but to the customer, it feels like zero."

She looked up, eyes gleaming. "Simple, smart, and everyone feels like they've won."

I nodded, impressed. "That's smart."

Vikram took a puff and said, "Yes. They'll think they're getting a 0% deal, and we still save our deal."

"Exactly, sir," Isha replied.

Sonu didn't say much—he didn't seem to follow all of it—but we didn't press him. This wasn't his thing.

As we were eating, Mr. Vikram wiped his mouth and said, "Alright, Isha, Arjun—we'll offer the customer ₹30,000 as a discount. I'll ask Rakesh to add ₹10,000 from the dealership. I'll arrange the rest from Rana Motors."

I was about to take a bite of paneer tikka, but paused.

"Sir, what if we give the ₹30,000 and 0% interest?" I asked.

Vikram put down his fork and looked at me seriously.

"Arjun, you've been in sales long enough. How can we afford both? If we give everything away, how will we run a dealership?"

I felt my face heat up. "Sorry, sir."

Sonu, who had been quiet till then, suddenly spoke. "You're giving the customer everything—what about my commission? If you don't keep my share, I won't let any vehicles sell in Jaigaon."

I tried to calm him. "Sonu, don't worry. Your commission is safe. I'll handle it."

Mr. Singh gave a small smile. "Look, either we give the discount or the 0% scheme—not both."

Isha nodded while chewing her biryani. "Got it, sir."

After lunch, we stepped outside. Sonu reached for the bill, but I stopped him. "Official trip, Sonu. I'll take care of it."

He shrugged, and we stepped out into the warm, sticky air of Phuentsholing.

We hurried—well, as much as four overfed people could—toward the Himalayan Construction Company. Inside the conference room, Mr. Karma Tshering was nowhere in sight. His laptop sat open on the table with the screen locked. A diary lay beside it, a pen jammed inside with the cap awkwardly stuck on the back, as if placed in a hurry.

The AC hummed gently, cooling the room. But it wasn't enough for Sonu. He did his usual routine—paced around, grabbed the remote, and turned the temperature down. Satisfied, he tossed the remote back on the table and turned to the TV, which was playing a random Hindi film song. A smirk crossed his face as he increased the volume slightly and leaned back, slipping into a lazy rhythm with the music.

Vikram didn't look amused. His face showed it, but he said nothing. He was busy typing furiously on his phone, probably unloading his irritation through emails.

Just then, the office assistant walked in with a tray of water. "Mr. Tshering will be here at 4:30," she said, placing glasses in front of us.

I looked at my watch—3:30 p.m. An hour to kill.

We quietly drifted into our own worlds. I pulled out my mobile and diary. Sonu stared at the TV, Vikram kept tapping on his phone, and silence settled in—a familiar kind of silence found in every meeting room when there's nothing to do but wait.

At 4:45 p.m., the door creaked open. Mr. Karma Tshering walked in, calm as always. Just behind him was Mr. Suraj Singh, the Managing Director, walking with an air of authority. He gave a quick wave, eyes scanning the room like his mind was already juggling ten things.

"Sorry to keep you waiting," he said briskly, his tone sharp but not unfriendly. "These days, the construction business is full of complications." He turned to Karma. "So, have you finalized anything? What's the outcome of the discussion?"

Before we could speak, Karma leaned back in his chair and said, "Nothing finalized yet. We're still looking at other vehicle options. But I did ask them for a one-year finance scheme—zero percent interest, no processing fee."

Suraj frowned slightly and scratched his forehead. "Did they give you the scheme?"

"They said they'd share it after lunch," Karma replied. Then he turned to Isha, who had been typing on her laptop. "Isha, is the scheme ready?"

She looked up from her keyboard. "Yes, sir. I've prepared it as per your request."

Suddenly, Vikram leaned forward, a concern in his voice. "Sir, I just have one doubt. Why are we considering a one-year plan? The EMI for ten vehicles will be too high."

In the corner, Sonu blinked, shaking off his nap. His eyes were red, but he was trying to focus as the conversation picked up again.

Karma shifted to face Vikram. "We don't want to pay interest on this deal, Mr. Singh. And honestly, we don't have the liquidity to pay everything upfront. So a one-year EMI plan makes more sense."

Vikram nodded. "Understood. That clears it up."

After lunch, the mood in the conference room was more relaxed, but an air of expectation lingered. Isha stood at the head of the table, projecting the finance scheme. Karma Tshering and Mr. Suraj Singh leaned back in their chairs, studying the numbers. Both seemed convinced.

But Suraj wasn't done.

"Isha," he said, his voice steady and firm, "we're not paying even a single rupee as processing fee. Please talk to the finance company and make that clear. Everything else looks fine."

He keyed some numbers into his calculator, the soft beeping breaking the silence. Then he looked at Karma. "What do you think, Karma? I'm okay with the advance EMIs and the monthly ones too."

I let out a slow breath, finally feeling some relief after hearing Mr. Suraj's approval. Sonu, now fully awake, straightened in his chair. Across the table, Vikram was waiting for the final word—just like the rest of us. And Isha—well, she was already celebrating inside. Her zero-interest scheme had hit the mark.

But of course, Karma Tshering wasn't the type to let things slide. His reputation as a sharp, meticulous purchase manager was well-earned.

"Sir," he said, turning to Suraj Singh with that usual composed tone, "before we finalize anything, we need to check again with the other manufacturer. They've proposed a compelling finance scheme, and their fuel efficiency looks solid too."

I didn't wait.

"Sir, the Turbo Cheetah has the best mileage in its category," I interjected, trying to steer the conversation back.

Karma turned to me, his gaze steady. "And how do you prove that? Every brand says the same. Why should we believe yours is any different?"

Suraj Singh nodded, leaning back slightly. "Good question, Karma. Fuel efficiency directly hits our bottom line."

And just like that, the air changed. The room, moments ago cordial, now bristled with quiet tension.

Silence settled in the Himalayan Construction Company conference room. Only the faint hum of the air conditioner filled the void—until Vikram Singh leaned forward, his deep voice breaking through.

"If there's doubt," he said calmly, "let's clear it the right way. We propose a mileage challenge. Let every competitor in the segment show up. Rana Motors will cover all expenses. I'm confident—our Turbo Cheetah will outperform them all."

Suraj raised an eyebrow. His fingers tapped the armrest in rhythm, as if testing the weight of Vikram's claim.

"You sound very sure of yourself, Mr. Singh," he said, his tone sharp. "If your truck underperforms in that test, we won't buy a single unit. That's final."

Vikram didn't blink. If anything, he sat taller.

"Understood, sir. Invite every brand in the segment. Let them bring their best. If we fall short, we'll walk away without asking you to reconsider."

Isha, seated across the table, had stopped typing. Her fingers hovered mid-air, her eyes fixed on Vikram with a flicker of curiosity.

Beside me, Sonu leaned in, whispering sharply. "What the hell is he doing? Has he lost his mind? We don't even know if we're the best. Say something before he kills this deal."

I whispered back, "Relax. Vikram's been in tighter corners than this. Let's hear him out."

Karma adjusted his collar and spoke again, calm but alert. "Mr. Vikram, it's a bold proposal. But how exactly will you conduct this challenge?"

All eyes turned to Vikram.

I hadn't seen anything like this before. Neither had Isha. But Vikram, a veteran in these corporate chess matches, didn't falter.

He smiled slightly. "Simple. We'll invite all manufacturers in the segment. Each vehicle gets its tank filled at the same fuel pump. Same driver route—a hundred-kilometre round trip. Identical conditions. We'll measure actual mileage. The top three will be awarded on performance. It's a clean, real-world comparison."

A beat of silence followed. Everyone processed the offer.

Suraj Singh finally spoke, arms crossed. "One concern, Mr. Vikram. Claimed mileage figures differ. Specs aren't standard. GVW varies. Some vehicles are built heavier, some lighter. How will you normalize the results?"

Karma added, "Exactly. We need clarity. How will you calculate and rank?"

Vikram leaned back, adjusting the cuff of his sleeve. That signature twirl of his mustache returned—a small tell that he was thinking.

"We'll take each brand's official mileage claim as baseline—call it 100. After the run, we calculate the actual mileage. If a vehicle delivers 110% of its claimed mileage, its score goes up. If it falls short, we deduct accordingly. It's proportional. Transparent. Objective."

The tension began to lift. Suraj exchanged a glance with Karma—both seemed less defensive, more intrigued.

The conference room returned to its professional stillness.

Then, Sonu broke it.

His face lit up like a child who had just heard about a school picnic. "It's going to be fun! A real mileage rally!" He turned to me. "Arjun, don't you think it'll be a blast?"

I blinked, caught off guard. Then smiled. "Yeah, sounds exciting."

Encouraged, Sonu leaned forward, enthusiasm bubbling. "We can even arrange a pandal, loudspeakers, refreshments—a proper event! I'll invite everyone I know. It'll be like a festival!"

Suraj chuckled faintly. Even Karma allowed himself a slight smile.

Vikram simply nodded. "Let's make sure we win it first."

But Suraj Singh, calm and composed as ever, looked at Sonu thoughtfully. His voice was steady, deep, and carried the authority of experience.

"Mr. Sonu," he said, "we can't make the mileage test results public. Some vehicles will do well, others won't. But we have to give every product a fair chance. We're a respected company, and we can't risk putting any brand down in front of others. That said, we still have the right to choose the best vehicle for our business."

Sonu's expression shifted. He looked down briefly, then raised his head. "So who's going to see the test?"

"Only our internal staff, and representatives from the manufacturers and dealers," Suraj replied firmly.

Sonu gave a small nod. He looked disappointed but understood. Vikram, who had been quietly observing, finally spoke.

"Yes, we need to keep things ethical," he said. "This test is for our evaluation only."

The conference room was quiet, except for the soft hum of the air conditioner and the rustle of papers. Suraj leaned forward and turned to Karma Tshering, his voice steady but urgent.

"Karma, when can we arrange this mileage test? We can't afford delays. If we don't get the vehicles in time, the next project will be affected."

Karma, sitting straight with his usual calm, nodded. "Next Sunday would be ideal, Sir. It won't disturb our work week, and our staff will be available."

"Good," Suraj said. "But check with the manufacturers. Make sure Sunday works for them too. What do you think, Vikram?"

Vikram Singh, seated across the table, smiled slightly. "We're okay with whatever you decide, Sir. I believe the others will be fine too."

Suraj returned the smile. "Let's hope so. We've always enjoyed working with you, but this time, the results matter. I hope your vehicles do well."

Vikram nodded. "Thank you, Sir. We're confident."

As Suraj began gathering his papers, Karma turned to me. "Arjun, today is Friday. I'll speak to the other manufacturers and confirm the date."

"Please confirm it by tomorrow," I said. "We need to start preparing."

"Of course, Arjun," Karma replied with a smile. "You'll have the update by tomorrow."

We stepped out of the conference room into the late afternoon sun. Shadows stretched across the parking lot in Phuntseoling. It had been a long day of hard discussions, and the tiredness showed on everyone's faces. Suraj Singh and Karma Tshering gave us polite smiles as we shook hands. But behind the formality, the doubt lingered—had we done enough to convince them?

The four of us—Sonu, Vikram Singh, Isha, and I—walked toward our cars in silence. Only the sound of gravel under our shoes and a few distant horns broke the stillness. Sonu was already ahead, lighting a cigarette. He blew slow smoke rings into the cool evening air, his face unreadable. Vikram followed, lighting one of his imported cigarettes—the kind he only used when things were tense.

Nobody spoke, but the pressure was thick in the air. The deal wasn't sealed yet, and we all knew it. Isha glanced at me, but even her usual sharpness seemed quiet.

Just before we reached the car, Vikram stopped and said, "Arjun, this won't be easy. The competition is aggressive. And they've done their homework. These guys know exactly what they want."

I nodded. "Yes, sir. They've been in constant touch with our rivals. They're well informed."

We stood by the car. The parking lot around us was busy, but for a moment, it felt like we were standing in our own bubble.

Isha finally broke the silence. "Sir, do you think challenging them to a mileage test was a good idea? Can the Turbo Cheetah really win?"

Vikram raised his eyebrows, a bit surprised by the blunt question. He took a long drag, tossed the cigarette into a dustbin, and looked directly at her.

"We've run this mileage test across the country, Isha. Turbo Cheetah has won most of them. It'll win this one too."

He didn't wait for a reply. He opened the door to his SUV and gestured for her to get in.

Before he climbed into the driver's seat, he turned to me. "Arjun, make sure the demo vehicle is serviced tomorrow. It needs to be in top condition."

"Sure, sir. I'll get it done first thing."

Vikram gave me a small, reassuring smile—rare, but genuine. “And don’t worry about the weekend. I’ll make sure Rakesh gives you guys some extra time off next month.”

I smiled. “Thanks, sir. We’ll give it everything in the competition.”

Sonu, already in the TCT demo vehicle, leaned out of the window. “Arjun, don’t stress. If the Turbo Cheetah doesn’t win, I’ll charm them into choosing your vehicle. Just make sure my commission’s ready.”

He laughed loudly as he started the engine and waved me in. We drove off into the fading light, the weight of the day still with us—but now, with a little more hope.

CHAPTER 31

# The Conference Room Confession

The door clicked shut behind me as I entered my hotel room. Vikram had gone back to his suite, and I'd dropped Isha home before heading here. Sonu, as always, was at the showroom, checking the day's walk-ins and following up on old car leads.

I changed into a loose T-shirt and track pants, then sank onto the bed. My legs felt heavy. The day had been a blur of meetings, endless discussions, numbers, and decisions in that freezing conference room. Now, in this hot, quiet room, the ceiling fan spun slowly above me, barely moving the stale air.

I picked up my phone. A long list of missed calls flashed on the screen. Most were from customers, but one name made my heart sink—Ma. I hadn't called her all day.

I felt the guilt. But I was too tired to act on it. I placed the phone down and closed my eyes.

Just as I drifted into sleep, the sharp ring of the phone jolted me awake. The room was dark now, thick with the smell of sweat. I grabbed the phone—Ma's call.

I switched on the light and answered, "Hello, Ma."

Her voice was soft, almost tired. "Arjun, where are you? I've been calling all day."

"I'm sorry, Ma," I said, rubbing my eyes. "I was sleeping. It's been a long day."

"You're sleeping now? Are you okay?"

"I'm fine, just exhausted. Work's been hectic."

She sighed. "You need to take care of yourself. I keep telling you, this job isn't good for you. You're always out, always stressed."

I pressed the room service bell and smiled faintly. "Someone has to do sales, right? Not everyone gets a chair and a desk."

But her tone didn't lighten. "You run around like a machine, Arjun. This isn't a life."

"I know, Ma. But I have bills to pay. I'll switch when something better comes up."

There was a long pause. I could sense something was wrong.

"Are you okay, Ma?"

"No," she said softly. "I've had this pain on the left side of my chest. It's been there for a few days now."

I sat up straight. My heart dropped. She was alone back in Maynaguri, and there was no one to check on her.

"Mom, I'll leave right now. I can be there in three hours."

"No, Arjun. Please don't. Finish your work. I'll manage," she said quickly.

"How can I work knowing you're unwell? I'm coming home."

But she stopped me again. "We need the money, son. And… maybe it's time you thought about getting married. At least then someone will be here to take care of me."

Her words hit me hard. Before I could reply, the call disconnected. I stared at the screen for a few seconds, heart heavy.

I quickly called my aunt and asked her to check on Ma until I reached home.

Room service arrived with tea. I took a sip, but the taste didn't register. My mind was far away—on Mom, on work, on everything that just didn't seem to let up.

The next morning, light filtered through the thin curtains. Birds chirped outside as I slowly opened my eyes. The exhaustion was still there, but the early calm gave me a few seconds of peace.

I had slept early after Mom's call, leaving the phone on vibration mode. The room felt cooler, the air quiet. I pulled open the window. A soft breeze came in, brushing against my face. I stood there for a while, trying to gather my thoughts. There was a lot to do.

My tea arrived. I took it to the small desk near the window and sipped slowly, watching the street below come alive. Shops opening. People rushing. Everyone is chasing something.

But I felt still. Like the world was moving around me and I was stuck.

After finishing my tea, I headed for a shower, hoping it would wake me up. The sound of the water hitting the tiles was soothing, but my thoughts were already racing again.

I called room service and asked them to bring breakfast quickly. There was no time to waste.

Back at the desk, my phone buzzed. It was Isha.

"What's your plan for today?" she texted.

I replied, "Sonu's office by 9:30."

I didn't mention the vehicle service—there was no need. Mr. Vikram Singh, staying in another hotel, hadn't called yet. But I knew he would, any minute now.

And so another day began.

By 8:30, breakfast was on the table. I scrolled through the news on my phone, half-distracted, when it rang again. It was him. My boss—S.K. Aggarwal.

I stared at the screen for a moment, tension tightening in my chest. I could already hear the tone in his voice: sarcastic, impatient. There was no avoiding it. I sighed and picked up.

"Good morning, Mr. Arjun," he said, voice slick with false cheer. "How's your grand tour of Bhutan and Jaigaon? Having fun?"

A flicker of frustration rose, but I held it down. "Good morning, sir. Everything's fine here."

The fake pleasantries vanished quickly.

"You're fine, huh? What about the business? Have you sealed the deal in Bhutan?"

"Yes, sir. Our meeting with Himalayan Construction went well. They've asked for a mileage test and a small discount."

He cut me off before I could finish.

"Arjun, this is becoming a pattern. Every deal—you want discounts, tests, brokerage fees. Ever think about the dealership's bottom line? Who's paying for all this?"

I took a breath, steadying myself.

"Sir, the mileage test was offered by Mr. Vikram Singh, and the discount was promised through Rana Motors."

"These manufacturer guys," he muttered bitterly. "They promise the moon and vanish when it's time to deliver. Don't trust them. They never back their words."

I stayed quiet. Mr. Vikram was dependable and always delivered—but there was no point arguing. I'd learned that the hard way.

Just another morning with Mr. Aggarwal.

Two days earlier, we had closed a deal at Rajakamal Dhaba with Mr. Rajesh Gupta. I had informed Mr. Aggarwal right after—gave him the full update, the loan status from the financiers. I was heading to Phuntseoling for the Bhutan deal, so I asked if he could handle the delivery. Just three vehicles after paperwork. Simple.

But from his reaction, you'd think I asked him to rob a bank.

"Sir, today we promised Mr. Gupta the vehicles. Could you please arrange the delivery?"

His voice exploded through the line. "Arjun, are you my boss or am I yours? Why are you asking me for updates?"

"Not at all, sir. I'm only asking since I'm out of town working on the next deal," I replied calmly.

He wasn't having it.

"Whose fault is that? Who told you to promise two-day delivery? You should've done it after Bhutan."

"That commitment sealed the deal," I said.

It made him angrier. He ranted about my planning, my "overcommitment," and then ended it with, "I won't deliver your vehicles. You come back and do it yourself."

I knew he wouldn't skip it—sales pressure would make sure of that.

The air was crisp when I reached Sonu's showroom. Jaigaon was just waking up—shutters creaked open, the streets buzzed softly with early customers. Inside, Sonu was checking a worn-out bumper while his office boy swept the floor, the broom's soft swish filling the quiet space. Sunlight filtered through dusty windows, casting a golden glow on the old vehicles.

Sonu glanced up and nodded. "Take a seat, Arjun Da," he said, waving toward the chair. "Oh, and don't worry. As soon as Karma Tshering confirms the date for the mileage challenge, I'll let you know."

I nodded and sat down, pulling out my Special Date Diary. Every morning, I checked for birthdays or anniversaries. Today—July

26—I saw three birthdays and two anniversaries. One of them was local. I made a mental note to call them first.

Just as I reached for my phone, it buzzed.

Mr. Vikram Singh.

"Good morning, Arjun. Where are you right now?" His voice was brisk.

"Good morning, Sir. I'm at Sonu's showroom, waiting for your instructions."

He paused. "I won't be able to join you today. Back-to-back conference calls and a pile of work."

My heart sank a little. With Vikram Sir around, things always felt smoother. But I masked it quickly.

"No problem, Sir. I'll take care of everything here."

"Good. Get confirmation from Karma Tshering. And have the demo vehicle serviced—we need top mileage."

"Absolutely, Sir," I said, nodding instinctively.

"Wishing you a productive day, Arjun." The line went dead.

I set the phone down, exhaled slowly.

Another day. Another challenge.

The showroom had just started to come alive. Sunlight slipped through dusty windows, glinting off the hoods of old classic models that sat like silent storytellers. The faint scent of polish mixed with the aroma of chai drifted in from the street.

I shifted in my chair, pretending to focus on the screen. But I knew she'd walk in any second.

And she did.

Isha stepped through the glass door, wiping a touch of sweat from her forehead. The sunlight caught her at just the right angle—her skin glowing, her damp hair brushing against her cheeks. She moved with quiet purpose, elegant yet efficient, and took the seat beside me.

"What are you doing?" she asked, her voice bringing me back.

"Good morning," I said, trying not to sound too eager. "Just sorting through customer data—birthdays, anniversaries. A little 'happy birthday' goes a long way."

She raised an eyebrow. "Still doing this birthday thing, Arjun?"

I smiled. "Why not? Everyone deserves to feel remembered. Even customers."

She gave me a look—half amused, half curious. Then her eyes dropped to my shoes.

"Arjun... again? You really need a new pair."

I quickly tucked my feet under the table. "Next month," I mumbled, with a small grin. "I'll get them next month."

She nodded, then switched gears. "So, what's your plan for the day?"

I leaned back. "Birthday messages first. Then hot leads, a check-in with financiers... the usual chaos."

She lifted her hand, cutting me off. "No, no. I meant Himalayan Construction. Karma Tshering?"

"Still no confirmation," I said. "Sonu's following up. After this, I need to take my vehicle for servicing."

Her eyes narrowed. "Okay, and after that?"

I leaned forward slightly. "Join me. To the service center. Could use a break from all this."

She rolled her eyes. "And what would I do at a service center?"

"I'm going to a client's place after servicing—it's his anniversary. Come along, it's still fieldwork," I said, glancing at her.

She tried not to smile, but it peeked through. A moment later, we were in the Turbo Cheetah, driving into the sunlit morning. The road felt open. The day ahead—unwritten.

The Darjeeling Auto Works service center was twenty kilometers away, a space humming with clanking tools and the smell of grease and diesel thick in the air. As we pulled in, the background buzz of engines and shouts from mechanics wrapped around us like a familiar soundtrack.

We walked into the small, non-air-conditioned conference room. It was stuffy—old upholstery, rubber, motor oil in the air—but somehow, it fit. Isha opened her laptop, focused as ever, tapping away with calm precision. Even in this faded room, she made things feel sharp, important.

I pulled out my diary and flipped through pages of leads. Month-end pressure pressed down hard. My sales target hovered like a storm cloud. SP Aggarwal's last scolding still echoed in my ears.

I clutched my phone, making call after call. Some unanswered. Some cold. A few polite refusals. I paced, slumped, paced again—desperation and caffeine pushing me forward.

Across the table, Isha stayed in her world—cool, concentrated, headphones in.

Engines growled outside. Horns blared in the distance. The smell of fuel clung to the walls.

And then—mid-call—I felt her eyes on me.

She looked up, clearly annoyed. But in that look was something else too—sharp, challenging… alive.

"Arjun," she said sharply, her voice edged with frustration, "can you lower your voice? Between your shouting and the engines outside, it feels more like a market than a conference room."

Caught off guard, I ended the call and slipped my phone into my pocket. “Sorry, Isha. It’s just… this month’s target…” I tried to explain, though even I could hear the stress in my voice.

She rolled her eyes, her irritation softening just slightly. “We all have targets, Arjun. But we’re professionals, right? So, maybe keep it down a little?”

“Right… sorry,” I said quietly.

A small smile flickered on her face—half amused, half forgiving. Her eyes met mine and lingered a little longer than usual. There was something in that look—a warmth, a quiet understanding—unspoken, but there.

Outside, the sound of tools clanking and engines revving continued. The air in the room was thick with the smell of grease, diesel, and old upholstery. It wasn’t glamorous, but somehow, it felt like the perfect place for truths to surface.

I sat across from her, nervously twirling a pen. Her fingers danced across her keyboard, steady and focused, while I watched in silence.

Then I cleared my throat. “Isha… there’s something I’ve been meaning to say.”

She didn’t stop typing. “Arjun, if this is about sales targets, I’m already juggling enough.”

I shook my head. “No… It’s not about work.” My voice lowered. “Isha, I… I love you.”

Her fingers paused mid-air. Slowly, she looked up. Her eyes held caution, but behind it, something softer. Something unspoken.

“Arjun…” she whispered. “You know my family wouldn’t accept this. They want someone stable. Someone secure. Someone with… a proper title.”

"I have a degree," I said gently. "I'm earning well here—with incentives. Rana Motors and Darjeeling Auto Works are solid names."

She sighed, conflicted. "I know. But my parents are strict. To them, stable means something bigger. A title. A future that's already set."

I nodded slowly, feeling the sting but not letting it show. I looked down and opened my phone, pretending to scroll through client names.

Then her voice broke the silence. "Arjun," she said softly, her hand brushing mine, "finish your MBA. Get a stronger position. Maybe then… they'll see things differently."

My heart skipped. "You think that's all it would take?"

She nodded, meeting my gaze. "And think about your family, too. I'm Nepali… that won't be easy for them either."

I gave her a small smile. "My mother would understand. I'd make sure of it. Isha, I'm not giving up on us."

Her cheeks flushed, and she gently pulled her hand back. "Then finish your MBA," she said, her voice barely above a whisper.

I leaned back, feeling a weight lift off my chest. "I'm in my final year," I said, almost shyly. "Just six months to go."

She blinked, surprised—then smiled. A real smile. Bright. Relieved. "Arjun… that's amazing," she whispered. "You just made everything feel… possible."

We sat there, in that worn-out room filled with diesel fumes and engine noise, surrounded by scratched furniture and faded posters. And yet, in that moment, everything felt still. Clear. Hopeful.

The silence between us no longer felt heavy. It felt like a promise.

Suddenly, my phone buzzed. It was Sonu, of course.

"Arjun Da! Where are you, man?" he asked, loud as always.

"I'm at the service center," I replied calmly, glancing quickly at Isha.

"Alone?" he asked instantly. Sonu never understands boundaries.

"Nope. Isha's here too," I added, making my voice extra formal for her sake.

"Oh-ho! You and Isha in a conference room?" His tone turned playful. I could almost see his smirk.

"We're working, Sonu," I said, already irritated. "The TCT's in for servicing."

He laughed. "Yeah, yeah, 'working.' Just you two, alone? What kind of servicing is happening there?"

I rolled my eyes, my face warming with embarrassment. "Cut the cheap jokes, Sonu. What do you want?"

Still chuckling, he said, "Okay, okay! Just… don't service anything else, alright?"

I snapped, "Enough!"

Isha looked up, one eyebrow raised, clearly picking up on my irritation. I turned away to avoid more questions.

Trying to change the topic, I asked, "Did you hear from Himalayan Construction?"

"Yup! Karma Tshering called. We need to reach the Hashimara petrol pump by 8 a.m. tomorrow for the mileage challenge."

"8 a.m.? That's too early."

"Everyone's coming, even the competition. You want them to beat us?"

I sighed. "Fine. I'll meet you at your office by 7."

"Got it," he said seriously before hanging up.

I put my phone down. Isha was trying hard not to laugh.

"Sonu?" she asked, smiling.

"Yeah, Sonu," I muttered, rolling my eyes. She chuckled quietly and went back to work.

Later, I spoke to her about tomorrow's mileage challenge in Phuntsholing.

"Arjun," she sighed, "we've done everything we can. Let's just hope it goes our way."

We grabbed a quick lunch at the service center, collected our freshly serviced vehicle, and left. Our destination was Mr. Jayprakash Prasad's house in Hashimara—just 10 kilometers away. He ran a rice wholesale business with his wife, who also managed a small grocery shop. He'd asked us to come after 4 p.m.—not realizing we were actually planning to surprise them. It was their anniversary. He probably didn't even remember.

After a short drive, we parked our **Rana Turbo Cheetah Truck** a little away from his home and walked up carrying a bouquet and a gift. Isha gave me a puzzled look.

"Why do you attend your customers' personal events like this?" she asked.

I smiled. "Because our customers are like family. When we show up for their special moments, it shows they matter to us."

She raised an eyebrow. "Is that connection—or just a strategy?"

I laughed. "Real connection isn't a strategy. It's the reason they stay loyal. They remember how we made them feel."

She nodded, thoughtful, as we reached the shop. It was buzzing with activity—laborers loading heavy rice sacks into two Turbo Cheetah Trucks I had sold him.

Mr. Prasad noticed us as we approached.

"Namaste, sir," I greeted.

He blinked, adjusting his glasses, trying to place us.

Isha stepped forward, holding the bouquet. “Happy anniversary, sir.”

He looked genuinely surprised. I handed him our gift.

“Thank you, madam… Arjun… Oh, I’d completely forgotten!” he said, a little embarrassed. “You really made our day.”

He dusted off two chairs and asked us to sit. He sent away a few customers and signaled for tea and water. Then he called into the house: “Shanti! Come quickly! Guests are here!”

His wife stepped out, looking surprised but happy. Isha got up, handed her the bouquet, and said gently, “Happy anniversary, ma’am.”

A soft smile spread across her face. Maybe she had hoped someone would remember. Now, here we were.

I asked Mr. Prasad to stand beside her for a photo. As they held the bouquet and gift, I clicked a picture and sent it to him. Their smiles said it all.

We were served sweets and tea, and we chatted for a while—no sales talk, just connection. When Shanti offered us lunch, we politely declined, thanking her for her kindness.

As we drove back, we stopped by the **Torsa River**. The sky had turned orange and pink, the breeze cool and quiet. We sat by the bank in silence.

I stole a glance at Isha. She was watching the water, lost in thought. Probably thinking about her MBA results, her future, her plans.

Then she spoke, her voice low. “Arjun… are you serious about us?”

I blinked. “About what?”

She looked down, a shy blush on her face. "What you said… in the conference room."

Her words hung in the air. I took a deep breath. "Isha, if you're willing to walk this path with me—I'm right here."

A small smile touched her lips. "But it's not just about us. My family is involved too."

We sat in silence, the sound of the river flowing beside us. In that moment, words weren't needed. What we felt was real—quiet, strong, and slowly taking shape.

CHAPTER 32

# A Gift to Walk Forward

It was already evening when we reached Vikram Singh's hotel room after the anniversary celebration. Isha, Sonu, and I waited outside, still laughing about a funny lobby decoration. I knocked on the door, and soon it opened.

There he was—Vikram Singh—in what had clearly become his unofficial "office."

The room was a mess. Papers were scattered across the table, chargers dangled from sockets, and the stale smell of cigarettes filled the air. Half-drunk cups of tea stood abandoned in corners, like he'd started each one but never finished. His laptop sat on the bed next to his wallet, and his headphones were in a tangled mess.

"Come in, guys," he said, waving us in. "Mind the mess—you know how it gets."

We took our seats while he called room service and asked for more tea. As we settled down, I gave him the update.

"Karma Tshering's confirmed the mileage challenge, sir."

"Good," he said, leaning back. "Where are we doing it?"

"At the Hashimara petrol pump. Round-trip to Falakata via Jateswar. They want a flat route for 'standard norms'."

He sighed, clearly already thinking about the logistics. "We need good roads and less traffic. No point if we can't get accurate numbers."

"No problem," I said. "I know the area well. Road's smooth, barely any traffic."

He nodded slowly, taking a sip of tea. Then he turned to me again. "We'll need a quieter petrol pump in Hashimara. Non-stop run—no interruptions."

"Sorted, sir," I said. "I've handled seven of these challenges last year."

He paused, then asked, "And who's driving? This is about precision, not speed."

Before I could reply, Sonu jumped in. "Sir, I'll drive. I don't want to lose the deal I got for you. If Arjun can't deliver top mileage, we'll lose everything."

The room fell quiet.

Sonu had driven my Turbo Cheetah Truck demo unit a few times before. But his driving was aggressive—speedy, not smooth. I wasn't sure he could deliver the fuel efficiency we needed.

Vikram Singh sat up, narrowing his eyes at Sonu. He tapped his fingers on the table, studying him.

"Sonu," he said, calm but doubtful, "how do you plan to win this mileage challenge?"

Sonu shifted, his usual grin fading. He straightened up.

"Sir," he said, "I might not know your technical terms, but back home we say—if you want good mileage, keep speed between 40 and 60 km/h. Don't overuse the clutch or brakes."

We all listened.

Vikram's expression didn't change. "Anything else? Tricks for better mileage?"

A small grin crept back onto Sonu's face. His red-stained teeth showed as he chuckled. "Sir, can't reveal everything now. I'll show you during the challenge."

Vikram raised an eyebrow. Curious, but not fully convinced.

Sonu added, more firmly, “Don’t worry. I’ll get you the best mileage.”

Vikram leaned back, thinking. Then he looked at me and nodded. “Arjun, let him drive. Let’s hope he delivers.”

The decision was made. I dropped Isha and Sonu off at home afterward. None of us said much—our minds were already on tomorrow. If we failed the challenge, we’d lose the deal.

Back in my hotel room, I tried to sleep, but the pressure wouldn’t let me. I lay on the bed, staring at the ceiling, knowing tomorrow was a make-or-break day.

At around 8 p.m., my phone rang.

“Hello Arjun, come outside your hotel. I’m waiting for you,” Vikram Singh said.

Surprised, I stepped out without asking questions.

His SUV was parked right outside. He rolled down the window.

“Come in,” he said.

I got in. The cool air from the AC hit my face. The car smelled of cologne and a freshener.

“Arjun,” he said, “is there any good shoe shop nearby?”

I thought for a moment. “Yes, sir, the VeerWalk store is just a hundred meters ahead.”

We drove there.

Inside the store, he asked the staff to show him some formal shoes. The salesman brought out a few polished leather pairs, all expensive-looking.

Then Vikram turned to me. “Try these.”

“Sir…?” I said, unsure.

“No need to be formal, Arjun,” he said gently. “Pick the one you like.”

"Sir, not necessary. I'll buy next month, once salary comes," I replied, my voice tightening.

He picked a pair and handed it to me. "Try this."

I slipped them on. They fit perfectly.

"How much?" he asked the salesman.

"₹3,500 after discount."

"Pack it," Vikram said, paying without a pause.

We stepped outside.

He started the SUV and glanced at me. I held the bag in my lap, speechless.

"Thank you, sir," I finally said.

He looked ahead, smiling faintly. "Don't thank me. You're my warrior, Arjun. You help me hit my targets. Keeping you motivated is my job."

With that, he drove away.

I stood there, looking down at the bag in my hands. The shoes were more than I'd ever spent on myself. I felt a lump in my throat—not just for the gift, but for the trust behind it.

CHAPTER 33

# The Mileage Challenge

The morning air at the Hashimara petrol pump was thick with diesel, petrol, and smoke from nearby tea stalls. A few cigarette kiosks added their own scent. The place was quiet except for five double-cabin trucks lined up like warriors ready for battle.

Mr. Binod Gurung from Pawan Auto, the Raftar Motors dealer, walked in confidently and slapped his truck. “Today you’ll see what real mileage looks like.” His driver, Debu, leaned against the truck, calm and silent.

Across from him, Tamal Chokroborty from Uday Wheels—representing StormX Automotive—paced nervously. “Guys, no fooling around. Stick to the plan—we have to win,” he muttered to his team.

Peter Lakra from Siliguri Motors, dealer of Tejas Automotive, smirked at me. “Turbo Cheetah, huh? Let’s see if it runs as well as it sounds.”

I forced a smile but felt tense. With Mr. S. P. Aggarwal absent, Vikram and I were representing Turbo Cheetah. “I was supposed to drive, but Sonu insisted,” I told Vikram quietly.

Sonu caught my look and grinned. “Come on, Arjun. Trust me—I’ll get us the best mileage.”

Vikram and Isha smiled reassuringly. “Alright, buddy. Turbo Cheetah’s in your hands.”

Isha walked over, eyes dropping to my shoes. “Nice shoes, Arjun—you’re looking handsome today.”

“Thanks,” I said, not mentioning they were a gift from Vikram.

Then Karma Tshering arrived with about twenty employees from Himalayan Construction. "Gentlemen," he began firmly, "this rally will decide which truck joins our fleet. It's not just about mileage—your vehicles must prove everything you've claimed."

Tamal raised a hand. "Sir, what's the rally process?"

"The route is a 100 km round trip—Hashimara to Falakata and back," Karma replied. "Each truck will be filled to the brim here and flagged off together—no stops unless it's an emergency."

"How do we make sure no one cheats?" Tamal pressed.

Karma smiled. "Each vehicle will have three people—your co-driver, one from our company, and one from a rival team. Patrols will monitor the route."

Binod winked. "No problem, sir. We'll play fair."

"Good," Karma said. "The winner is the truck with the best mileage. Stick to the route and play clean."

Engines rumbled to life. Karma raised a sheet. "Transparency is key. Check every vehicle before starting. After the trip, we'll record odometers and calculate mileage."

Vikram leaned toward me. "Arjun, look how he turned our small idea into a full process."

I nodded. "Yes, sir. He's handling it like a pro."

Karma called out again, "Follow the rules and stay honest."

Binod smirked. "Rules? My Raftar truck doesn't need them—it's built for efficiency."

Peter shot back, "We'll see about that."

Soon, trucks lined up at the pump. Teams checked engines, tires, and tanks as Karma walked around with his clipboard.

Standing beside Sonu, I said, "This isn't a race—drive smart, not fast."

Sonu chewed his paan, lit a cigarette, and grinned. “Relax, Arjun. I know how to get good mileage—we’ll win.”

“Don’t get overconfident,” I warned. “Keep speed steady, 40–60 km/h. No sudden braking.”

Mr. Vikram joined in. “Just follow Arjun’s instructions.”

“Did you check the tire pressure?” he asked.

“Yes, sir. Perfect levels,” I replied.

“Good. What about load?” Sonu asked.

“All trucks carry standard load—no extras.”

“Got it. No extra weight.”

“Perfect,” I said. “Light and steady—that’s how we win.”

The sun climbed higher. Diesel fumes mixed with the heat. Vikram adjusted his sunglasses and looked at Sonu, still leaning casually against Turbo Cheetah, chewing paan.

“Sonu,” Vikram said firmly, “keep the windows shut during the drive.”

“Why, sir?” Sonu frowned.

“Wind drag. Open windows reduce mileage. Don’t use AC either—it wastes fuel.”

Sonu nodded. “Alright, sir.”

Engines were running. Three trucks stood ready, tanks gleaming. Raftar Motors finished checks, Himalayan Construction team shouted for urgency.

“Sonu,” I called, trying to stay calm, “no speeding, no hard braking, no clutch-riding. Just drive steady.”

He straightened. Mischief replaced by focus.

“Relax, Arjun. I’ve got this. Your truck will give the best mileage.”

I smiled and clapped his back. "I'll be in the co-driver's seat. Let's see what you can do."

Vikram and Isha waved. "Best of luck!" Their voices rose above engine noise and diesel fumes.

The rally was about to start. Trucks lined up, tanks full, windows closed. Drivers tightened seat belts, adjusted mirrors, waiting for the signal. Nervousness and confidence mingled—but everyone was ready.

Just before 8 a.m., chatter stopped. A black SUV rolled in. Mr. Suraj Singh stepped out, sunglasses on, calm and serious. Everyone straightened.

He walked to the front, voice steady.

"Good morning, everyone. Thank you for being here. Today isn't just a competition—it's a chance to prove something. Every vehicle is built with a purpose. There are no bad vehicles, only different strengths. Today, we'll see which fits our needs best."

He paused, then added with a small smile, "The driver who gets the best mileage today will win a brand-new smartphone. A small reward for great driving."

Applause followed. Drivers nodded, pressure rising. Trucks roared to life.

I climbed into the co-driver's seat next to Sonu. In the back, representatives from Himalayan Construction and Raftar Motors held notepads, observing. Isha checked the Load Max Motors vehicle, ensuring no cheating.

Vikram Singh drove his SUV, face unreadable. Everyone exchanged glances—nervous but ready.

Karma Tshering raised his whistle. Silence fell. Mr. Suraj Singh lifted his hand. The whistle blew.

The challenge began.

Sonu adjusted his hands on the steering wheel. The morning sun lit the Hashimara crossroads in a soft golden glow. Engines hummed, birds chirped, and traffic moved steadily. Sonu stayed calm, driving smoothly—braking and restarting would hurt mileage. This wasn't just about reaching the end; it was about driving smart.

Binod Gurung, Sales Manager of Raftar Motors, pushed up his glasses, watching Debu. The engine ran steadily as Debu kept the right speed, hands firm on the wheel, blue T-shirt soaked in sweat.

"Slow and steady, Debu. Don't rush. Focus," Binod said quietly.

Debu nodded, eyes on the road.

A sudden engine roar broke the calm. Tamal Chokroborty leaned forward, waving at his driver.

"Anthony! Go faster! We're falling behind!"

Anthony shot a side glance. "You said slow and steady before. Now you want fast?"

"Yes! But don't mess it up. Raftar Motors can't beat us!"

Anthony sighed and pushed the gear. Their truck shot forward, passing Binod and Debu.

"Show-offs," Binod muttered.

Another truck overtook them, horn blaring. Peter Lakra from Tejas Automotive, grinning, leaned out and spat betel juice.

"Sonu!" he shouted. "Don't let them win! Stick with me. You worked for me yesterday, today you're here, and tomorrow—who knows?" His laugh echoed as he sped ahead.

Sonu shook his head. "He talks too much," he said, focusing on the road.

Past Hashimara, his usual overconfidence was gone. Every gear change is perfect, every brake is gentle. Two brakes in ten kilometers, I thought. Impressive.

"Sonu," I said, "I didn't know you could drive like this."

He grinned. "This isn't about a trophy, Arjun. It's about that twenty-truck deal. I can't lose."

Near Jateswar, my phone buzzed. Vikram's voice came through, excited.

"Shakti Singh was caught refueling in the jungle to cheat on mileage!"

"What? Seriously?" I said.

"Arjun, no cheating. Tell Sonu to drive properly. Himalayan Construction is watching. If we get caught, we're out."

"Don't worry, sir. I won't let anything happen."

Sonu whistled softly. "Knew someone would try to cheat."

Isha sent an update. "Tamal took a shortcut. They caught him. He's still allowed to continue."

"Unreal," I murmured.

Now it was just us, Peter, and Binod. Sunlight reflected off the trucks as we moved ahead.

Peter's truck came close. "Keep up, Arjun! Or fall behind!"

Sonu didn't react. He turned up the music and shifted gears smoothly. "Patience. I've got this," he whispered.

The road narrowed, with green tea gardens on both sides. Peter veered onto a rough side road. Sonu stayed on the main path.

"Hold tight, Arjun," he said.

With one clean move, he overtook Peter's truck, leaving a trail of dust and Peter's angry shouts. Tension rose as we neared Falakata crossroads.

"Take a U-turn here, Sonu," I said.

"I know, Arjun. Don't worry," he replied, eyes locked on traffic.

Even a kilometre out, he slowed early—no hard braking, no clutching, no engine restart. Just a clean, fuel-efficient turn.

Ahead, Binod's driver made his turn smoothly. The vehicle crowd grew, but Sonu stayed focused.

Suddenly, a Himalayan Construction vehicle darted through and took a sharp U-turn, chaos erupting behind it. Mr. Vikram Singh leaned out from his SUV, flashing a victory sign.

Then, a massive truck cut across the intersection, stopping abruptly. Horns screamed, brakes squealed. Cars, buses, and rickshaws jammed every inch. Sonu tapped the brakes gently, trying not to stall, frustration darkening his calm face.

Engines idled. Time dragged. Peter restarted and made his U-turn cleanly, speeding away.

Sonu restarted the Turbo Cheetah, jaw tight.

"This damn jam ruined my mileage," he muttered.

He turned sharply and got us back on the road.

Trying to lift the mood, I leaned forward. "It's just a hiccup, Sonu. Stay focused. We can still finish strong."

He gave a silent nod, eyes on the road, determined. The engine hummed gently; tyres rolled steadily over tarmac. Silence helped more than words.

Peter's truck whizzed past. He waved. I smiled and waved back, dialing Isha.

"Isha," I said, "what's this I heard about Shakti Singh from Load Max Motors getting disqualified?"

Her voice came through, annoyed and surprised.

"You won't believe it, Arjun. That guy suddenly told his driver to take a detour—a narrow lane by the highway. They stopped near a jungle."

"What? Why?" I asked.

"I asked the same! I confronted him, 'Shakti, what's going on? Why stop here?' And he lifts his little finger, grins, and says, 'Relax, Isha. The driver just needs a bathroom break.' Then both got down with a water bottle!"

I burst out laughing. "Seriously?"

"Yeah, but that's not all," she said, voice dropping. "The Himalayan Construction team stopped too. I stayed inside—I had a weird feeling."

"What happened next?"

"After a few minutes, shouting broke out. I got out and saw Shakti and his driver arguing with the Himalayan guys. They were sneaking diesel into the tank—trying to cheat on mileage."

I sat up. "What?! Shameless!"

"I know. Mr. Karma showed up, furious. He told Shakti, 'If you can't be honest, how can we trust your company?' Boom—disqualified."

I leaned back, shaking my head. "Good for Karma. Cheaters like that need to be thrown out."

"Exactly," she said.

"I'm heading toward the Hashimara petrol pump," I said.

"You too, Arjun. Drive safe."

We hung up. Sonu gave a small nod, hands steady on the wheel. Silent agreement. My mind stayed with Isha's story as we drove.

Twenty minutes later, we reached the Hashimara petrol pump. It was crowded. Peter Lakra was refueling; Binod Gurung pulled in behind him. Sonu parked carefully, conserving fuel. Tamal Chokroborty arrived shortly after. Engines were off—no one risked extra fuel consumption.

By 2:30 PM, all teams had gathered. The air was tense. This wasn't just numbers—it was deals, reputations, and futures. The rally's outcome would decide the Himalayan Construction Company contract.

Peter's vehicle went first. His truck, claimed at 16.5 kmpl, clocked 16.3. Slightly under, still impressive. Binod Gurung's Raftar Motors, rated 15.5, came in at 15.7—better than expected, but not enough to lead.

Our turn came. Sonu, previously relaxed, straightened. The Rana Turbo Cheetah Truck, rated 15.9, was refilled. The reading: 16.2. A new benchmark. Isha cheered; Sonu remained calm, eyes quietly proud.

Tamal's StormX, rated 16.9, clocked 16.4—not enough. Shakti Singh stood aside, arms folded, disqualified, bitter.

Mr. Karma Tshering called, "Please have lunch. Results shortly."

An hour later, the teams gathered. Karma and Mr. Suresh Parikh joined. Sonu's truck led, but numbers weren't everything—relationships, brand perception, and trust mattered.

Karma stepped forward. "Thank you all. Each vehicle has strengths, but mileage affects operations and profitability. The winner is based on the announced method. You may review the calculation sheet afterward."

He paused, looked at Parikh. Parikh nodded.

"I now invite our MD, Mr. Suresh Parikh, to announce results."

Parikh adjusted sunglasses and read aloud:

"Third-highest mileage: Tejas Automotive, Peter Lakra. Well done."

"Second: Raftar Motors, Binod Gurung."

"And the highest—16.2 kmpl, surpassing the manufacturer claim: Sonu Kumar, Rana Turbo Cheetah Truck. Congratulations. This vehicle will be considered for our fleet."

There was an unexpected twist. Earlier, Mr. Suresh Parikh had announced that the winner would receive just a smartphone. But now, with a smile, he made a surprising change. "First place receives a gold chain instead of a smartphone, courtesy of Himalayan Construction Company."

Sonu's face lit up. Isha clapped. The crowd joined in. Binod received a smartphone, Peter Lakra a smartwatch. Handshakes, laughter, pats on the back—it was a defining moment.

Tamal, upset, raised a concern.

"Can you explain how the champion was selected?"

Parikh smiled. "Fair question. Karma?"

Karma explained: vehicles ranked by how actual mileage compared to manufacturer claims. In some cases, trucks outperformed claims. "We judge based on improvement, not raw numbers," he added, handing the sheets to Tamal and Peter.

Tamal frowned. "But claims differ across companies. How is that fair?"

"We calculated the percentage difference from claimed mileage. This ensures fairness and transparency," Karma said.

Once things were cleared up, we slowly packed up and left Hasimara and Jaigaon, all of us waiting eagerly for the final decision from Himalayan Construction Company.

CHAPTER 34

# I Love You, Over and Out

Returning from Jaigaon, I walked into the house, expecting things to be normal. But one look at my mother told me it wasn't. Her eyes were sharp, her lips pressed into a thin line.

"You're never here," she snapped. "What kind of job is this? It's ruining your life. You've forgotten this is your home."

I took a deep breath. She wasn't wrong. But how could I explain the pressure, the endless hours, the chaos that came with this job? Still, she deserved an answer.

"Ma, I know it's hard," I said quietly. "But I'm doing my best. Things will get better."

I meant it. Or at least, I wanted to believe it.

The next day, I pushed the guilt aside and got back to work. It was the end of July—always the most stressful time of the month. The leads I had followed up on for weeks had to close now. Every sale counted. Customers hesitated, bosses shouted, and targets hung over us like dark clouds. Somehow, with sheer effort, I managed to meet my numbers. Was I relieved? Maybe. But happy? Not really.

In all the chaos, one issue stayed buried: Hamid Alam's vehicle repossession case. He didn't call. Mr. Vikram Singh didn't ask. It was like the problem had disappeared—swallowed up by the pressure of closing sales. I wanted to fix it. But in our line of work, old problems often became someone else's burden.

On August 2nd, 2014, Mr. S.P. Aggarwal called for the monthly review meeting. July's performance had been poor, and with the festive season coming up, August needed to start strong. The meeting room felt tense, the air thick.

One by one, the managers scolded us. Targets missed. Follow-ups delayed. No one was spared—not even Mr. Aggarwal. Mr. Rakesh Chetri even questioned his planning. By the end, the room was silent. No one said a word.

As soon as the meeting ended, Mr. Chetri stormed off to check the service numbers. I saw a chance and went up to Mr. Aggarwal.

"Sir, about the Hamid Alam case—"

"Later," he said sharply, not even lifting his eyes from the laptop.

But later never came. He went straight into another meeting—August target planning, marketing discussions. Every time I tried to step into his cabin, he waved me away. "Not now."

It was clear—he didn't want to deal with it.

That evening, I left the office drained. The weight of my mother's words, the Hamid issue, and the constant pressure all sat heavily on me. The house was quiet when I walked in. But inside me, things were far from calm.

It was 7 PM. I stepped in, tired and looking forward to a bit of peace. After a quick shower, I lay down on my bed. The ceiling fan spun slowly, and a news anchor spoke in the background. My mother entered, holding a cup of tea and some snacks.

She sat next to me, looking worried.

"Arjun, did you get your salary? There's hardly anything left at home. I need to buy groceries."

I took the tea and said gently, "Not yet, Ma. You know how it works. We get paid after the 7th. Today's just the 2nd."

She sighed but didn't say anything else. After a few quiet minutes, she left the room.

I lay back, flipping through TV channels without watching anything. My phone buzzed. It was Isha.

"Hey, Arjun!" she said in a playful voice. "Back from work already?"

"Yeah, just reached."

Not wanting my mother to hear, I quietly walked out of the room. The door creaked.

"Where are you going, Arjun?" she called out.

"Just stepping out for a walk," I said.

Isha giggled on the other end. "You're sneaking out to talk to me, aren't you? Naughty!"

I smiled as I stepped onto the porch. Trucks roared past on the highway.

"Ugh! That noise is horrible," Isha said. "Anyway, how was your day?"

"Okay, I guess," I replied. "But that Hamid Alam case is still troubling me. I tried speaking to Mr. Aggarwal, but he didn't listen."

"What about the GM?"

"He was busy all day. I couldn't get through."

"Don't worry. Mr. Vikram Singh will handle it," she said kindly.

"Yeah. He always looks out for us," I said, feeling a little better.

"Guess what?" she said suddenly, excited.

"What happened?"

"I passed my MBA! Results came out today!"

"That's amazing, Isha! Congratulations!"

"Thanks, Arjun," she said warmly.

"So, when's the treat?" I teased.

"Whenever you want. Just name the place."

"How about a five-star dinner tomorrow?" I grinned.

She laughed. "You're dreaming big, huh?"

Lowering her voice, Isha said, "Oh, and I might get promoted soon."

"Seriously? That's amazing! Don't tell me—you're replacing Mr. Aggarwal? That would be the best news ever!" I laughed.

"Stop it, Arjun!" she said, pretending to scold me, but I could hear the smile in her voice. "Mr. Rakesh told me that if I pass my MBA, I'll be promoted to Assistant Sales Manager—personal vehicles."

"That's double the reason to celebrate! Now I want two parties. And from tomorrow, it's 'Madam Isha,' right?" I teased.

"You're impossible," she sighed, pretending to be annoyed.

There was a pause. Then her voice softened. "By the way, when's your MBA final exam?"

"End of December," I said, a little more serious now.

"Are you preparing properly?" she asked gently.

"I'm trying," I replied. The sound of trucks passing by made my voice feel far away. "But who knows how it'll go."

"You'd better do well, Arjun. I'm waiting for your results," she said firmly.

"I will, Isha. I won't let you down."

Lately, Isha had started talking more seriously about our future. Our bond was a strange mix—part romance, part chaos—with love tangled up in sales targets, diesel, and daily deadlines.

She kept pushing me to finish my MBA. She believed it would lay the foundation for a better life—for both of us. And for the first time, I gave her a real promise.

"I'll give it everything, Isha. This time, I mean it," I said, holding the phone a little tighter.

There was silence.

Then she said, "Arjun, I want to tell you something."

I braced myself. Maybe another sales update or some new target.

"What is it, Isha?"

"Arjun... I love you."

I froze.

The loud highway suddenly felt quiet. The trucks passing by became just a low hum. A cool breeze touched my face. Those three words—I had been waiting for them.

"Isha, I love you too," I whispered, standing under the coconut tree outside my house.

Even the vehicles on the highway seemed to celebrate with us. The lights, the sounds—it all felt magical, like the world had quietly said "yes" to us.

Then she added, "Next week, I have to take a customer for a test drive. He's an army officer. We'll be driving the SUV from Gangtok to Nathula Pass. Can you come with me?"

"Sikkim? That sounds amazing! Of course, I'll come. Just give me two days' notice."

"Done. I'll inform you," she replied, her voice cheerful.

"It'll be a trip to remember. Goodnight, Isha."

"Goodnight, Arjun. Sweet dreams. I love you."

Her words made me pause for a moment.

"Goodnight… Isha. Same to you."

I ended the call and walked back into the house. Mom was setting plates on the dining table.

"Who was that?" she asked with a playful smile.

"Work call," I said, trying to hide my grin.

"Hmm," she said knowingly. "Come on, let's call your cousins. You haven't spoken to them in a while."

That was Mom's thing. Staying in touch with everyone—no matter how far—was her way of keeping relationships alive.

We sat down with our phones and made conference calls to relatives. She led every conversation, asking about everyone's health, work, children—everything.

After the calls, she looked at me and said, "Arjun, always remember—relationships matter the most. No amount of money can replace them."

We ate dinner—dal-chawal, simple and warm. We talked about work, old family stories, and her plan to visit the temple next week. These small moments meant more than I could explain.

Later that night, lying in bed, I kept hearing Isha's voice in my head. I love you.

It lit something inside me. For the first time, my thoughts weren't filled with engines, invoices, or deadlines. I saw a glimpse of a life with her—our dreams, our future.

And I fell asleep with a smile.

My dream was vague, like a half-finished movie. Isha had been in it, laughing.

Her laughter echoed faintly as I opened my eyes in the morning.

I dragged myself to the washroom. A splash of cold water woke me up. From the kitchen came the smell of spices and the sound of utensils clinking. Mom was already busy—just like every other morning. A soft classical tune played in the background, calming the noise around.

Still half-asleep, I walked into the kitchen.

"You're up late again," Mom said sharply. "Seven o'clock is not morning! I told you—wake up at five. Early risers succeed in life."

"Good morning, Ma," I mumbled, reaching for the tea she handed me.

She looked tired. There were lines on her face, carved from years of managing everything on her own.

"You know what would help? A wife. Get married, Arjun. I'm tired. Let her take over this house," she said.

I laughed, sipping my tea. "I'm working on it, Ma. One day, someone will make you really happy."

Her eyes narrowed. "Someone? Who? That receptionist?" she teased, pulling my ear. "I'm your mother—I know everything. Now go get ready for work."

Blushing a little, I laughed and ran off to the bathroom.

CHAPTER 35

# The Knock at 9:15

By 9:15 a.m., I was ready for the day—bag on my shoulder, shoes polished. That's when the knock came. Firm. Steady.

I opened the door. Inspector Sanjeev Singh from Maynaguri police station stood there with two constables. My heart skipped a beat.

"Inspector Singh," I greeted, trying to smile. "Please, come in."

He shook his head, serious. "Arjun, I'm here on official duty. There's an arrest warrant against you. Mr. Hamid has filed another case. It's serious. I have to take you in."

The word "arrest" hit me hard. My chest tightened. "Arrest?" I asked, barely able to speak. My head spun. My job, my reputation, my future—all flashed in front of me. I hadn't done anything wrong. This was my boss's mess. But I was the one being punished.

From behind me, my mother's voice broke through the silence. "What has my son done, Inspector?" Her voice trembled with both fear and anger.

Inspector Singh softened. "Don't worry, Ma ji. Your son is innocent. But he represents his company. I'm just doing my duty."

"Innocent? Then why arrest him?" she cried. Tears rolled down her cheeks. "His life will be ruined. Our name will be dragged through the mud. Please, don't do this."

I placed a hand on her shoulder. "Ma, it'll be okay. The office will handle it. Don't worry."

But she wasn't calm. She turned on me, furious. "I told you this job would bring trouble! And now this? Jail?" Her voice cracked as she looked at the inspector. "Take him! Let him see where this job leads."

Neighbours started gathering, whispering, watching the scene unfold. My mother walked inside, crying. I sighed and followed the inspector to the police van, her words still ringing in my ears.

The police station smelled of damp concrete. A sleepy constable sat at the gate. Inside, the lockup was dark, its metal bars casting long shadows on the floor.

"Do I have to stay in there with them?" I asked, panic rising.

"Yes, Arjun," Singh replied. "But don't worry. I'll tell them not to bother you."

He opened the cell door. Four men lay on the floor, their faces tired and cold. One looked straight at me—his stare unsettling.

"Listen up!" Singh barked. "This man is not one of you. Don't disturb him."

I stepped in and sat on the cold floor. The door clanged shut behind me. My thoughts were a mess. How had things come to this? How would I get out?

For the first time in years, I had nothing to do. No calls to make. No targets to chase. Just silence.

And in that silence, my own thoughts caught up with me.

Is this the life you wanted, Arjun?

Is this job worth it? Fifteen-hour workdays, constant pressure, and now this? Is this what success is?

The questions hit hard. I thought of my mother's angry tears. Of Isha's soft laughter, now just a memory. I had always kept moving, pushing forward no matter what. But now, it felt like the road had disappeared.

Tears welled up in my eyes. I turned away so the others wouldn't see. But two of them looked at me—blank, unreadable. Were they judging me? Pitying me? I didn't know.

All I knew was that I had hit a wall.

Still, I wasn't ready to give up.

Maybe life had thrown mc into first gear. Maybe I was stuck for now. But I would move again. Somehow.

The clock showed 10:30 a.m. when I walked up to Inspector Sanjeev Singh. My voice shook a little, but I kept it steady.

"Sir, may I use my phone? I need to inform my office."

He looked at me over the rim of his teacup.

"Why?"

"To let them know I'm in custody. It's about the Hamid Alam case."

He placed the cup down without changing his expression.

"Yes, they should know."

A constable handed me my phone. Around me, the lockup was waking up—one man groaned for tea, another asked to call his family. I blocked out the noise and dialed Isha.

She picked up on the second ring, her voice cheerful.

"Good morning, Arjun! How was your night? Let me guess—you didn't sleep, just kept thinking about targets and Mr. S.P. Aggarwal, right?" She laughed, teasing.

I paused. I couldn't match her energy.

"Isha, I'm in—"

She kept going, still laughing.

"I know, I know. You're under pressure again. What's new?"

"No, Isha, listen—"

"Okay, okay," she joked. "No pressure this month, huh? Overachiever Arjun's on track!"

"Isha," I said firmly. "Don't joke. This is serious. I'm in police custody."

That stopped her. Her tone changed at once.

"What? What do you mean?"

"I'm at Maynaguri Police Station. It's about Hamid Alam's case."

There was silence for a moment. Then her voice came back, softer.

"I'm sorry, Arjun. I didn't know. I shouldn't have joked."

Then her tone turned sharp.

"This is all because of Aggarwal and Rakesh Chetri! They're the ones who left you to deal with this mess."

"Isha, stop," I said gently. "It's complicated. Maybe they tried and couldn't solve it."

"You're too honest for this job," she snapped. "Winning hearts is great, but being too soft in front of people like them will only get you hurt."

"Please, Isha. Don't lose your temper. Just let Mr. Aggarwal and Rakesh know."

"I will," she said, more calmly. "But I'm not holding back this time. You're always the 'good guy,' Arjun—but being good isn't always enough. Just watch what I do."

She hung up. I looked down at the phone, unsure of what she meant.

Inspector Singh came over with a kind look.

"Arjun, have some tea," he said, nodding to the chaiwala nearby.

The tea was lukewarm, served with a few biscuits on a small plate. Even though I was an accused, the inspector showed me respect. He knew my name in the market and understood this wasn't a black-and-white case.

"You'll need a lawyer for your bail," he added. "Do you know someone? Or should I arrange one?"

His words reminded me of the 24-hour rule—I had to be presented in court soon. I thought of Anup Roy, my lawyer friend. I had told him about this situation before I went to Jaigaon.

Taking the phone from Mr. Sanjeev, I took a sip of tea and dialed Anup. The cold steel bars in front of me felt heavier with every ring.

"Hey, Arjun! Back from Jaigaon or still chasing trucks?" Anup joked, his voice full of energy.

"Anup," I said quietly, "I'm in Maynaguri… in police custody."

"What?" His voice jumped. "What happened? Are you okay?"

"It's Hamid Alam's case," I explained. "The company didn't act. Hamid and his son kept threatening me. I informed everyone—nobody helped. Now I'm here."

"Damn it, Arjun! Don't worry. I'm coming right away."

He hung up before I could say anything more.

A little later, my mother arrived with my aunt and a few neighbors. When she saw me behind bars, she broke down. Her cries filled the small room.

"Ma," I tried to calm her, "Anup is coming. I'll be out soon. I've done nothing wrong."

She didn't speak. Instead, she walked straight to the inspector.

"Sir, he's innocent," she said, voice shaking. "When will you let him go?"

"Ma ji," Singh replied gently, "you'll need to arrange bail. It's a cheating case filed by a customer. But your son has already called his lawyer."

She nodded and sat down, wiping her tears quietly.

By noon, Isha arrived at the station. She looked serious, her usual confidence a bit shaken. She wasn't alone—Partha and Bikash were with her.

"Arjun," Isha said softly, stepping close to the bars. "We're here. Don't worry. I've spoken to the bosses. They agreed to cover all your bail expenses."

"Thank you," I said. My throat was dry.

Partha, always the one to speak his mind, added, "We know who messed this up. That customer was ignored, and now you're paying for it. But we'll talk about that later. Right now, we'll get you out. When is your lawyer coming?"

"He's on his way," I replied.

I looked at Isha. "What about Mr. Aggarwal and Mr. Chetri? What did they say?"

She crossed her arms. "Aggarwal locked himself in his cabin. Didn't say a word. But Chetri helped. He sent his car and told me to bring you out. At least someone understands how serious this is."

Bikash shook his head. "Arjun, you work too hard. I've told you—this company won't back you when things go wrong. Just look at Aggarwal now—silent, hiding."

I didn't reply. They weren't wrong. A part of me knew it. But still, some part of me wanted to believe in the bigger picture—in the job, in the mission.

Finally, Anup arrived and handled everything. By 3 p.m., I was out on bail.

As I stepped outside, even the sunlight felt like judgment.

The ride home was quiet. No one spoke. When I reached my room, I lay on the bed, staring at the ceiling. The day had left a mark—not just on my career, but deep inside me.

For someone who had always taken pride in doing the right thing, being arrested felt like a scar that wouldn't fade.

A little later, Ma walked in with a plate of food. "Eat, beta," she said gently. "You need your strength."

I nodded, but I couldn't eat. The heaviness inside me didn't let go.

Around 6 PM, my phone buzzed. It was Isha.

"Hello, Arjun. How are you feeling?" Her voice was soft, tinged with concern.

"Better," I lied, though the truth pressed heavily in my chest.

"There's a meeting tomorrow at 11 AM about the Hamid Alam case. You'll need to come prepared. Aggarwal will try to pin everything on you."

"Of course he will," I muttered, barely hiding the tension in my tone.

"Don't let him. Keep your backup data ready," she said firmly, almost like she could shield me with her words.

"I will," I said, trying to sound confident.

There was a pause. Then, quietly, almost fragile, she added, "Arjun… you'll get through this."

"Thanks, Isha. I mean it," I whispered.

When the call ended, I stared at the dark screen. Her belief in me felt like the only solid thing amid the chaos.

But the moment I closed my eyes, the weight of it all came crashing back—tomorrow I'd face my bosses, my colleagues, the aftermath of that arrest. I had to be ready. I couldn't let them break me.

CHAPTER 36

# The Anatomy of a Blunder

The next morning, I woke up early.

I couldn't sleep much. My mind was still restless from everything that had happened. My arrest in the Hamid Alam case had badly hurt my image. Even after breakfast, I felt a knot in my stomach.

At 8 a.m., I left for the Siliguri office. I turned the key and started the Turbo Cheetah Truck. The engine roared, almost like it was angry for the way I had been treated. I pressed the accelerator harder. The speedometer climbed to 120 kmph. It felt like the truck was feeding off my frustration.

By 9:30 a.m., I reached the showroom.

Isha was already at her desk, deeply focused on her work. Without looking up, she asked me to wait. One by one, Partha, Bikash, and other colleagues walked in. The housekeeping staff was busy cleaning the floor. The polishing team was working on the vehicles to make them shine for customers.

Mr. S. K. Aggarwal was alone in his cabin, flipping through files with a cigarette in hand. His face looked unusually serious.

Partha and Bikash joined me, and we began discussing our respective market performance. We compared our last month's targets versus actual achievements.

After some time, the three of us walked to the canteen to have tea and a smoke.

At 10:45 a.m., Isha called.

"Hey Arjun, it's 10:45. You need to report to the director's cabin in five minutes."

"Okay, I'm coming," I replied.

Bikash asked, "What's going on?"

"Isha said I need to meet the MD," I said.

Partha leaned forward. "If they're planning to terminate you or Aggarwal wants to trap you in front of everyone, just say the word. I'll take care of it."

"Relax, Partha," I told him. "I'll handle it."

At exactly 10:55 a.m., I entered the MD's cabin.

Mr. S. K. Aggarwal was already there, sitting on a sofa with a stack of files in front of him. Two finance assistants sat beside him, checking data and making notes in their diaries. He glanced at me for a moment, then returned to his work without a word. I quietly took a seat in the corner.

Two minutes later, Mr. Vikram Singh and Mr. Rakesh Chetri walked in. I stood up and greeted them.

"Good morning, sirs."

They nodded and returned the greeting. After settling into their revolving chairs, they opened their laptops. Mr. Rakesh was preparing his data, likely anticipating tough questions from our managing director, Mr. Sanjay Mittal.

Mr. Vikram Singh greeted Mr. Aggarwal politely, "Good morning, Mr. Aggarwal."

Aggarwal responded with a tight nod, "Morning, Mr. Vikram."

"When is the MD expected?" Vikram asked.

"He's on his way," Aggarwal replied.

About ten minutes later, Mr. Sanjay Mittal entered the cabin.

Isha followed, holding a stack of files and notebooks. After brief formal greetings, the meeting began without delay.

Mr. Mittal got straight to the point.

"Mr. Aggarwal, tell me what exactly happened in the Hamid Alam case."

Aggarwal's usual arrogance was gone. With a tense face, he replied, "Sir, Hamid Alam's payment was due, so we repossessed the vehicle."

"Which payment was due? EMI or down payment?"

Aggarwal hesitated for a second, then said, "Down payment, sir."

He looked nervous. It was probably one of the toughest questions he had faced, and he chose to lie to protect himself.

Mr. Mittal turned to Rakesh Chetri.

"How are vehicles getting delivered without a full down payment?"

Rakesh, despite being an experienced manager with an MBA, was clearly struggling. He looked trapped between his duty to the company and the need to protect his team.

"Sir, at the time of delivery, the down payment wasn't pending. This issue came up later due to a retail finance complication," he said, trying to sound confident.

Mittal's face turned red with anger. His voice rose.

"What are you all doing here? Delivering vehicles without proper payment? Is that your job? You're making a mess of my business!"

He immediately dialed his chief accountant, Mr. Debashis Paul.

Isha quietly picked up the AC remote and lowered the temperature. The soft hum of the air conditioner filled the room—adding to the growing tension in the cabin.

A few minutes later, Mr. Debashis Paul entered with his laptop and some files.

Mr. Sanjay Mittal turned to him sharply.

"Debashis, are you aware of the Hamid Alam case?"

"Yes, sir," Debashis replied nervously. "The vehicle was delivered after receiving the bank's delivery order. All documentation was complete."

"Then where is the payment?" Mittal snapped. "My audit team reports that the bank hasn't transferred a single rupee yet."

Debashis scratched his head with his pen. It was clear he knew more than he was letting on. He glanced toward Mr. Aggarwal and Rakesh Chetri, silently asking for help. But before either of them could speak, Sanjay Mittal cut him off.

"Debashis, I don't pay you to cover for your colleagues—I pay you to protect my business. Why didn't you audit this properly? Why didn't you tell me who's responsible for this mess?"

The pressure was getting to Debashis. His loyalty to Aggarwal was cracking. He looked directly at Mr. Aggarwal and said politely,

"Aggarwal ji, you're more familiar with the Hamid Alam case. Please explain what really happened."

Mr. Aggarwal cleared his throat. "Apologies, sir. There were some discrepancies in the payment settlement. We're doing our best to resolve the issue."

Sanjay Mittal wasn't satisfied. "How long will you keep trying, Mr. Aggarwal? Someone from your team was already locked up by the police over this. How many more days will it take?"

"Very soon, sir," Aggarwal said, looking down.

Sanjay Mittal was a powerful businessman. He ran five dealerships across brands, along with road construction and other ventures. Because of his scale, he couldn't go deep into every operational matter—something his managers often used to their advantage.

But this time, the issue had gotten too big to ignore.

Suddenly, Mr. Vikram Singh raised his voice.

"Aggarwal, Debashis, Rakesh—stop hiding the truth from Mr. Mittal. Admit that this issue exists because of your mismanagement."

He looked straight at Rakesh Chetri.

"This isn't a small matter anymore. Our brand reputation in the region is at stake."

Rakesh replied weakly, "Vikram, we're working on it. We'll resolve it soon."

Vikram's tone grew harsher.

"You've had enough time. You've failed to fix this. Are you playing with the name of Rana Motors? Because of this one case, our credibility in the market is suffering. If this isn't resolved today, I'll escalate it to the higher management at Rana Motors."

Sanjay Mittal's expression changed immediately. He grew tense. He knew that if Vikram reported this to the manufacturer, he'd be answerable. And with Rana Motors already struggling in the small truck segment, this could hurt further.

Still, Rana Motors remained a major brand—especially in heavy and light commercial vehicles. Even in the personal vehicle category, they had a decent hold. Thanks to that, Darjeeling Auto Works was doing good monthly sales.

Mittal understood the risk. He couldn't afford trouble with the manufacturer.

He turned sharply to Rakesh.

"When exactly are you going to fix this?"

"Sir, we're working on it. It should be resolved soon," Rakesh said.

Mittal wasn't convinced.

"Rakesh, tell the truth. What really happened with Hamid Alam? Don't protect anyone. One of your teammates landed in jail over this, because the customer thinks he was at fault. But the real problem lies elsewhere."

Mr. Vikram Singh added pointedly, glancing at Mr. Aggarwal and me,

"We all know who really caused this."

I stayed quiet. It wasn't my place to speak while my seniors were talking.

Mittal turned on Aggarwal again.

"Aggarwal ji, what are you doing here? Did I hire you to run this dealership or create this mess?"

Aggarwal looked like he was struggling to control his temper. His usual arrogance was simmering just below the surface. But instead of owning up, he tried to redirect the blame towards me.

He said,

"Yes, sir, the Hamid Alam case has turned serious. But the customer's profile was weak. Arjun collected the customer details but didn't properly evaluate the profile or ensure the finance process was followed."

Vikram Singh interrupted him.

"If the customer's profile was so poor, why was the vehicle delivered? Was it just to meet your sales targets? And how did the finance team approve it?"

Aggarwal tried again to shift responsibility.

"I told Arjun multiple times to make sure the payment was cleared by the finance company. But he ignored it."

At that moment, Sanjay Mittal looked directly at me.

His eyes were searching for answers.

At that point, Isha spoke up. It was clear she was angry—especially at Mr. S.K. Aggarwal. His behavior in front of everyone, directly blaming me, showed his poor leadership and lack of basic decency.

"Enough, Mr. S.K. Aggarwal," she said firmly. "You should be ashamed. You've been harassing Arjun nonstop about this case. I know everything that happened. I don't care if I lose my job today—I'm going to speak the truth in front of everyone."

I tried to calm her down.

"Isha, please stop. Relax. Let them handle it. I still have faith in my managers."

But Isha snapped back.

"You keep quiet, Arjun! This isn't like your good customers who come back to you with a smile. You need to learn to stand up against unethical behavior. You're following all the rules—but is everyone else?"

I tried again to stop her, but she continued,

"If this isn't resolved today, you'll either end up in jail for cheating or get attacked by that customer's son. So let's bring it all out now."

She looked at Mr. Sanjay Mittal and began to explain,

"Sir, I'll tell you exactly what's going on."

Mr. Mittal looked at Rakesh, then turned to Isha and said gently,

"Isha, let's talk about this later."

He didn't want to expose internal dealership issues in front of Mr. Vikram Singh, the territory manager from Rana Motors. Any negative impression could hurt Darjeeling Auto Works' standing with the company.

But Isha didn't stop. She understood Mr. Mittal's concern, but she also knew that if she didn't speak up now, the truth would once again be buried under office politics.

She continued, this time with a bold tone that challenged the leadership,

"Sir, let me tell you what really happened. And yes, I know this could cost me my job. But if you decide to fire me, at least do it honestly. Don't cook up some story to hide the truth."

Her words shocked the room. Rakesh looked uneasy. Mr. Aggarwal lowered his head and started flipping through his file to avoid eye contact.

Mr. Vikram Singh finally spoke up,

"Isha, don't hold back. Go ahead. Tell us everything."

She looked at me. I kept my eyes down, silently giving her permission.

"You can go ahead," I said quietly. "Say what you feel is right."

She took a deep breath and began,

"Sir, the case started with Hamid Alam. His loan was initially approved by Rana Higher Purchase Finance Company (RHPFC), a sister concern of Rana Motors. Arjun followed all the required steps—completed the paperwork and submitted the file to Mr. Aggarwal. Based on the finance company's approval letter, Mr. Aggarwal delivered the vehicle to Hamid Alam. But the trouble started after that."

"What happened next?" Mr. Mittal asked, clearly interested.

"About fifteen days later, the government's central bank issued new guidelines. RHPFC changed its policy and also changed its name to Rana Financial Services Ltd," Isha explained.

"Yes, I know that," Mr. Mittal said. "What happened after the change?"

I looked at Mr. Aggarwal. For the first time, he looked nervous. This was serious—his job was on the line, and Mr. Mittal paid him one of the best salaries in the industry. Rakesh also looked tense—this was a clear failure of leadership under his watch. Meanwhile, Mr. Vikram Singh sat silently, observing like an investigator.

Isha continued, speaking directly to Mr. Vikram Singh,

"After the company changed, Mr. Aggarwal forgot to collect the payment from RHPFC. Then, under the new rules, Rana Financial Services Ltd rejected Hamid Alam's loan."

Mr. Mittal frowned. "Isha, this is confusing. Can you explain more clearly?"

Before she could respond, Mr. Vikram Singh stepped in to clarify for Mr. Mittal.

"Sir, the vehicle was delivered to Hamid Alam on July 25, 2013, after all documentation was completed. The delivery was based on a principal approval letter from the finance company. But after August, RHPFC changed its policy and became Rana Financial Services Ltd. Before the transition, RHPFC had sent multiple reminders to the dealership to settle the case and collect the payment. The final deadline was October 25, 2013—but no one at this dealership followed up. After the transition, Rana Financial Services rejected all pending cases from RHPFC. Their new rules were much stricter. Hamid Alam's profile didn't match the new criteria, so his case was cancelled."

Hearing this, Mr. Mittal's face turned red with anger. He looked straight at Mr. Aggarwal.

"Aggarwal, is this true?" he asked sharply.

Mr. Aggarwal kept his head down. He didn't say a word.

"Moreover, sir, since RHPFC had outsourced the EMI collection to Darjeeling Auto Works, their team was collecting payments in auto mode and issuing receipts directly to customers," Isha explained.

Mr. Mittal's eyes narrowed. "Who authorised the file transfer to the collection team?" he asked, irritation seeping into his voice.

"As per standard procedure, the back-office team forwarded it with Mr. S. K. Aggarwal's signature," she replied calmly.

Mr. Mittal slammed his hand on the table. "God! What kind of bloody mismanagement is going on in my organisation?"

Then Mr. Mittal turned to Rakesh.

"Rakesh, what nonsense has been going on here under your leadership?"

Rakesh Chetri was trying to defend himself—and his manager, Mr. Aggarwal—in front of their boss, Mr. Sanjay Mittal.

"Sir, on behalf of my team, I take full responsibility. We'll fix the issue soon," Rakesh said professionally.

Mittal didn't waste time. "How will I recover the payment for Mr. Hamid Alam's vehicle?"

"Sir, we're trying to get a new financier to fund the vehicle again," Rakesh replied.

Mittal leaned forward, his tone sharp. "How can that happen? The vehicle is already registered. The money came from Darjeeling Auto Works, but the owner on paper is Hamid Alam. No financier will touch this case now."

Vikram Singh, who had been silent, added, "Sir, Mr. Aggarwal already approached five financiers. All of them refused because of Hamid Alam's poor credit history."

Mittal turned to Aggarwal. "Then what's your solution? Why didn't you collect the DO and payment from RHPFC before it merged with Rana Financial Services?"

Mr. Aggarwal had no answer. His usual arrogance was gone. He stared at the floor, silent.

Mittal raised his voice, "Rakesh, I want an answer—why didn't he collect the payment after several reminders from RHPFC?"

Rakesh turned to Aggarwal. "Aggarwal, please respond to the question."

But Aggarwal remained silent, visibly uncomfortable.

After a few seconds, Isha quietly spoke, "Sir, Mr. Aggarwal forgot to send the file to RHPFC for payment."

Mittal exploded. "Because of your negligence, I've suffered a huge loss—and Arjun paid the price."

Vikram added, "Sir, our brand's image has been damaged locally due to this mistake."

Isha, with emotion in her voice, said, "Sir, Hamid's son Harun kept chasing and threatening Arjun. His life was in danger. Even then, Arjun kept asking for help. He didn't get support from his seniors or the customer. Finally, he was arrested after Hamid filed a cheating case."

She looked directly at Aggarwal and Rakesh. "You didn't even show basic courtesy. He got stuck because of your mistake—and you didn't stand by him."

Mittal turned to Rakesh again. "Now tell me—how will you solve this?"

"Sir, we're trying to find a new financier to fund the vehicle," Rakesh replied.

Mittal snapped, "Five already rejected it. You think someone else will take it now? Find another solution."

He faced Aggarwal. "What's your plan?"

Aggarwal, now visibly shaken, said, "Sir, I'll try to arrange a private local financier."

That pushed Mittal over the edge. "I've tolerated enough. This is a business—I'm here to make profits, not to lose money because of your negligence."

He looked at Rakesh again. "Hold back anything we can legally—gratuity, bonus, pending incentives, leave encashment. Use that amount to cover the vehicle payment. If needed, deduct the rest from his salary."

Hearing this, Aggarwal stood up with folded hands. "Sir, please don't touch my gratuity, bonus, or pending incentives. My daughter's wedding is in six months. I was depending on that money. If you deduct my salary too, I won't be able to manage. Please give me some time—I'll arrange the finance."

The room fell silent. Aggarwal's pleading voice filled the cabin. He looked broken—this was punishment enough. For the first time, I saw a different side of him.

For the first time in an official meeting, I decided to speak up. My conscience told me it was time to stand by my boss. No matter what had happened, he had once supported me. Now it was my turn.

I looked at Mr. Sanjay Mittal and said,

"Sir, the issue with Hamid Alam is not as simple as it looks. His case originally fit the norms of RHPFC. But after RHPFC merged into Rana Financial Services, the financing rules changed, and his case got rejected. This was a result of shifting business policies. Still, I'm willing to take responsibility and will try to arrange new financing for the vehicle. So, I request you—please don't impose this heavy penalty on Mr. Aggarwal."

Hearing me, Rakesh Chetri also stepped in, "Yes, sir. I'm equally responsible in this matter."

Mr. Mittal looked at both of us, unimpressed. "If that's the case," he said coldly, "then all three of you—Aggarwal, Arjun, and Rakesh—will share the cost. I'm not going to bear the loss."

Just then, as always, Mr. Vikram Singh stepped in. His calm voice often brought direction during tough situations.

He said, "Mr. Mittal, it's true that Mr. Aggarwal mishandled the customer's case. It led to serious dissatisfaction and hurt our brand image. On top of that, Arjun has already suffered a lot."

Mr. Mittal turned to him, "Then what's your suggestion, Vikram?"

"Please finance the vehicle temporarily from your dealership's reserve. Ask the team to recover the EMI directly from the customer," Vikram proposed.

Mr. Aggarwal let out a visible sigh of relief. Rakesh leaned back in his chair.

But Mr. Mittal, cautious about his own finances, asked Vikram,

"Can Rana Motors offer some financial support for this vehicle?"

Vikram paused, his face tightening. "It won't be easy, but I'll try," he said.

Just then, Mr. Mittal got a phone call. As he stood up, he told Rakesh,

"Send Vikram an official email requesting the support. Let's see if Rana Motors can help resolve this."

Before leaving, he said to Vikram,

"Please do whatever you can. Let's try to settle the Hamid Alam issue once and for all."

I quietly returned to my desk. Now, I could only wait for our dealer principal's final decision.

One Week Later:

We were all busy with the new month's targets. The daily rush of leads, customer calls, and follow-ups had begun again. But deep down, my mind was restless.

Hamid Alam hadn't withdrawn the complaint. He was firm—until he received his vehicle from Darjeeling Autoworks, he wouldn't take back the legal case against me and the dealership.

Mr. Rakesh Chetri tried to keep me hopeful. "Don't worry, Arjun. Our dealer principal is reviewing it. I believe he'll approve the financing soon."

I nodded silently and went back to work—knowing one unresolved case still held my fate in its grip.

CHAPTER 37

# *Love, Loaded with Targets and Torque*

Isha had recently been promoted to Assistant Sales Manager in the personal vehicle division, recommended by Mr. Vikram Singh.

That Sunday, she asked me to accompany her to the Sevoke temple, a famous shrine in the Darjeeling district. We didn't take the demo truck this time. I rode my bike to Siliguri and picked her up. The thirty-kilometer ride through forest roads felt alive with wind and sunlight breaking through trees.

Isha sat behind me, arms around my waist. Her warmth made everything else fade—the road, the heat, even my targets. Her soft voice and laughter turned the ride into something unreal. For once, life wasn't about sales numbers. It was just her.

Halfway through, she leaned close and whispered,

"Arjun, I love you. I don't want to stay away anymore. Please take me with you, always."

Her words froze me. My throat tightened. I slowed down and stopped under a line of tall trees. I wanted to say something true—but my mind, trained to talk about trucks and targets, betrayed me.

"Isha," I began nervously, "I love you like I love my Turbo Cheetah Truck. And just like I hit my sales targets, I promise to achieve every target you give me in our relationship."

Silence. Her smile faded.

“Did you just compare me to a truck?” she asked, hurt. “Is that how you express love?”

I tried to explain, but the words fell apart. She turned away.

“Forget it. Let’s go. We’re getting late for the puja.”

The rest of the ride was silent. Her arms no longer held me, her warmth gone. I had ruined it.

At the temple, she prayed quietly, barely meeting my eyes. Even the breeze around the Sevoke bridge felt cold. The Teesta river roared below, but she seemed far away.

I finally said, “I’m sorry, Isha. I’m not good with words. My life’s been all about selling, convincing—but with you, it’s different. I don’t want to sell love. I want to live it—with you.”

For a moment, she just looked at me. Her expression softened—not quite a smile, but close.

We stood there in silence, the wind in her hair, the hills watching us. For once, I wasn’t chasing a target. I was standing beside the one I didn’t want to lose.

But she turned away again, walking down the slope. “Arjun,” she said sharply, “before you propose to anyone, learn the language of love. You’re still stuck in your profession—talking about trucks and journeys like that’s romance.”

She walked toward the river, steps firm and fast. I followed, still trying to reach her with words that kept failing.

Finally, she sat on a stone bench near the water. I sat beside her. Our shoulders touched. The wind carried the scent of the hills and her perfume. Her hair danced in the breeze, her eyes fixed on the river. And I sat there, knowing silence was all that was left between us.

I felt she was waiting—maybe for something real, not mechanical.

"Isha, I'm sorry," I said softly. "Maybe I don't know how to express love the right way, but every word I say comes straight from my heart—like pure fuel to a vehicle."

She burst out laughing. "Arjun, you're impossible," she said, eyes sparkling. "Nothing can stop me from loving you. You're as pure as your 'pure' vehicles!"

Her laughter faded into a softer tone. "Arjun, it's getting really cold."

"Why didn't you bring a sweater?" I asked.

Ignoring the question, she whispered, "When will you take me home forever?"

I smiled lightly. "Whenever you say."

She frowned. "Don't joke. I'm asking about us."

"Soon," I said. "We'll marry, and you'll stay with me—always."

The wind picked up. She leaned closer. "After marriage, when will we sleep?"

"Usually, my mother sleeps by ten. I sleep late."

She pouted. "No. We'll sleep early—together."

I nodded, still staring at the river. "Okay. As early as you want."

Then she asked, tracing her finger on my shirt, "Arjun, will our first child be a boy or a girl?"

I blushed. "That depends on biology—chromosomes decide it."

She laughed. "You know science but not romance. You duffer of love! Let me teach you your first lesson."

Her voice turned gentle. "Come close and hold me. I'm freezing."

I hesitated. Then, slowly, I wrapped my arms around her. She leaned in, eyes closed.

It was the first time I felt the softness of a woman in my arms. The wind rustled through the trees, the river hummed, and everything around us seemed to pause.

Then she kissed me—light, trembling, real.

Something inside me whispered to stop. To stay grounded. I pulled back gently.

"Isha, it's getting late. We should go."

Her lipstick was smudged, her hair slightly messy. I smiled. "Fix your makeup."

She blushed, adjusting her hair. Before we left, she teased, "Arjun, wipe the lipstick off your lips."

I laughed, wiped my mouth, and started the bike.

We rode through the cool evening, the hills fading behind us.

That night, after dropping Isha at her PG, I reached home around eight.

CHAPTER 38

# Trust Delivered. Case Closed

The next morning, I was getting ready for the office like any other day. Ma, as usual, was in the kitchen making breakfast. While chopping vegetables, she kept talking—more to herself than to me.

"Arjun, you need to get serious now. This sales job is not taking you anywhere. You should start preparing for a government job. Something secure, something steady," she said firmly.

I just nodded, not saying much. I didn't have the heart to argue.

At 9 AM, just as I was about to step out for my sales visit, my phone rang. It was Mr. S. K. Aggarwal—the first call from him since the heated argument over Hamid Alam's case.

I picked it up.

His voice was calm, almost polite—something I had never heard from him before.

"Good morning, Arjun. How are you doing today?"

"Good morning, Sir. I'm doing fine. How are you?"

"I'm fine," he replied briefly.

Then he got straight to the point.

"Our dealer principal has approved financing for Hamid Alam's vehicle using funds from Darjeeling Auto Works. Mr. Vikram Singh has also approved 25% support from Rana Motors. So go ahead and prepare the documents. Ask them to come on Monday to take the vehicle delivery."

I stood silent for a few seconds, soaking it in. It felt like a huge weight had been lifted off my chest. For months, this case had been haunting me. Finally, a solution.

"Thank you so much, Sir. I was really under pressure because of this case."

"Be there early on Monday with Hamid Alam," he added, then disconnected the call.

The moment the call ended, I dialed Harun Alam's number. After several rings, he finally answered. His voice was as rude as ever.

"Hello?"

"Harun, this is Arjun. How are you?" I asked politely, even though the memory of his last assault was still fresh in my mind.

"I'm fine. Say what you have to—quickly."

I stayed calm.

"Harun, our company has found a solution to your case. Please come on Monday, 18th August 2014, to our Siliguri showroom. Your vehicle will be delivered."

He didn't believe me.

"Oh, really? Another trick? We've already filed a police complaint for cheating. Don't think you'll get away this time."

"Harun, please trust me. Come with your father. This time, everything is sorted. I promise there won't be any issues."

He paused for a moment.

"Okay. I'll speak to Abba. Let's see what happens." Then he hung up.

I told both Ma and Isha that the issue was finally resolved. Over the next few days, I worked with new energy. For the first time in a long while, I felt light — hopeful.

Finally, the day arrived: 18th August 2014. I left early in the morning for our Siliguri showroom.

Before leaving, I called Mr. Hamid Alam to confirm.

"Yes, Arjun, we are coming. But listen, don't trick us again. Enough is enough," he said in a serious tone.

I understood where he was coming from. He didn't know the technicalities of dealership financing. All he knew was that he trusted me — and I had let him down.

Now, I had to earn that trust back.

"Sir, please come. This time, you will leave happy," I assured him.

At exactly 11:30 AM, Mr. Hamid Alam arrived — with his son Harun and seven other drivers from their vehicle stand.

Their faces were grim. Their body language was stiff, almost like they had come prepared for a fight, not a delivery.

I went to welcome them, with Isha by my side. We greeted them and led them to the customer lounge. I asked the pantry staff to serve tea and snacks.

We exchanged greetings, but the mood was cold. Their replies were short — just yes or no. They weren't there to smile or talk. They were waiting. Watching. Ready — in case anything went wrong again.

But deep down, I could sense something else too — a flicker of hope.

And this time, I was determined not to let it go to waste.

After a few minutes, Mr. S. K. Aggarwal and Mr. Rakesh Chetri entered the customer lounge. Everyone exchanged pleasantries, but the response from Hamid Alam's team was cold—tense, like volcanoes just before an eruption.

Suddenly, Harun stepped forward and snapped at Mr. Aggarwal.

"Why are you not returning my vehicle?"

Mr. Aggarwal kept his composure and replied calmly,

"Actually, there were some financial issues. That's why your vehicle was kept at the showroom."

Harun's voice rose, trembling with anger.

"Financial issue? What kind of issue? I paid the full amount! Even the EMIs were cleared on time. You repossessed the vehicle—and I'm still paying the loan!"

His honesty made the outburst sting even more. None of us had a clear answer. Mr. Aggarwal turned toward Mr. Rakesh Chetri, seeking help.

Before Mr. Chetri could speak, Harun's rage turned to me.

"This guy—Arjun—your sales executive is a fraud. He lied to us, again and again. He escaped us once, but this time we won't spare him."

One of Hamid Alam's driver friends joined in, shouting,

"If Harun's vehicle isn't returned, we'll make sure no vehicle from Rana Motors is sold in our area again!"

Another man, darker-skinned with a prominent tilak on his forehead, pointed at me and screamed,

"Enough, Arjun! Don't show your face in Dhupguri again. If you step in, you won't return alive. No one will even find your dead body!"

Within moments, the customer lounge turned into a battlefield. Tension crackled in the air. Angry words flew like sparks. Our Darjeeling Auto Works team rushed in to assess the situation. Security guards arrived, trying to calm things down.

Mr. Rakesh Chetri finally stepped forward. His voice was calm but firm.

"Please, sit down. We understand your frustration. But this wasn't Arjun's fault. It wasn't even Mr. Aggarwal's. A sudden change in financial policy caused this. But we've found a solution. Please, let us explain."

But Mr. Hamid Alam was still furious.

"You've been offering 'solutions' for six months now. Nothing but lies. That's why I had to file a police complaint against Arjun."

After a long pause, Harun exploded again—his voice sharp, eyes burning.

"Don't think you're safe just because you got bail. We'll put you behind bars. And this time, we'll make sure you don't get out."

Just then, Mr. Vikram Singh entered.

Tall, confident, and composed, he carried an aura that made everyone pause. Even Hamid Alam's team fell silent. Mr. Singh smiled, walked over, and shook hands with each of them.

He sat beside them and, folding his hands, spoke with quiet dignity.

"We're truly sorry for everything you've been through. We understand how much pain this has caused. Please accept our apology."

He then turned to me and said,

"Arjun, please arrange tea, snacks, and lunch for our guests."

After refreshments were served, the atmosphere slowly shifted. Mr. Vikram Singh explained the entire situation transparently. Then he turned to Mr. Chetri.

"Prepare the vehicle for ceremonial delivery. I've personally ensured the finance has been settled by the dealership from its own funds. You'll only need to continue regular EMI payments on time."

Despite this, I could still sense doubt in Hamid Alam's eyes. He and Harun exchanged glances, as if wondering if this, too, was just another trap.

Ten minutes later, the delivery manager rolled out the vehicle. It stood in the delivery bay, freshly washed, decorated with balloons, ribbons, and flowers. The green paint still shimmered under the light.

Harun's eyes lit up.

"Abba, look! Our truck! It still looks brand new—the green's still shining!"

Mr. Hamid Alam walked around the vehicle slowly, inspecting every inch. A faint smile appeared on his face.

He turned to Mr. Rakesh Chetri and asked,

"When will you deliver it?"

"Right after lunch, sir," Mr. Chetri replied with a smile.

He then asked Isha to escort the entire team to lunch.

After the meal, the formal handover took place. Mr. Aggarwal stood in front, handing the keys to Mr. Hamid Alam. Mr. Chetri offered a bouquet. Isha presented the documents. Harun and his friends double-checked everything—no room for further mistakes.

I stepped forward, folded my hands, and bowed slightly.

"Sir, I'm truly sorry for everything. For all the pain and loss you faced because of us. Please forgive me."

Mr. Hamid Alam didn't speak, but his eyes softened. There was something in them—regret, maybe even peace.

Harun came up to me and placed a hand gently on my back.

"Brother, I hurt you. We all did. You tolerated everything we threw at you—our anger, our words. Still, you stood firm and tried to help us. You never gave up. You're not just any sales executive. You're a real Mushkil Aashan—a man who eases troubles. You're our saviour."

The others echoed him, smiling.

"Arjun Da, we're with you now. Our stand will always support your trucks. Yours will be our first choice."

Harun climbed into the driver's seat, with Mr. Hamid Alam beside him.

Before leaving, Mr. Alam turned to me and said,

"Thank you, Arjun, for returning what was ours. I'll withdraw the police case tomorrow. You have my full support."

With a gentle rev of the engine, their truck rolled out of the showroom—leaving behind not just anger, but a sense of restored faith.

19th August 2014 — 12:30 PM

Mr. Sanjeev Singh called me.

As always, seeing a police inspector's name on my phone made me nervous. I felt tense but picked up the call.

"Hello, Sir…" I said in a shaky voice.

But to my surprise, Mr. Singh sounded kind and cheerful.

"Hello, Arjun! I have good news for you. Hamid Alam has withdrawn the case."

I smiled with relief. "Really, Sir? Thank you so much. That's great news. I feel so relaxed now."

Even though Hamid had told me earlier that he would withdraw the case, hearing it officially from the police made me feel safe. I also respected Mr. Singh and wanted to show that I valued his support.

He continued, "Arjun, I know you're an honest sales guy. You just got stuck in a business issue. But if a customer files a case, we have to follow the law. Still, you handled it well. In the future, be more careful. You have a bright future ahead—just make sure to keep your record clean."

"I understand, Sir. I will be careful," I said.

Then Mr. Singh ended the call.

I sat quietly, thinking about everything that had happened. The case was serious. Harun had beaten me badly—he could have even killed me. But I never fought back. I stayed calm and tried to solve the problem peacefully.

The customer was satisfied. The case was closed.

Now, I wondered—how would this incident shape my journey ahead?

CHAPTER 39

# *Whispers at Café Kanchenjunga*

Isha's army officer customer postponed his test drive to the 4th of September, 2014. I'd promised to accompany her. During the business planning meeting on the 3rd, I reminded her.

That evening, we went to Café Kanchenjunga, Siliguri's most popular spot for young couples. The air smelled of roasted beans and melted chocolate. Waiters darted between tables, balancing trays of coffee and sizzling snacks. The café buzzed with laughter.

Luckily, I had booked a table. We slipped into our seats as couples around us leaned close, sharing food and secrets. For a moment, I felt out of place.

I swore not to talk about sales tonight. Isha sat with her usual calm grace. My shirt clung with sweat; my shoes shone, but they told their own story—I couldn't afford better. Still, I tried to look confident, even as I worried about the bill.

"I'm ordering coffee first, okay?" I said.

She smiled. "Yes."

I leaned forward. "So, how are you?"

She laughed aloud, her voice carrying above the hum. "Arjun, again that funny question?"

I laughed too, awkwardly. "What would you like—momos, noodles, brownie?"

"Just coffee," she said.

But I insisted and called the waiter anyway, hoping she'd see care, not foolishness.

As we sipped, warmth spread through me. The noise faded; her smile felt like quiet light. Yet soon, work crept back into our talk.

"Who's this army officer taking the DronX test drive?" I asked.

"Major Kiran Thapa, posted in Nathula," she said. "He loves adventure—needs an off-roader."

"Yes, DronX suits him," I said.

"Exactly why I offered it," she replied.

I teased, "Let's see what happens tomorrow, Assistant Sales Manager madam."

She frowned slightly. "Arjun, not here. No official talk."

"Then should I talk romantically?" I grinned.

She leaned closer. "Are you preparing for your MBA?"

The air shifted. "Yes. Exams in January. I'm trying."

Her voice softened. "You have potential, Arjun. Work hard. A management degree will open doors."

Her words stayed with me. Amid coffee, laughter, and candlelight, something in me changed. She wasn't just a colleague; she believed in the version of me I hadn't yet seen.

The waiter brought our food. I smiled to ease the moment. "Let's eat now."

But her face turned serious. "Do you know Sahil Kumar? He's been disturbing me."

I froze mid-bite. "What do you mean?"

Lowering her cup, she said, "He's a fraud—and a womanizer."

I nodded grimly. "He cheated ten customers—two lakh rupees. Mr. Rakesh confirmed it."

Her voice was tight. "Five of those customers yelled at me. I had to face them."

I sighed. "When we count coins for coffee, he lives rich—on lies."

She looked down. "He even tried to lure me with money. Thought he could buy me. But I refused. I won't let anyone touch my dignity."

Hearing this, my blood boiled. My fists clenched.

"Isha, just say the word. I know people in the police—even politicians. I won't spare him."

She shook her head calmly. "No, Arjun. Don't worry. I can handle it."

I exhaled, still restless. "And after the fraud case?"

"Customers filed complaints. He was in custody for a while, then got bail," she said, anger flashing in her eyes.

"So that's why he's vanished from the dealership," I muttered.

"He's been terminated," she replied. "Management kept it quiet to protect the company's image."

I nodded. "Good. If people like him stay, we'll never reach our Mission 51%—winning back trust."

She finally ate a few momos. When we finished, I went to pay, but she stopped me and handed over the cash.

"Isha, at least let me pay," I protested.

She smiled. "Arjun, use that money to buy something for Ma ji. Send me a photo of both of you enjoying it. Think of it as my gift to her."

I couldn't argue. "Thank you, Isha. I'll do that—and treat this as your promotion party."

"Welcome, Arjun," she said softly as we left the café.

The next morning, sharp at seven, we started from Siliguri in the gleaming DronX. Isha gripped the keys, her face glowing with nervous excitement. This wasn't just a test drive—it was her first long one as a licensed driver.

"Arjun, I'll drive today. Don't touch the wheel," she warned, fastening her seatbelt.

I nodded, hiding my fear. To me, she wasn't the confident Assistant Sales Manager—she was Isha, my friend, my secret love.

The DronX roared to life, its diesel growl echoing in the crisp morning air. The SUV glided over rough patches as we headed toward Gangtok. Isha drove with steady hands; still, my heart leapt at every bend.

"Arjun, don't act scared," she laughed. "Trust me. Today, DronX is my partner."

Her laughter eased my nerves. Wind swept through the windows, tossing her hair. Between gear shifts, we joked and forgot the world. It was just the road, the machine, and us.

By afternoon, we reached Gangtok. Major Kiran Thapa waited—tall, disciplined, every inch a soldier. After introductions, Isha said with quiet pride, "Major Saab, this machine is made for your adventures."

He smiled, adjusted his aviators, and took the wheel. The DronX surged forward. Every gear shift felt like a command; every curve, a test of balance. Isha explained each feature—hill hold, suspension, differential lock—with the ease of someone who believed in the machine.

Finally, at Nathula, the tricolor snapped in the icy wind. Major Thapa stepped out, hand on the bonnet. "This isn't a car," he said. "It's a companion for the mountains. Isha ji, you've given me what I wanted."

Her face lit up. "The day after tomorrow," he added, "come to my home in Darjeeling—we'll finalize everything."

On the way back, Isha was quiet, lost in thought. "What happened?" I asked.

She smiled faintly. "Arjun, today was more than a test drive. It was the beginning of something bigger—for me, for us."

I looked at her, holding that moment close. The DronX rolled down the winding road, carrying more than us—it carried our dreams.

CHAPTER 40

# The Day the Mountains Wept

It was 2:30 p.m. The monsoon sky over Nathula hung heavy with dark clouds, the mountains wrapped in mist. At 14,000 feet, the air was thin, every breath sharp in my chest. The road ahead was narrow, wet, and always at risk of landslides.

Yet between Isha and me, the mood was different. There was a strange romance in the storm, a quiet closeness in stolen words as we sipped coffee at the viewpoint.

But the mountains don't let peace last.

A deep growl of an engine came from behind. Out of the fog appeared a massive off-roader, its lights glowing like a predator's eyes. I knew it at once—the Tejas Xtor, Tejas Automotive's flagship beast, built for rough terrain. And at the wheel was the last person I wanted to see—Sahil Kumar, once our colleague, now a rival sales executive.

He stepped out, his grin sly and sharp. A fair-skinned man with pointed features came with him, scanning the road with mischief in his eyes.

Isha stiffened. "This bastard," she muttered. "Thrown out of Darjeeling Auto Works, now crawling here with Tejas."

Sahil walked up, voice oily with mockery.

"Hi, Isha. And you…" He looked at me, smirking. "Mr. Mushkil Aasaan. First, you ruined Hamid Alam's life. Now you've brought Isha here to ruin hers?"

I clenched my jaw, but Isha cut in:

"We're here for a test drive with our customer, Sahil. Don't start your nonsense."

"Ah, Major Kiran Thapa?" Sahil sneered. "Sorry, sweetheart. He's our man now. The Tejas Xtor is made for soldiers like him. Why don't you pack up and leave? I'll take this deal."

Isha's eyes burned. "Sahil, don't cheat him. You've already cheated ten customers and got thrown out of Darjeeling. Don't try that with an army officer. He won't spare you."

The grin faded from Sahil's face. His anger spilled out.

"I told you not to report me to Rakesh and Sanjay Mittal. Because of you, I was in jail. I lost my job. And today, I've got you alone here with this fool. No one can save you. The Nathula wind is cold… but your body can keep me warm."

"Inside. Now!" Isha snapped.

We rushed into the DronX. The engine roared to life as Sahil lunged forward. Tires screamed as Isha hit the accelerator, the SUV leaping ahead. Behind us, Sahil and his man jumped into the Tejas Xtor. Its headlights cut through the fog as it gave chase.

The mountain road twisted like a serpent. On one side, sheer rock. On the other hand, a drop into an endless valley. Rain lashed harder, the road slick and deadly.

The Xtor closed in, its bumper flashing in our mirror. Sahil leaned out, laughing:

"Run, Arjun! Run, Isha! Let's see if your toy can beat a real off-roader!"

Isha's grip tightened. "Hold on, Arjun."

She downshifted and pressed harder. The DronX growled and pulled out of a sharp curve with surprising force. Gravel flew, stones tumbling into the abyss.

The Xtor rammed from behind. The jolt threw me against the dashboard, breath knocked out.

"Damn it!" Isha gasped, wrestling the wheel. The DronX skidded close to the edge but steadied just in time.

Sahil's SUV drew level, almost scraping us. His partner jeered, taunting Isha. My fists curled, but I knew—Isha was the one in control.

"Trust me, Arjun," she said, eyes fierce. "The DronX and I—we won't lose today."

Up ahead, an army supply truck crawled uphill, blocking most of the road.

"We'll hit it!" I shouted.

But Isha's reflexes were faster than fear. She swung the DronX against the mountain wall, sparks flying as metal scraped stone. Somehow, we slipped through with inches to spare.

Sahil tried to follow, but his heavier Xtor struggled. Tires screeched. He lost ground.

Isha seized the moment. She floored the accelerator. The DronX leapt forward, agile as a mountain goat. For the first time, hope flickered in me.

But Sahil's voice cut through the storm, venomous:

"You can't escape me, Isha! Not here. Not ever!"

Her eyes shimmered—not with fear, but with fury.

The storm outside mirrored the one within. This was no longer just a chase. It was a duel—between old betrayal and present courage, between Sahil's greed and our fight for dignity.

The mountain would decide who survived.

But fate is merciless in the mountains.

By the time we crossed Kyongnosla, the storm had grown furious. Rain hammered the windshield like shards of glass, the road a trembling ribbon clinging to the cliffs. And then, through the blur of rain and fog, I saw them again — the blinding headlights of Sahil's Tejas Xtor.

He was back.

This time, his eyes weren't just angry. They were hungry — a predator closing in. It wasn't a rivalry anymore. He wanted Isha. The fraud she exposed, the proposal she rejected, his humiliation at the dealership — it had twisted him into obsession.

"Isha, let me drive," I pleaded, voice breaking.

Her hands were locked on the wheel, knuckles pale. "No, Arjun… no time to switch. Hold on. I won't let him win."

Her words were steady, but her trembling shoulders betrayed her fear. She pushed the DronX harder, its engine howling as we shot around a curve. For a while, she held her ground, her eyes fixed like a soldier's in battle.

But Sahil was relentless. The Xtor stormed after us, tires crushing gravel, horn blaring like a war cry. He wanted us rattled. And we were.

Isha's breath came fast. She pressed the accelerator again.

"Isha, slow down! Please!"

She didn't.

In a flash, the DronX skidded. The wet road betrayed her grip. Tires screamed, the barrier cracked, and then there was nothing beneath us — only air.

The world spun.

Metal tore, glass shattered, my body thrown against steel again and again as we rolled down the abyss. My scream tangled with hers — until hers was swallowed by silence.

Then, blackness.

When I opened my eyes, rain and blood blurred my sight. Pain stabbed through me. My legs… twisted, useless.

"Isha…" Her name slipped out like a prayer.

I dragged myself with my elbows, every movement fired through my bones. The storm roared, drowning everything but my heartbeat.

And then I saw her.

Her hair — once alive in the wind, glowing under café lights — now tangled, heavy with mud and blood. Her body lay bent against a jagged rock, her face pale, lips drained of color.

"No… no, no…"

I crawled to her, every inch tearing me apart. I lifted her head into my arms, rain mixing with tears and blood.

"Isha… say something. Please… look at me."

I pressed my ear to her chest. Silence. Her wrist — limp, cold. No pulse.

Still, I called her name, again and again, each time weaker:

"Isha… Isha… Isha…"

Only the rain answered.

I rocked her in my arms, praying the gods would return her breath. My blood soaked into hers, staining the rocks. My vision swam, half with tears, half with the blur of blood loss.

Her phone was still in her pocket. With shaking hands, I pulled it out. By some miracle, it worked.

I dialed the only number I could remember.

"Major Thapa… help… please," I rasped. "Our vehicle… fell from Kyongnosla… three hundred feet. Isha… she's not moving. Please… hurry…"

His voice was steady, urgent. "Arjun, hold on. Don't give up. We're coming."

Hold on. Courage.

I looked at her face, tilted toward the sky, as if already beyond these mountains. Courage felt like a cruel word.

The rain poured harder, turning the earth into a grave. My strength drained away. My eyelids sank, breath shallow.

I rested my head on her shoulder — my friend, my inspiration, my unspoken love — and prayed that if I closed my eyes, I would wake somewhere else. Somewhere, she was alive.

Darkness took me again.

When my eyes opened, the first thing I felt was the hum of the air-conditioner above me, its steady rhythm cutting through the silence of the cabin. The air smelled faintly of antiseptic and wet cotton. I realized I was lying in a hospital bed in Gangtok. My body felt foreign—heavy, stitched, broken.

A nurse in a white apron hovered beside me, checking a file. Her face was calm, her voice firm but not unkind. "Don't move too much. You've already been given the maximum dose of painkillers. I cannot give you more."

But the agony inside me was unbearable. Both of my legs were wrapped in thick plaster, suspended carefully on supports. My torso was tight with layers of bandages. Each time I tried to lift even a finger, a ripple of pain shot through me, raw and electric. I clenched my teeth, but finally a scream tore out of me, echoing against the sterile white walls.

The door opened sharply. Boots clicked on the floor. Major Kiran Thapa entered—straight-backed, his olive-green army uniform neat even in the hospital's dim light. His presence brought discipline into the room, but his eyes softened when they met mine.

"Arjun, take rest," he said firmly, yet with empathy. "You are badly injured. Don't worry—I will take care of everything here."

His assurance was strong, but my heart was restless. In that fog of pain, a single name beat inside me like a wound. "Where… where is Isha? How is she now?" My voice cracked, trembling as if I already knew the answer I dreaded.

The soldier hesitated. His jaw tightened. He looked at me not as a Major, but as a man carrying news too heavy for words.

"I'm sorry, Arjun," he said at last, his tone quiet but unflinching. "We tried our best… but Isha did not survive. She expired on the way. The doctors confirmed her death."

The words crashed over me like a landslide. My chest tightened, breath caught in my throat. For years, I had held myself together in storms, never one to cry easily. But this time, I broke. My cries filled the cabin, raw and helpless, reverberating off the sterile walls. Every moment with her—our coffees, our laughter, the long road to Nathula—rushed back like shards of glass cutting into me.

Major Thapa placed a steady hand on my shoulder, his voice low but resolute.

"Be strong, Arjun. You have to accept this. Take care of yourself now. Time will heal you."

But time, in that moment, felt cruel.

Through my tears, I asked, almost pleading,

"Sir… when will I be shifted to Siliguri? I want to see Ma… I need her."

He shook his head with calm authority.

"Not now. This is an army hospital. I have already arranged for fifteen days of your treatment here. Travelling down in your condition is dangerous. You must first be stable."

His discipline steadied me for a moment, but inside, my heart clawed for comfort.

"Sir… could I use your phone?"

"Why?" His voice was sharp, instinctive, like an officer protecting a patient.

"I… I want to call my mother." My words quivered, my throat tight.

His eyes softened again. Without another word, he handed me his phone.

My fingers shook as I dialed. When Ma's familiar voice came through, my throat closed. I forced a cough, clearing it, trying to sound normal.

"Ma… I am stuck in Gangtok… for a big deal," I lied, my voice breaking between syllables. The truth was too cruel to tell.

But mothers always know. Her voice carried both love and anger. "Arjun, how many times have I told you not to vanish like this? I am tired of your sudden trips. You don't need to do this job. I am growing old, son. My body aches every day. I need you at home. Please… leave this work."

Her words pierced me deeper than any injury. In my heart, a voice whispered: *Enough, Arjun. Now the time has come to quit.*

Suppressing the tears, I whispered back,

"Ma… let me return home. Then I will decide." And before my sobs betrayed me, I ended the call.

Major Thapa stood silently, watching. Then, in his steady voice, he added,

"Your office has already been informed. We used Isha's phone to reach them. They are coordinating with us. Don't worry. No one will disturb you here for the next fifteen days. Just heal."

Major Thapa's question cut through the sterile silence of the hospital ward.

"Who attacked you, Arjun?"

My throat was dry, but the name burned on my tongue.

"Sahil Kumar, sir."

His brows drew together. “Sahil Kumar? I think I know him.”

“He’s a sales executive of Tejas Automotive,” I said, each word heavy with rage.

Recognition flickered in his eyes. “Ah… yes. Now I remember. He gave me a test drive of the Xtor.” His voice hardened, clipped with a soldier’s discipline.

I told him everything—the chase, the collision, Isha’s death, Sahil’s threats. Each detail spilled out like poison, and with every sentence, his jaw clenched tighter.

When I finished, he rose from his chair, pacing once, twice, the way a soldier restrains his fury before it breaks discipline.

“That man…” His voice was sharp, low, and dangerous. “He must be stopped.”

He turned to me, his eyes burning with a commander’s resolve. “I will inform the Sikkim Police and the West Bengal authorities immediately. He won’t escape the law. Not this time.”

I nodded, but inside my mind, another thought was already taking shape—dark, relentless.

Justice by law might take years. But the wound in my chest was raw, bleeding. Sahil Kumar had to pay. Not just in courtrooms and files. He had to feel what I felt when I held Isha’s lifeless body in the storm.

With that, he gave a final nod and stepped out of the cabin.

The familiar hum of machines filled the room again. Leaning back on the pillow, I stared at the ceiling fan, its sluggish rotation echoing the weight of passing time. Outside, Gangtok’s September rain tapped gently against the windows. Inside, I was drowning in a storm far louder than the one in the mountains.

After fifteen days in Gangtok Army Hospital, I was shifted to Siliguri.

Mr. Rakesh Chettri and Mr. S.K. Aggarwal themselves arranged the ambulance and stayed by my side throughout the journey. When we reached the hospital, I was wheeled into a clean white room. My body ached with every movement, but my heart ached even more — because this time, Isha was not by my side.

Mr. Rakesh sat beside my bed and placed his hand on my shoulder.

"Arjun, don't worry about the hospital bills. Darjeeling Auto Works will manage everything. You just focus on your recovery."

His words gave me relief, but nothing could fill the emptiness inside me.

Mom came rushing in with her sister. Her saree hung carelessly, reflecting the chaos she felt inside, her face swollen from sleepless nights, and her hands trembling. The moment she saw me, she broke down completely. She hugged me tightly, her tears falling on my right shoulder.

"Arjun!" she cried. "I told you to leave this job. I told you, this job will kill you one day. But… you are saved. My son is saved."

Her pain pierced me. With my own tears running down, I whispered,

"Ma… Isha is no more."

She froze, her hands gripping me even tighter. After a moment, she spoke softly, her voice breaking,

"I know, Arjun. I know everything about you and Isha. She had already become a part of our family."

Her words shook me. I hadn't realized Ma had accepted Isha so deeply.

"But be strong, my son," she continued, wiping her eyes. "I know you will overcome everything. Talk to her family. Send them my condolences, too."

I nodded through my tears. "Yes, Ma, I will."

Before I could say more, the hospital security guards came.

"Visiting hours are over. You will have to leave the patient's cabin now."

Mom gradually loosened her grip on me. She turned to go, wiping her eyes again and again, looking back at me as if she feared I would disappear. Watching her leave was harder than enduring my injuries.

After she left, I turned to Mr. Aggarwal and spoke hesitantly.

"Sir… this month I will not be able to meet the target. Give me one month; I promise I will cover it again."

Aggarwal patted my back gently.

"You don't have to worry about targets, Arjun. Just take care of yourself."

Mr. Rakesh added firmly,

"Arjun, you don't need to worry for the next three months. Heal yourself — both physically and mentally. We will take care of everything else."

Tears welled in my eyes again. "Thank you, sir… for all your support."

I told Rakesh everything—every twist of the road, every flash of headlights in the fog, every taunt Sahil Kumar hurled at us. My voice cracked when I spoke of the moment Isha fell silent in my arms.

"For his lust, his arrogance… we lost her, sir," I whispered, my throat burning. "Please… do something. Punish him. Don't let Sahil walk free."

Rakesh leaned closer, his face grim, eyes heavy with the weight of my grief. For once, the usual calm in his voice was replaced with steel.

"Yes, Arjun. We've already moved against him. Fraud. Attempt to murder. The FIR has been filed. He will not be spared this time."

Beside him, Aggarwal nodded, jaw set like stone.

"We will pursue this until the end. He won't escape. Sahil Kumar will go to jail—and this time, permanently. Rest assured."

Their words brought a flicker of relief, but deep inside, my chest still ached with a hunger the law could never satisfy. Isha's laughter would never return; no verdict could bring her back. Justice might be written on paper, but my wounds bled ink no court could read.

Yet in that sterile hospital room, hearing my seniors promise retribution, I felt the first shadow of resolve settle over me. Sahil's fate was sealed—whether by law or by something far darker, he would answer for Nathula.

The next morning, around 11 a.m., my phone rang. It was Mr. Vikram Singh.

"Hello, Arjun. Good morning. How are you now?" His voice was calm but filled with concern.

"Good morning, Sir. I am fine now," I answered, trying to sound confident though my body still ached.

There was a pause, then his tone grew heavier.

"Arjun, I am deeply sorry for the incident with you and Isha. Both of you are very important to me. Isha played a vital role in Darjeeling Auto Works. Her death is not just a personal loss to you but also a great loss to Darjeeling Auto Works and to Rana Motors."

I swallowed hard. "Yes, Sir… Isha's death has left a vacuum in my life. It will take me a long time to return to normal."

"I understand, Arjun," Vikram said softly. "This will take time to heal — both mentally and physically. But I know you. You will return to your old form soon. When will the doctors release you?"

"Sir, doctors said after fifteen more days. Then I'll need at least three months' rest at home for my broken legs and injuries to heal."

"Good," Vikram replied. "Take that rest. Heal yourself. And then get back to your old self."

I drew in a deep breath. "Sir, I have not forgotten Mission 51%. I will achieve this target for my territories. And I will also keep my promise to Isha. Alongside, I'll prepare for my MBA exam — my final semester is in January next year."

There was silence for a moment, then Vikram spoke warmly.

"I have full trust in you, Arjun. You will manage everything, and you will come out a winner."

"Yes, Sir. Just allow me to work from home during these three months. My market is ready. I can manage them over the phone. I assure you, I will achieve every target and deliver Mission 51%."

"I know you will, Arjun. I have complete faith in you," Vikram said. "Now get well soon."

"Thank you, Sir," I replied, my voice steady but my heart still carrying the weight of loss.

As the call ended, I stared at the ceiling. Isha's face flashed again before my eyes. She wasn't there to hear my promises, but I knew — every step forward I took from here was for her.

CHAPTER 41

# When Empathy Returns

On the 7th of October, I left the hospital behind. At home, my mother had arranged the bed exactly as the doctors prescribed—her care precise, almost ritualistic, as if order itself could heal me. Both legs were in plaster, heavy reminders that time would now move slowly. The doctors had said three months or more. My mother, anxious, hired a nurse. Even water, food, and medicine had to pass through other hands.

Beside me lay two things that defined my world—my phone and my diary. Through them, I convinced myself Mission 51% was still mine to chase. Rana Motors wanted numbers, and numbers didn't pity broken bones.

I called Mr. Aggarwal to assess the gap. September had left its scars—on both the balance sheet and my body. Once, my strategies lived in the dust of highways and the sweat of truck stands. Now, confined to bed, my war would be fought through calls and notes. Each name in my notebook felt like a bridge to the world I couldn't walk upon.

Then the phone rang. Harun. His voice carried weight.

"Hello, Arjun. How are you?"

"I'm fine, Harun."

"I heard… about Isha. I'm sorry. Be strong. Are you still in the hospital?"

"No. At home now."

"When will you return to work?"

"Three months, maybe more. Both legs broken."

He paused, then said firmly, "You have our support. I'll tell the stand secretaries to send you leads. You won't fight alone."

Something eased inside me. "Thank you, Harun."

"You were always honest," he said. "You took our anger without fault. Now every driver and owner stands with you. We'll help you close deals. You're not alone."

After the call, I turned to my diary. Isha's face lingered between the lines—her laughter, her scolding, her quiet faith in me. The silence pressed in; a tear fell, smudging the ink. I wiped it quickly. I had to stay steady—for her.

My MBA books sat by the bed, January's exams looming like another mountain. Between calls, I opened them, reminding myself there was still a future beyond plaster and pain.

I spoke to financiers to handle deliveries. Aggarwal and Chetri promised support. The system began to move, as if my stillness had set others in motion.

Each day, I made calls, my hand trembling from fatigue. Selling trucks without touching the soil felt unreal—like trying to feel rain through glass. Yet I pressed on.

Three days later, I called a familiar name—Mr. Pintu Haldar, the chicken wholesaler whose life I'd once saved in a storm.

"Arjun Da! How could I forget you?" he said warmly.

"Pintu Da, I've had an accident—both legs broken. I'll be in bed for months. If you know anyone needing a Turbo Cheetah, please send them my way."

After a pause, his voice softened. "How is your mother? And… the receptionist, madam?"

My throat tightened. "Mother's fine. Isha didn't survive."

Silence followed. Then, breaking slightly, he said, "Oh God… that's unbearable. Don't worry. I'll help you. You saved my life—now let me repay it. I'll tell everyone in the chicken trade to buy from you."

His promise steadied me. I reached out to Rajesh Gupta from the tea growers' union; he, too, pledged support. One by one, old customers and brokers responded with warmth. Gratitude turned them into allies. Leads began flowing again.

The notebook, once just paper and ink, became alive with voices and hope. My customers were no longer just buyers—they were my messengers. From this bed, broken but unbowed, I felt the strange power of connection. Mission 51% was no longer mine alone—it had become a shared cause.

News of my accident and Isha's death spread across the market like light spilling over a dark valley. Those I had once stood beside—in hospitals, in crematoriums heavy with smoke—now came to stand by me. What I had given as empathy returned multiplied.

Even Mr. Aggarwal, never known for softness, surprised me. He didn't say, "It's your responsibility." Instead, he appointed a man to handle deliveries himself, ensuring no customer felt neglected. His usual sternness was replaced by quiet, steady action.

At home, my mother managed everything—the nurse, my dressings, medicine, and meals. She built order around my broken body, as if the rhythm of care could keep despair away.

Confined to bed, I lived on calls. The phone became my road, my marketplace. Each voice carried a chance, a thread to the world outside. From this unlikely space, a new way of selling emerged—built not on travel, but trust. October ended with targets met. By November, I'd crossed forty-five percent.

When the monthly meeting came, they held it in hybrid mode so I could join. Sitting with plastered legs, I listened as they praised my results. But I knew numbers told only part of it. What truly drove me were the bonds I'd built—turning anger into trust, unhappiness into loyalty, small gestures into lasting ties. My colleagues began to see what I'd learned: connection could be as powerful as any discount.

On December 7th, Mr. Vikram Singh called.

"Arjun, what's up?"

"I'm good, sir. Preparing for today's deal."

"From home? You're still closing deals?" His tone held surprise—and respect.

"Yes, sir. As you once said, I've taken an alternate route."

He chuckled. "And what route gives forty-five percent of Jalpaiguri's share?"

I paused. Since 2013, I'd tried to be more than a man chasing numbers. I'd helped in storms, shared families' joys and griefs, and stood with them quietly when words fell short. Those moments had tied us together. And when my accident came, those same threads pulled people back to me—not from pity, but belonging.

"So your empathy created theirs," Vikram said softly. "And that brought you sales."

As he spoke, my mother placed breakfast beside me. The ceiling fan stirred the air.

"Yes, sir," I said. "I don't know the theory—but it works."

"Well done, Arjun. You turned tragedy into strength. Join us for the January 5th review and share your learnings."

When the call ended, I looked at my breakfast but felt only emptiness. Around ten, the silence grew heavy. It was Isha's hour to call. The screen stayed blank. My chest tightened. Tears came before I could stop them.

My mother touched my shoulder. "If you truly love her," she said, "prepare for your MBA. Let your success be her tribute." Her voice was steady. Mine wasn't.

That evening, Bikash called. Sahil had been sentenced to ten years. I sat still, letting the news settle. Justice—late, but real. It couldn't bring her back, but it leveled the weight inside me. Peace, fragile and quiet, finally came.

Work resumed slowly. My colleagues visited, shared leads, and lifted my spirits. "Friends," I told them, "I'll manage my own territories, but your support means everything."

Customers came too—Pintu Haldar, Hamid Alam, Harun, and even Rajesh Gupta. It felt as if every driver, broker, and mechanic had become my sales team. Financiers brought delivery orders themselves.

Only one person I hadn't called—Sonu. I feared his recklessness might stir trouble. Yet he learned from Mr. Aggarwal and came anyway.

The moment he entered, Sonu broke down. His voice trembled as tears rolled down his face.

"I'm so sorry about Isha. She was like my sister. I still can't believe she's gone."

I placed a hand on his shoulder and guided him to a chair.

"How's your health now?" he asked.

"I'm better," I said. "Working from home these days."

"Arjun, why didn't you call me?"

His words stung. I knew his concern was real, but his reckless ways—too much drinking, chasing women—worried me.

"Sonu, I didn't want to disturb you," I said quietly.

He shook his head, eyes wet. "Don't ever say that. I'm your brother. I'll always be here."

"Thank you, Sonu," I said. "If I need help, I'll tell you."

Inside, though, I hesitated. I feared his help might cause more harm than good. Still, he insisted,

"No, Arjun. I'll bring you three customers every month. Your health won't stop your success."

His conviction surprised me. For the first time, I saw a steadier side of him.

"Thank you, Sonu," I said softly.

He stayed another hour. We talked about everything. Mother served fish curry with rice and vegetables. When he left, my heart felt lighter.

Life had changed. My home was now my office. Deals were closed from my bed while Mother cared for me with quiet strength.

The new year brought another challenge. On 5th January 2015, our online meeting began at 10 a.m. Though I had crossed my targets, I was tense—the final market share was still unknown.

Faces lit up on screen. My name blinked on the list. Then came Vikram Singh's voice—steady, commanding.

"Good morning, team. Today, we measure what we've built. Every mile, every late night, every customer—it all comes down to this. Mission 51% isn't just a number. It's who we are."

The screen shifted to Mr. S. K. Aggarwal. Slides flashed, voices came and went—praise, critique, numbers.

My pulse raced. Jalpaiguri. Alipurduar. My territories.

"Arjun tops the dashboard," Aggarwal announced. "Despite the challenges, he's crossed our target. His market share stands at fifty-two percent."

For a heartbeat, silence. Then applause burst through the speakers.

"Remarkable," said Mr. Rakesh. "A big hand for Arjun."

The figures glowed on my screen like medals:

Turbo Cheetah Truck Market Share

Arjun – 52%

Raju Roy – 45%

Rahman – 43%

Others – below 40%

At the bottom, one bold line:

Overall Market Share – 42%

Each number carried sleepless nights, long roads, and quiet endurance.

Vikram Singh spoke again, his tone softer.

"For Arjun, 51% isn't just a target—it's a story of survival. Despite the case with Hamid Alam, losing Isha, and being confined to bed, he found another way."

Silence returned, deeper this time. Then the regional manager, Raj Kapoor, appeared on video.

"Team," he said, "Rana Turbo Cheetah's 42% share reflects your effort. My special thanks to Arjun, and to Raju Roy and Rahman."

Then he looked straight at me.

"Arjun, tell us—how did you achieve Mission 51% so early?"

I unmuted the mic. The pause before I spoke felt like the stillness before rain.

"Sir… Mission 51% was never just a number. It was survival. It was resilience. It was empathy—and dignity."

The words wavered, then steadied.

"When I began, I wasn't only selling trucks. I was fixing broken engines at night, rescuing customers in the jungle, and sitting beside drivers when they cried. I shared their weddings, their funerals, their storms. When financiers panicked, I stood with them. When brokers demanded dues, I made sure they were paid. I wasn't just a salesman—I became part of their lives. Those small acts, over time, built the strongest kind of sales—trust."

I drew a breath.

"And when my own life broke—when Isha was gone, when both legs were in plaster—those same people became my legs, my voice, my team. My home turned into my office. My mother, my silent manager.

So, if you ask how I achieved Mission 51%, the truth is—I didn't do it alone. What I gave in drops, the world returned in a river. That 52% is proof that empathy sells more than any scheme or discount. Beyond dashboards and targets—it's humanity that wins."

I lowered my gaze. Silence filled the meeting.

Then Vikram Singh unmuted. His voice, usually crisp, softened.

"Arjun… this isn't performance. It's history. You've shown us what Mission 51% truly means."

Applause followed—first a few hands, then a wave. Faces smiled, some moved, even Raj Kapoor's stern features eased into a faint smile. On my screen, the number 52% glowed like a medal—like Isha's unseen hand on my shoulder. For the first time in months, I felt whole.

But celebrations end fast. Raj Kapoor's tone turned cold.

"And at the bottom," he said, "is Partha's territory. What happened, Partha?"

Partha froze. "Sir, I've overachieved my target."

"I'm asking about market share," Kapoor snapped. "You're at thirty-one percent."

Partha stumbled through excuses—bad reputation, cold calls, road shows, digital marketing. Kapoor cut him short.

"Enough. We're not here for excuses. I want 51% from your region. Engines, tyres, service vans—we've given everything. What else do you need?"

Bikash spoke gently, "Sir, the damage was serious. The old reputation still haunts us."

"Then how are Arjun, Raju, and Rahman selling?" Kapoor shot back. Silence answered.

He turned to Aggarwal.

"Set targets based on market share, not comfort zones."

"Yes, sir," Aggarwal said quickly.

"Rakesh," Kapoor continued, "watch every customer concern. No complaint should reach Rana Motors. Fix it before it festers."

"Yes, sir."

"Vikram, raise the marketing budget. No block, no village untouched. This quarter is war."

"Yes, sir."

"Get competitor registration data from every district," Kapoor added. "Know the ground before you fight."

Then his voice rose like a general before battle.

"Crush the competition before they're born. Every deal is a warfront. I want 51%."

He paused, then thundered, "Go all out—march forward! Victory is ours."

The line crackled as everyone unmuted. Applause roared through the speakers—half praise, half relief.

Soon, the discussion moved to other products, but I stayed silent.

Two years had passed since I entered the automobile world. From a temporary executive, I had become permanent—one of the best. I had won trust, solved tough cases like Hamid Alam's, and reached the dream of Mission 51%. Yet three months still remained in the financial year. I had to hold the line—or go further.

But beneath the pride, one wound never healed—Isha's death. Her presence still lingered in every corner of my life. Her perfume, her smile, her restless hair—they returned like ghosts of memory.

Silently, I promised her:

Isha, I'll prepare for my MBA. I'll pass. I'll create the future we dreamed of.

To honor her, I had to succeed—in studies and in the market.

By January 2015, I buried myself in exam prep. Sonu became my right hand, managing deliveries and handling Aggarwal. I had doubted him once, fearing betrayal, but he proved loyal—steady when I needed him most.

The last quarter of 2014–15 turned electric. Raj Kapoor's words—"Crush the competition before they're born"—became our war cry.

The market turned into a battlefield. Before competitors reached a customer, we were already there. Finance schemes became our missiles, service support our shield. Within 24 hours, every issue was fixed. Satisfied customers became allies, even spies, warning us of rival moves.

Competitors—Raftar Motors, Tejas, LoadMax, StormX—fought hard. Our managers—Aggarwal, Rakesh, Vikram Singh—raced through markets in Turbo Cheetah trucks, helping us close cases. The showroom was empty. The field was our office.

It wasn't just sales anymore. It was war. And Mission 51% was the victory we bled for.

CHAPTER 42

# The Trophy and the Stick

But my battle to uphold Mission 51% was unlike any before.

The plasters were gone, yet walking still hurt. Physiotherapy became my daily ritual, each stretch teaching my legs the forgotten rhythm of movement. The stick beside me was a quiet reminder—I wasn't whole, but my resolve had to be.

Even during recovery, my mind refused rest. I searched for business in new ways. Relationship-building—once my strength—became my survival tool.

I had once read that in hard times, we must evolve to endure. Those words now found their meaning.

Pintu Haldar kept his promise. He connected chicken wholesalers and helped close deals. The goodwill earned that stormy night of 22nd July 2014 returned to me now, when I needed it most.

Harun, too, became my unseen ally. His grip over the pickup stands was absolute. Every driver and secretary became my eyes and ears, feeding me leads from the field.

Then, on 25th January, my phone rang—Karma Tshering from Himalayan Construction.

"Arjun," he said, "Sonu told me about your condition. I'm sorry for Isha… and for your injury. We were very impressed with her presentation."

His words reopened an old wound.

"Yes, sir," I said quietly. "We lost Isha in that accident."

"I'm sorry, Arjun," he said softly, then added, "But I also have some good news. We've decided to place an order for twenty Turbo Cheetah Trucks."

For a moment, I couldn't breathe. Hope rushed in like fresh air.

"Thank you, sir," I said, voice trembling.

"Deliver by the fifteenth. Send Sonu—I'll hand him the documents. Payment in cash."

After the call, I informed Sonu and Aggarwal. That single deal felt like a lifeline.

Even from bed, I worked the market by phone, convincing customers and coordinating deliveries. To my surprise, Mr. Aggarwal had changed—he arranged deliveries himself and even assigned a new executive to help me.

Through Rajesh Gupta, I reached tea growers in Jalpaiguri, adding new business. But our biggest challenge remained—the truck itself.

Turbo Cheetah was infamous: seized engines, cracked chassis, poor mileage. Selling it felt impossible. Yet the manufacturer had invested heavily; failure wasn't an option. So we carried the burden, turning flaws into promises.

When the target was 51% market share for such a product, it seemed absurd. Still, our sales tripled. Somewhere deep down, we felt—we might have done it.

The year ended in tense silence. No celebration, only waiting.

I called Rakesh Chetri. "Any update, sir?"

"Working on it," he said. "You should hear good news soon."

On 8th April 2015, at 4 p.m., the message arrived:

"Congratulations, team—Darjeeling Auto Works has achieved Mission 51%. Turbo Cheetah holds 53% market share. Arjun, 67% in your territory. Raju Roy 55%, Rahman 53%. This is history."

The group erupted. Messages poured in.

Mission 51% was no longer a dream. It was done.

And yet, amid the celebration, one presence was missing—Isha. From the beginning, her spirit had been stitched into this mission. She was gone, yet her work lived on in every number, every victory.

Mother sensed my silence. She placed her hand on my head and whispered,

"Now it's time to fulfill Isha's dream."

"Yes, Ma," I replied softly. "I must."

On 15th April, our dealership held its annual function at a four-star hotel in Darjeeling. The ballroom shimmered with chandeliers, music, and laughter. The scent of flowers mingled with polished wood and glass. Colleagues in crisp suits and saris stood tall with the pride of a team that had achieved the impossible.

When my name was called, applause surged like a wave. I rose slowly, leaning on my stick. Each tap echoed through the hall, louder to me than the cheers. Colleagues guided me to the stage. The trophy—Top Performer of the Year—gleamed in my hands.

But its weight felt uneven. In one hand, polished metal; in the other, the stick scarred by struggle. Together they told the story—of sacrifice and survival, loss and victory.

Raju Roy, once the unbeatable star, took the second prize. His smile was polite, but his eyes betrayed defeat. Pride and pain crossed paths in silence. I felt both triumph and guilt.

The evening sparkled—music, speeches, clinking glasses—but for me, it was hollow. My limp marked every step, my stick tapping a rhythm of endurance. Their words lifted me, yet I still listened for the one voice that would never return.

Amid the celebration of Mission 51%, the stick reminded me of the true mission I now carried—to live, work, and dream for Isha too.

By May, I was back in the field. My legs had just healed, and I drove the demo Turbo Cheetah Truck with care, each gear shift echoing months of struggle.

Around then, my MBA results arrived. I had passed—not brilliantly, but well enough. A distance degree, paired with hard-earned experience, would help me move forward.

CHAPTER 43

# *Mission Accomplished, Yet Incomplete*

On 12th May, while meeting a customer in Dhupguri, I received a call from Mr. Vikram Singh around 11 a.m. I thought it was routine business.

"Hello Arjun, where are you?" he asked.

"I'm in the Dhupguri market, sir."

"Have you passed your MBA exam?"

The question, sudden and personal, caught me off guard. Standing in the heat and traffic, I replied quickly,

"Yes, sir. Cleared it a few days back."

"Oh, excellent. Then you have a good opportunity ahead," he said in his calm, professional tone.

I stepped aside, curiosity rising. "What kind of opportunity, sir?"

"Don't share this with anyone. You're the first I'm telling. I got an offer from Tejas Automotive Ltd—India's leading SUV and small truck manufacturer. They appointed me Regional Sales Manager for Bihar and Jharkhand. I joined just a week ago."

Hearing that, a wave of happiness swept through me. Mr. Vikram Singh truly deserved it—capable, kind, and respected by all.

"Many, many congratulations, sir! I'm so happy for you," I said warmly.

"Thank you, Arjun. It's because of the team's effort and your support. We performed well together, and this chance finally came my way." His voice was full of joy.

I pressed my foot into the dusty roadside soil, hiding the heaviness in my chest. First, Isha had left; now Vikram Singh—my second pillar—was moving on. In a quiet voice, I said,

"But sir, the pain is… I'm losing you as my best territory manager. You've been a true support."

"So what, hmm?" he laughed lightly. Then asked, "Arjun, do you want to be a manager?"

"Yes, sir. Anyone would. But I don't know if I'm capable. By the way… which dealership, sir?"

"This isn't a dealership role," he said, serious now. "It's a Territory Sales Manager position at Tejas Automotive, under me. You'd be posted in Patna."

I froze. For a moment, I thought he was joking. Tejas Automotive was a dream company—young graduates prayed for its offer letter. They hired only engineers with MBAs from top institutes. My profile didn't fit at all. It felt like life's cruel humour.

Memories flashed—my first interview at Darjeeling Autoworks, when Mr. S. K. Aggarwal had insulted me; the times friends mocked my job; my mother's disappointment; the failures in tutoring, insurance, and even early sales. Yet through all of it, I had kept moving—and somehow achieved Mission 51%.

But a sales manager's role? That felt beyond reach.

"Sir," I said softly, "thank you for considering me. It's like a dream. But… I don't think I'm eligible. I don't even have the courage for that interview. Still, thank you for thinking of me."

Vikram's tone grew firm, as if he knew my doubts too well.

"Arjun, stop underestimating yourself. You think Tejas Automotive only cares about your college or accent? That's where people go wrong. Do you know why I see you as the right candidate?"

I stayed silent.

"You have what most MBA graduates don't—real scars," he said. "You didn't just earn a degree; you carried it into the mud of the market. For two years, you've lived as a sales executive, learning every frustration of a customer, every trick of a dealer. That's not classroom learning—that's survival."

His words brought back those endless days under the sun and rain, walking roads others never would.

"You built relationships, Arjun—not just transactions. Customers in villages know you by name. They call you when they're in trouble. How many MBAs can claim that? You risked your safety in Hamid Alam's case, when most would have run. You stood your ground. That's leadership."

I gripped the phone tighter.

"And don't forget," Vikram continued, his voice softer now, "when you broke your legs, everyone thought you'd vanish. But you didn't. From your bed, you still led the numbers. You achieved Mission 51%. Who does that, Arjun? Only an underdog with the heart of a fighter."

My breathing quickened—caught between disbelief and a rising pride I'd never allowed myself.

"Underdogs are dangerous," he said. "Once they taste success, they never stop. That's why I trust you with this role—not despite your struggles, but because of them. You've already lived the toughest lessons a Territory Sales Manager will face. Now it's only about wearing the title."

I swallowed hard. "Thank you, sir… for believing in me. Please give me some time to talk to my mother."

That evening, after freshening up, I sat with my tea, flipping through TV channels. But my mind stayed elsewhere — circling around Vikram Singh's proposal.

I finally told my mother everything.

"Ma, you know Vikram Sir from Rana Motors?"

"Yes—the manager who gave you that costly shoe," she smiled.

"Yes, that's him. Today he offered me a position with Tejas Automotive—as Territory Sales Manager."

Her face turned serious. "Where will they post you?"

"If I'm selected, probably Patna," I replied.

Her expression fell. "What? Patna… Bihar?"

"Yes, Ma. It's the capital, a big city."

She shook her head anxiously. "Arjun, don't go so far. Try for a small government job and stay here. I don't want you under this stress again."

"Ma, this would be a company payroll job. Salary could be close to one lakh a month," I explained gently.

But she looked at me with worry. "I don't want money or titles. I just want my son to be safe. Look—there are ads for school teachers in the paper. Apply for that instead."

"Ma," I said softly, "we need money to keep the house running. I can't even give you proper treatment. I'm already in debt. Please understand."

She sighed. "Do what you think is right, Arjun. But think carefully. Don't let this become another burden for me."

It was her way of saying yes. She had lived a government employee's life — she believed only in steady jobs, not the chaos of corporate battles.

The next morning, I called Vikram early.

"Good morning, sir."

"Good morning, Arjun. How are you?"

"I'm ready to face the interview," I said, trying to sound steady.

"That's the spirit of an underdog," he encouraged. "Underdogs don't think about winning or losing. They just keep fighting."

"When and where will the interview be, sir?"

"Me and my boss, Mr. Animesh Chatterjee, the Zonal Head, will be in Mumbai from 3rd to 6th June. Come to our Mumbai office on the 5th. It'll be tough—prepare well."

"Yes, sir. I'll be there," I said, though I silently wondered how to afford the travel.

Perhaps he sensed it.

"Arjun, send me a photo of your ID card."

"Why, sir?"

"I'll book your flight from Bagdogra to Mumbai and back."

"Not required, sir. I'll manage."

"Don't worry. Once you get the job, you can return it," he said with a smile in his voice.

And just like that, he booked my tickets and a hotel.

I took a week's leave from Darjeeling Autoworks and boarded the flight on 3rd June. Ma blessed me, reminding me once more to apply for that government job later. I only smiled.

When I landed in Mumbai, I felt the weight of a new chapter pressing on me. This interview wasn't going to be easy. It was going to be a battle. But I carried hope.

On the 5th June morning, I entered through the tall gates of Tejas Automotive's corporate office. After a few security checks, I reached the sales and marketing department with Vikram's help.

The office was cool, the air faintly smelling of machines and coffee. Rows of desks hummed with quiet focus; glass cabins gleamed with managers at work. The place felt different—polished, distant—and something inside me began to change.

Vikram welcomed me with a smile and tea. For half an hour, he briefed me. Then he looked at me with quiet seriousness.

"Arjun, your interview is at 2 p.m. with Mr. Animesh Chatterjee, our Zonal Head. Senior managers will be there too. Be strong. Give your best. Rest, I'll manage."

"Yes, sir. I'll try my best," I said, hiding my nerves.

By 2 p.m., my heart was racing. My palms were cold. Still, I told myself—I had to win. For Isha. For my mother. This was not just an interview; it was an underdog's fight.

I knocked softly. "May I come in, sir?"

"Come in," a calm voice said.

Inside, four officials sat around a table. A middle-aged man with kind eyes smiled first.

"Good afternoon. Are you Arjun?"

"Good afternoon, sir. Yes—I'm Arjun Chowdhury."

"Please, have a seat," he said warmly. "I'm Animesh Chatterjee. Vikram told me a little about you. Now, tell me something about yourself…"

The interview began—professional, yet polite, so unlike Mr. S. K. Aggarwal. But I could tell it wouldn't be easy.

Then Mr. Chatterjee leaned forward, eyes steady.

"Arjun, your résumé shows two years in a dealership. That's it. Now tell me—why should we risk millions on you, with no manufacturer experience at all?"

For a moment, time stopped. The hum of the AC faded; even the city noise outside seemed to disappear. My throat went dry.

Every failure, every insult, every sleepless night flashed before me — Darjeeling Autoworks, the long roads, the endless rain, the faces that once doubted me.

And there I was again — the underdog standing at the edge of another impossible chance.

I took a slow breath, straightened my back, and met his gaze.

It was time to answer.